EAST ASIAN SOCIAL SCIENCE MONOGRAPHS

STREET STUDIES IN HONG KONG

STREET STUDIES IN HONG KONG

Localities in a Chinese City

FRANK LEEMING

HONG KONG
OXFORD UNIVERSITY PRESS
LONDON NEW YORK MELBOURNE
1977

Oxford University Press
OXFORD LONDON GLASGOW
NEW YORK TORONTO MELBOURNE WELLINGTON
IBADAN NAIROBI DAR ES SALAAM LUSAKA CAPE TOWN
KUALA LUMPUR SINGAPORE JAKARTA HONG KONG TOKYO
DELHI BOMBAY CALCUTTA MADRAS KARACHI

Filmset by T.P. Graphic Arts Services
Printed by Windmill Printing Co.
Published by Oxford University Press, News Building, North Point, Hong Kong

To my wife

Je meurs de seuf auprès de la fontaine,
Chaud comme feu, et tremble dent à dent;
En mon pays suis en terre lointaine;
Lez un brasier frisonne tout ardent;
Nu comme un ver, vêtu en président,
Je ris en pleurs et attends sans espoir;
Confort reprends en triste désespoir;
Je m'éjouis et n'ai plaisir aucun;
Puissant je suis sans force et sans povoir,
Bien reçeuilli, débouté de chacun.

FRANCOIS VILLON

The peasants also had their traditions... They had the ability to reduce theory to the essentials of practice, to work in combination with little apparent leadership, and to climb rapidly from lower to higher levels of organisation and the use of resources when free of pressure from above.

OWEN LATTIMORE

Contents

Figures

Plates

Foreword

THE essence of these studies is an attempt to fuse the visible reality of the high-built, noisy streets of the great double city of Hong Kong with the invisible reality of the social, economic and administrative pressures which operate within the community. It arose out of my own attempt, on returning to Hong Kong in 1969 after more than twenty years, to assimilate and rationalize the visible complexity and no less visible orderliness of the common street landscapes of busy working-class districts. It has developed into an attempt to identify the characteristic forces which make and maintain the physical and social fabric of localities in Hong Kong; to show how these forces operate, in what ways people use them and in what ways they are limited; and to show how they relate to the triple inheritance of the community from China, from the world outside China, and from its own past.

My method of working has been somewhat unorthodox. I began by isolating, through observation, talking and thinking, a group of about ten areas which appeared to display characteristic features or characteristic groupings of features, and then went on to collect sufficient factual and interpretive material about these features to be confident that I had come to an understanding of them and the localities to which they belonged. This understanding I have then tried to convey, reducing the number of localities to the seven for which the original insights and subsequent investigations proved the most rewarding. Unlike most researchers on Hong Kong, I tried to work not from the top (the government and the excellent government documentation) downwards to the people, but from the limitless detail represented by the streets and the people towards an intellectually satisfying level of generalization and understanding. On the whole I tried until a late stage in each phase of the work to avoid deciding which particular categories of information were most relevant to my purposes and in what ways—in fact, I have as much expected my own purposes to emerge from the materials which the community provided, as expected my own prior thinking to govern the selection of materials. By these means, it is hoped, an authentic and unforced account of each locality, comparatively free from academic jargon in both word and thought, may have emerged.

The day-to-day and year-to-year life of communities of working people is not well known to students in any field, by comparison with its importance. In the study of these topics in non-Western situations, including

Chinese ones, the detailed factual matter to be found in Western or even vernacular sources is often extremely sketchy and may be virtually non-existent. At the same time, the advance of thinking about human society demands more and more information about working people—failing which, the need for knowledge is filled by analogy, guesswork and conceptualization. But on the ground, limitless information may be gathered by any student who is willing to seek it out—and this information can and should include the interpretations of their circumstances which working people themselves make. It is this task to which I have addressed myself in these studies. I have tried to work towards the ideal of an account of localities in the city which should be true at the level of day-to-day life among the people who live there. The studies arise, with as much directness as has proved possible, out of the experience of the resounding streets and crowded lifts, the busy markets by day and night, the vertical landscapes of the high factory buildings and mixed tenements, and the vast, peaceable housing estates of this remarkable city.

There is much in Hong Kong that is astonishing, and materials can be found to illustrate many kinds of superlatives. I have tried less to astonish the reader than to describe and interpret the facts; and I have tried to preserve a sense of proportion about what is superlative. The Hong Kong which emerges from these studies is less a showcase of the West or a corrupt capitalist slum, less a political anachronism or an economic miracle, than a place where labourers, musicians and bureaucrats, businessmen and electricians, housewives and factory-girls, policemen and waiters live close together in a close-knit, complicated, tense, shy and energetic Chinese community. This Hong Kong is a great Cantonese manufacturing city and seaport, crammed with ordinary human beings bringing up families and holding down jobs.

Acknowledgements

I came to Hong Kong first as a young soldier in 1945, and returned in 1969 as a visiting lecturer in the United College of the Chinese University of Hong Kong. I am glad to acknowledge my debt to the Chinese University and the Vice-Chancellor, Dr C.M. Li, and to the United College and the President, Mr T.C. Cheng. The University of Leeds gave me leave and helped to finance my visit: in Leeds, I have to thank particularly the then Registrar, the late Dr J.V. Loach, Professor J.W. Birch and Professor O. Lattimore for making my visit possible, and for encouragement.

In 1971 a generous grant from the Leverhulme Foundation enabled me to complete my basic field-work and to begin to bring the project into a coherent form. I returned to Hong Kong in 1974 for a visit financed in part by the University of Leeds, which made it possible for me to bring the whole enterprise up to date.

My debt to Hong Kong people is evident on every page of the book. Part of it is owed to my friends, including colleagues and students, who talked about their city with me and showed me warm hospitality. Part of it is owed to people in all walks of life whose names I did not know even at the time of our conversations—people at street corners and on squatter footpaths, people in shops, factories, offices and resettlement estates. Part of it is owed to officials of the government of low rank and high, both European and Chinese, especially in a number of offices where I was received with special warmth. Part of it is owed to businessmen and women who with great kindness explained the rudiments of their trades to me.

It is a pleasure to thank by name Miss M. Au, Mr W.H. Au, Mr Y. Chan, Mr H.S. Cheng, Mr Y.F. Cheung, Mr S.C. Cho, Professor D.J. Dwyer, Professor D.M.E. Evans, Mr K.K. Fung, Mr W. Higbee, Mr K.C. Lam, Mr Y.T. Lau, Mr Y.C. Lee, Mr C.S. Leung, Mr F.C. Lo, Miss M.Y. Ma, Mr H.C. Mok, Dr K.Y. Wong, Mr S.L. Yang and Mr S.L. Yeung, for various forms of kindness and help, and particularly Mr C.Y. Poon who more than any other individual guided me in evolving an independent style of approach to Hong Kong people. I am also happy to thank the library of the University of Hong Kong for hospitality. I am grateful to my friend and colleague, Mr G.C. Dickinson, for reading and commenting on some chapters, and a number of other friends and colleagues for constructive and perceptive comments. I am glad to thank Mrs M. Welsh and Mrs R.J.P. Whitehead for their patience in typing my manuscript. I also thank my wife for comments at many points, and at some my children.

Figures number 6, 7, 13, 15, 19, 20 and 23, and Plate 25, are reproduced from or based on original maps and air photographs by the Crown Lands and Survey Office, with permission, © Hong Kong Government. I also acknowledge the Government Printer for permission to reproduce Figure 3 and Plate 1; Her Britannic Majesty's Stationery Office for permission to reproduce Figure 14; and the Government Information Services, Hong Kong, for permission to reproduce Plates 8, 12 and 24.

University of Leeds,
January 1976

FRANK LEEMING

Sources

THE greater part of the book has been written from field observation. Extensive notes, interpretative as well as factual, were collected during repeated visits to the streets discussed and to many other places. Where contemporary information is produced without a named source, it has been gathered in the field—and this includes discussion with local people in many cases.

But it is of the nature of direct observation that it raises questions of interpretation which have to be answered from other kinds of information. Two kinds of information have predictably been of particular value in this respect: that collected and published for internal business purposes, and that collected and preserved by the government. Both kinds have contemporary and historic dimensions.

Among contemporary business compilations, the most useful for background material has been the *Hsiang-Kang ching-chi nien-chien* (*Hong Kong Economic Yearbook*), an annual work with an unconcealed left-wing bias, which contains summaries of conditions in many business and manufacturing fields. For contemporary distributions, the Yellow Pages (subscribers classified by kinds of business) in the Chinese and English telephone directories have been most valuable. Business subscribers are allowed only one free entry (Chinese *or* English) in the Yellow Pages; hence the two versions differ in some degree.

Trade directories have provided valuable insights and materials from the past. Old trade directories for Hong Kong are however very scarce, and recourse has had to be had to those which could be bought. Those which have been used consistently are shown in the list below.

The official materials of which most use has been made, both for contemporary conditions and conditions in the past, are the splendid records of the office of the Commissioner for Rating and Valuation. I am particularly indebted to the Commissioner and to members of his staff for allowing me access to them. The excellent contemporary maps of the Crown Lands and Survey Office have been a constant standby; I gladly acknowledge my debt to them. Finally, I have drawn very much background and corroborative detail from the informative and often thoughtful publications of the government, both the *Annual Reports* and a number of *Annual Departmental Reports* of recent years, and some earlier publications.

STANDARD REFERENCES

The following have been used as standard sources. They are referred to in the ways indicated. In the case of the commercial directories, material introduced in the text for the relevant year comes from the directory named for that year, unless otherwise stated. The same is true for the *Valuation Tables* for 1870 and 1871.

1877 Directory. Chronicle and directory for China, Japan and the Philippines, 1877. (Hong Kong, 1877). English (also other years).

Chance's Directory for 1915. Anglo-Chinese commercial directory, probably *1915.* (Hong Kong, n.d.). Published by Jan George Chance. English and Chinese. Victoria only.

1927 Directory. Business guide and directory, 1927. (Hong Kong, probably 1927). Published by the Chinese General Chamber of Commerce. English and Chinese. Victoria; also suburbs including Kowloon.

1940 Directory. Hong Kong and Macao Business classified directory, 1940. (Hong Kong, 1940). Published by the Hong Kong and Macao business classified directory publishing company. Chinese. Victoria and Kowloon without differentiation.

1951 Directory. Hong Kong commercial yearbook of 1951. Published by the Chinese General Chamber of Commerce. English and Chinese. Also other years. Victoria and Kowloon without differentiation.

HKCCNC. Hsiang-Kang ching-chi nien-chien (*Hong Kong Economic yearbook*) Annual. Published by *Hsiang-Kang ching-chi tao-pao* (*Hong Kong Economic Reporter*). Chinese.

Yellow Pages. Hong Kong telephone directory. Annual. Published in English and Chinese by the Hong Kong Telephone Co. Ltd.

Valuation table, 1870, 1871. Valuation table of tenements at Victoria, in the Colony of Hong Kong, as valued for purpose of police, lighting, water and fire brigade rates for the year 1870. Also *1871.* Unpublished records held in the office of the Commissioner of Rating and Valuation.

CHINESE NAMES AND EXPRESSIONS

It is impossible to be both realistic and consistent in the use of romanized forms of Chinese names and words in the Hong Kong context. I have preferred realism to consistency. Where an English name has general currency, I have used it. Apart from these cases, I have used local, Cantonese forms for place-names, written for preference as one word. These are not always the same as the official forms. For names of authors and titles of books, I have used the customary Mandarin forms. For Chinese expressions, I have in principle preferred Mandarin forms but in practice used Cantonese where the latter appeared much more natural.

HONG KONG CURRENCY

Values and prices are expressed throughout this book in Hong Kong dollars. Standard rates of exchange with the pound sterling and the United States dollar in 1971 and 1974 respectively were as follows:

1971 Hong Kong \$ 6.06 = United States \$1
\$14.55 = £ sterling 1

1974 Hong Kong \$ 5.085 = United States \$1
\$11.87 = £ sterling 1

A standard lower-paid skilled or semi-skilled wage in 1971 was of the order of \$600 per month; in 1974, \$900 per month.

1 Time, Place and Community in Hong Kong

THE GROWTH OF THE CITY, 1841–1974

HONG KONG as a colony came to Britain in 1841, in the form of Hong Kong island, at that time sparsely inhabited and with no town, but protecting on its north side the splendid harbour.

Hong Kong as a city began life at the foot of the steep north-facing slopes of Victoria Peak, and on the foreshore below. As early as 1843, a Chinese town was coming into existence, occupying streets in Sheung Wan most of which are still quite recognizable. The Hong Kong of the British and other foreign communities was at that time less a town than a rather scattered group of precincts, including business premises, barracks and the naval yard, centred on the modern Central District. This composite settlement, Chinese and colonial, was called Victoria. During the first twenty years of its history, most of the modern streets of Central District and Sheung Wan were laid out, together with Chinese mixed industrial and residential peripheries at Saiyingpoon to the west and Wanchai to the east, and some European houses on the slopes above the town. Important reclamations were also undertaken (Figure 2). Fine waterfront streets (then called *prayas*, in imitation of Macao) were built in Central District, Sheung Wan and Wanchai, which have since become (as des Voeux Road and Hennessy Road) main traffic arteries for Victoria. The population of the whole colony is recorded as 119,321 in 1861, of whom 2,986 were non-Chinese.[1]

In 1860, two miles of the tip of the peninsula of Kowloon, on the Chinese mainland across the harbour, was added to the colony. Here, barracks were built, and on the west-facing coast the new Chinese town of Yaumati began to take shape, partly on reclaimed land, with wharves and docks to south and north. On a point of land to the east, the docks and dock village of Hunghom were built. By the end of the nineteenth century, occupation of the west coast of the peninsula was still discontinuous and far from complete, but nevertheless fairly general. In Victoria at that time, tenement building was extending towards its present limits in the west at Kennedy Town, whilst in the east tenement, suburban and industrial development were all taking place in various parts of the coastal strip and group of valleys centred on Causeway Bay. The

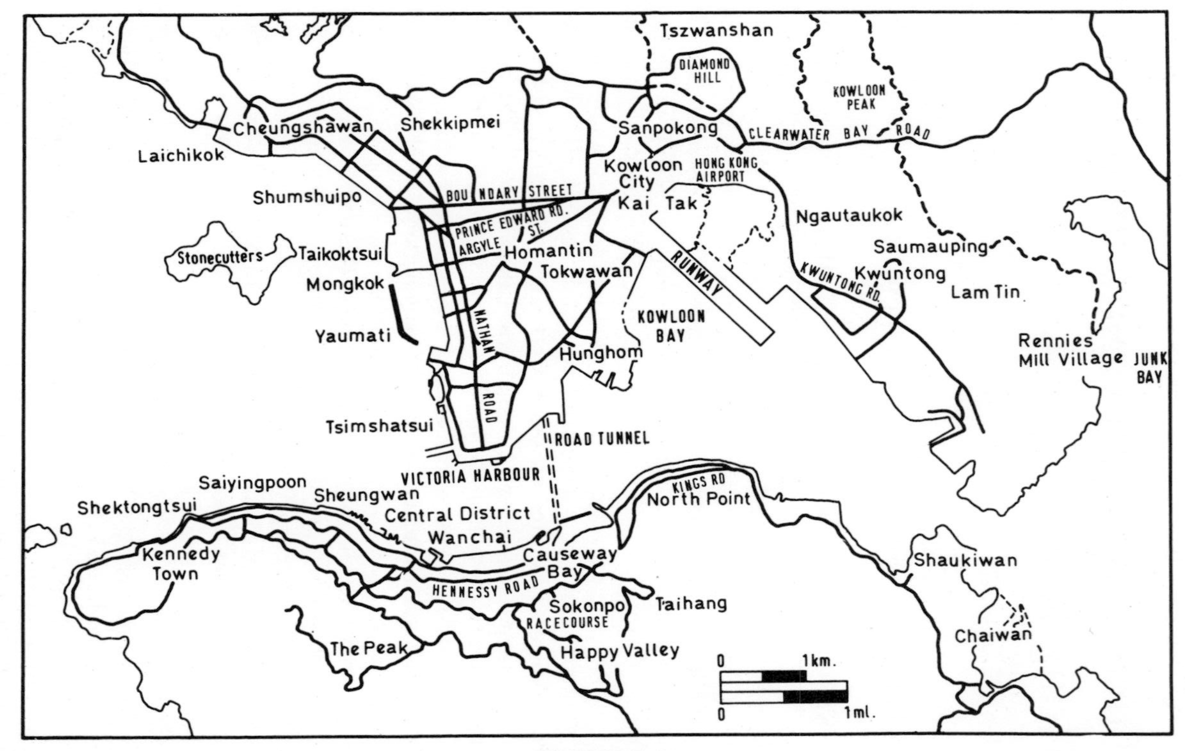

FIGURE 1

GENERAL MAP OF URBAN HONG KONG SHOWING PLACE-NAMES

population of the whole colony in 1891 was 224,814, 10,494 of them non-Chinese. At that time the population was growing at a standard rate of about 5,000 per annum.

In 1898, the rural hinterland and a number of islands, collectively called the New Territories, were added to the effective area of the colony, in accordance with the terms of a 99-year lease negotiated with the Chinese government. The old frontier, which juridically but in no other way separates Old Kowloon from a New Kowloon which has grown up beyond it, is represented by Boundary Street. In New Kowloon, the first of a long series of reclamation projects were started both on the west coast at Shumshuipo and on the east at the head of Kowloon Bay. The west coast was promptly drawn into the growing northwards expansion of Yaumati, much of it industrial, through Mongkok and Taikoktsui. The eastern side of New Kowloon, focused on the little walled town and former administrative centre of Kowloon City and its associated villages on the shores of Kowloon Bay, remained relatively isolated, in spite of the reclamation works.

In 1931, including the New Territories, the population of Hong Kong was 840,473, including about 20,000 non-Chinese.[2] During the 1920s, the population rose by an average of 21,500 per annum, due mainly to immigration. Development took no radically new course during these thirty years to 1931. Important fresh reclamations extended parts of the Central and Western sections of Victoria seaward by about 200 feet, and much of the Eastern by 500 feet. The crowded Western and Central Districts, with their wharves, tenements, offices and both Chinese and international central business districts, experienced some rebuilding and evolution of localities but little real change. The eastern section of Victoria, in Wanchai, Causeway Bay and North Point, separated from Central District by the barrier of the naval dockyard and the Victoria Barracks, remained much less crowded. In north-west Kowloon, a big new industrial suburb was growing up beyond Boundary Street in the dreary new tenement streets of Shumshuipo. At the same time, north-east Kowloon remained relatively undeveloped, except for the airport which after 1936 occupied the reclaimed land in the bay. Tsimshatsui, at the tip of the peninsula, developed as a centre for shipping and as an urban residential suburb.

During the 1930s, growth in Hong Kong gathered a fresh kind of momentum. Increasingly disturbed conditions in China led to increasing immigration which became a torrent after 1937. The population probably grew by half a million between 1937 and 1940 to reach the pre-war peak of 1,800,000 in the latter year—more than double the figure for 1931.[3] Further building, a great deal of increased crowding, and some squatting appear to have been the means by which these vast numbers were accommodated.

During the Pacific war and the Japanese occupation, business and industry in Hong Kong were virtually at a standstill, and the city experienced acute distress. The population fell, perhaps to 650,000.

With the end of the war, people began to flow into Hong Kong again.

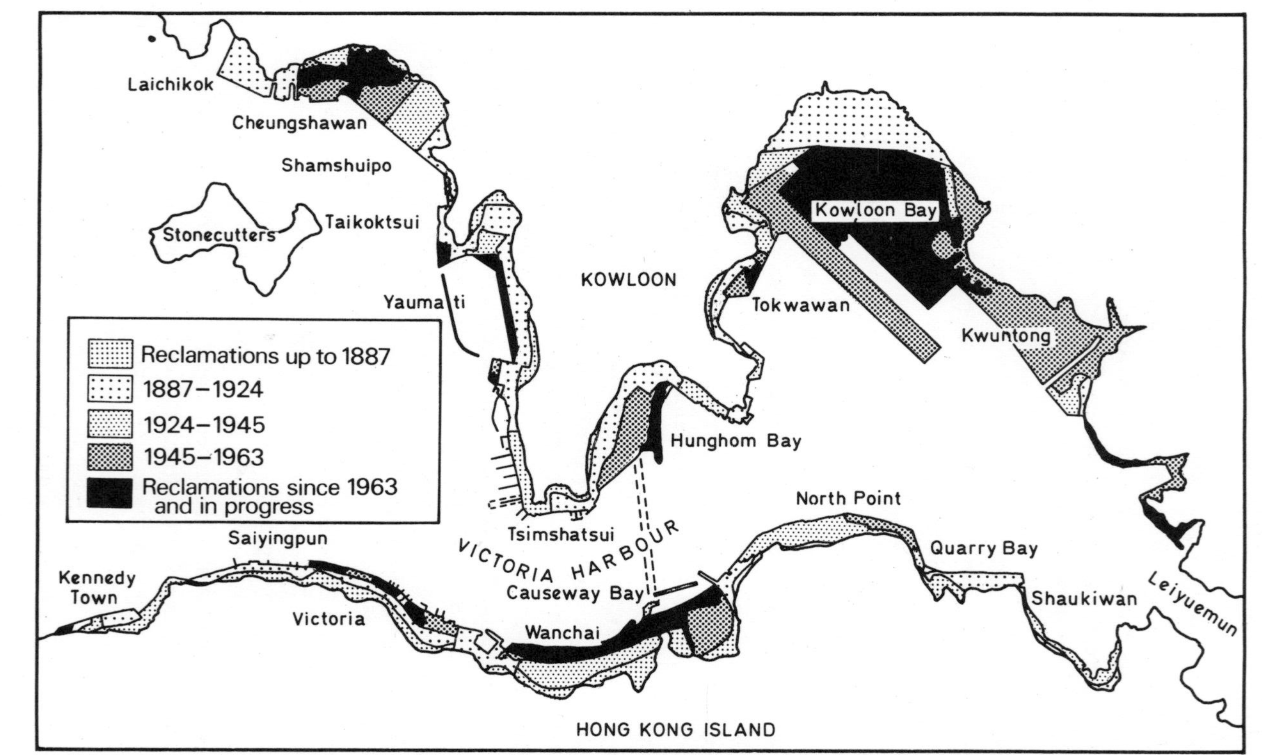

FIGURE 2

MARINE RECLAMATIONS IN URBAN HONG KONG, SHOWING MAIN HISTORIC PHASES OF RECLAMATION

(Based on a map in *Annual Report*, 1963, pp. 20–1)

The official estimate of the population of the colony in 1951 is 2,015,300. Crowding reached astronomical levels, squatting became a standard feature of the city, and there was rapid infilling of vacant lots in the street grids. Immigration practically ceased after 1950, but the standard rate of growth of the population remained about 120,000 per annum. From 1954 onwards multi-storey government housing became a standard feature of many districts of the city, and in some the dominant. In the same phase, new towns were planned at Tsuen Wan on the mainland coast beyond north-west Kowloon, and at Kwuntong on the eastern coast of the harbour. Building and rebuilding continued on an unprecedented scale during the 1960s, with only brief phases of slacker activity. During the same decade, Kwuntong was virtually completed. By 1970, the two sides of the harbour were almost completely filled by the city. Apart from a few specific localities which still await development, such as the new reclamations in Kowloon Bay and the unfinished Tsuen Wan complex, big-scale future growth is expected to take place away from the harbour, for instance at the new town of Sha Tin across the watershed to the north.

One result of the tremendous growth of the past forty years has been a fundamental change in the relative size and importance of the component parts of the city.

The following table for populations summarizes these changes.

TABLE I

POPULATION OF HONG KONG BY MAJOR AREAS, 1911–1971

	Hong Kong Island	*Old Kowloon*	*New Kowloon*	*Urban Marine Population*	*Total Population of the Colony*
1911	244,323	56,186	13,205	51,943	456,739
1931	409,203	240,386	22,634	51,631	840,473
1941 (Est.)	709,000	580,000		n/s	1,640,000
1951 (Est.)	900,000	800,000		120,000	2,015,300
1961	1,004,875	725,177	852,849	90,343	3,129,648
1971	996,183	716,272	1,478,581	61,200	4,064,400

Source: Figures for 1911, 1931, 1961 and the total for 1951 are taken from *Hong Kong Statistics, 1947–1967,* Table 2.3, p. 15. Those for 1971 are from the *Hong Kong population and housing census, Main report,* (Hong Kong, 1972), Table 2, p. 22. Figures for 1941 are A.R.P. estimates quoted by D.J. Dwyer in 'Housing provision in Hong Kong', in D.J. Dwyer (ed.), *Asian urbanisation, a Hong Kong casebook* (Hong Kong, 1972), p. 33. Figures for 1951 are estimates based mainly on figures given by R.H. Hughes in 'Hong Kong, an urban study', in *Geographical Journal,* 117, i (1951), p. 12.

Between 1911 and 1971, the population of Hong Kong island expanded by more than four times. But that of Old Kowloon did so by more than twelve times, and that of New Kowloon by more than one hundred times. In 1961 the populations of the three great areas were most nearly alike. Relaxation of the highest densities in old property in Victoria and Old Kowloon, and ceaseless government building in New Kowloon, have led to the present increasing disparities. In 1970, 1,161,000 people lived in government housing in New Kowloon,[4] nearly 80 per cent of the whole population of the area. In the 1960s, population totals in Victoria and Old Kowloon finally began to fall. Hong Kong island now has slightly less than one million people, not all of them in Victoria. Kowloon as a whole has more than two million, and in demographic terms easily dominates the double city.

The growth of the whole city during the twentieth century may be compared in general orders of magnitude and time-span with that of Shenyang (Mukden) in north-east China, or with that of Los Angeles. These parallels are apt. During these seventy years Hong Kong has been transformed from an important and individual but undistinguished colonial merchant town into a vast industrial metropolis.

THE MANUFACTURING ECONOMY[5]

The extent of Hong Kong's dependence on manufacturing industry is best illustrated by the trade figures. Between one-fifth and one-sixth of total imports in 1973 were financed by invisible earnings and capital flows.[6] The rest was financed by domestic exports, almost entirely manufactured goods. Ninety per cent of the city's output of manufactures is exported. The state of exports and of the manufacturing industry which sustains them dominates the state of prosperity in the community, mainly through the demand for labour and its effects on wages: as industrial wages rise, prices in the tertiary sector rise to take advantage of the increased spending power among the people. The factories are by any standards the heart of the economy.

Table II shows the distribution of industry in the city among the three major areas. New Kowloon has three-fifths of all industrial workers, and its proportion is still growing. A group of concentrated factory areas in New Kowloon—Sanpokong, the industrial zone at Kwuntong, and Cheungshawan, each with more than 90,000 industrial workers, or nearly 20% of the city's total—is responsible for this situation. The nearest rival to this group in Old Kowloon is Taikoktsui, with over 40,000 workers. It is clear that the scale of industrial areas in New Kowloon is quite out of the experience of the rest of the city.

New Kowloon dominates in manufacturing industry in Hong Kong by reason of these vast groups of factories, no less surely than it dominates in resettlement and low-cost housing developments. Like the flood of resettlement building, the flood of factories came to New Kowloon in the decade of the 1960s. Sanpokong was airport land until about 1960: the industrial area at Kwuntong and part of that at Cheungshawan were reclaimed only in the 1950s. In the 1960s, during a period of time no

TABLE II

INDUSTRIAL EMPLOYMENT IN THE CITY AREA, 1968–1973

	Victoria	*Old Kowloon*	*New Kowloon*	*Total*
1968				
Establishments	1,958	3,105	5,059	10,122
Workers	74,910	100,715	223,722	399,347
Workers as a percentage of Total Workers	19%	25%	56%	
1971				
Establishments	3,062	4,930	8,014	16,006
Workers	93,773	120,890	293,668	508,331
Workers as a percentage of Total Workers	18%	24%	58%	
1973				
Establishments	4,493	8,128	12,080	24,701
Workers	79,465	115,692	302,059	497,216
Workers as a percentage of Total Workers	16%	23%	61%	

Source: Labour department. Figures for employment by areas are recorded only since 1968. The figures given are for jobs—that is, for employment plus vacancies. They relate to registered factories only (factories which use power-driven machinery or which employ more than 19 workers). The city areas alone are represented in the table. This includes Kwuntong (in New Kowloon), but excludes Tsuen Wan and the three southern districts of Hong Kong island.

longer than a decade, a series of wholly new complexes of factories and public housing developments has sprung into existence in New Kowloon, to the north-west, north-east and east of Old Kowloon town and the new Nathan Road and Mongkok. As housing developments and factory areas they display abundant force and vitality. They do not carry equal conviction as towns—a weakness which is not critical if the new developments are reckoned one by one, but which assumes more importance when it is realized how great is the area and how vast the population which lives in essentially industrial environments which lack the general diversity and specific facilities which the community likes to have at its disposal. The exceptional vitality of Mongkok, the capital city of all this vast industrial territory, owes something—perhaps very much—to the comparative deprivation of Tsz Wan Shan. The Chinese habit of following precedent in locating a business (and in patronizing one), the government's liking for physical orderliness and the separation of differing kinds of land use, and the extreme rapidity of growth of these complexes themselves, have all contributed to the relative lack of provision for entertainment and social life of all kinds in New Kowloon. To take the single case of restaurants, the most important of all, 23 per cent of restaurant jobs in the city in 1971 were in New Kowloon, 77 per cent in Old Kowloon and Victoria. Otherwise expressed, these figures reveal that there were 111 people living in New Kowloon for every restaurant employee, but only 39 in Old Kowloon and Victoria.[7]

The emergence of the great specialist industrial areas of New Kowloon as dominant in the industrial figures would have been more rapid and more complete but for a second remarkable feature revealed by the table —that is, the continued vitality displayed by Old Kowloon and Victoria. Industrial employment in New Kowloon in 1974 was 135 per cent that of 1968, but the figures for Victoria and Old Kowloon were 106 per cent and 115 per cent respectively. In part this represents the opening of new sites in the older areas, such as Chai Wan on Hong Kong island, which are really analogous to New Kowloon. In part it reflects the redevelopment of old factory sites in areas like Taikoktsui.

Something remains to be said about the history of industry in Hong Kong. It is clear that since the end of the Pacific war Hong Kong has made a decisive transition from the status of an international seaport and business city with an important manufacturing fringe to that of a great manufacturing city with an important seaport and business side. This transition has been cumulative. Enough has already been said to show that industrial Hong Kong experienced radical change in the 1960s, in terms of both scale and distribution. Change of an even more radical kind took place in the years from 1945 to 1960. In this phase, particularly as a result of the fresh wave of labour, capital and skill which entered the city from China in 1947–51, manufacturing industry expanded rapidly. Szczepanik shows that in the period 1947–55 the total of invisible earnings and capital inflow amounted on average to 40 per cent of the national income. This permitted the financing of industrial investment on such a scale 'that the rate of growth of the economy had revolutionary dimensions indeed'.[8] At the end of the 1950s, moreover, re-exports fell decisively as domestic exports rose sharply; this marked the end of the old merchanting era in Hong Kong, and the coming of age of the new industrial economy.

It has been conventional to represent this industrial transformation as almost wholly a creation of the post-war expansion.[9] There is however abundant evidence to push the foundation of the industrial era back before 1947, and there is evidence of an industrial tradition in the city which goes back to its earliest days. As a result of the Japanese attack on China in 1937, many manufacturing businesses migrated to Hong Kong, and there was a marked growth of industry which must have been of the highest importance in providing work for the greatly increased population of the same years. Evidence from the 1940 Directory shows conclusively that the official figures greatly understated the scale of industry at the time.[10]

Szczepanik, Endacott and others quote low official figures for industry in 1940—800 factories, with 30,000 workers, 16,000 of them in the shipyards. The *Blue Book* for 1940 enumerates 1,142 factories in Hong Kong in that year, just one-half of the number given in the *Blue Book* for 1927. But the *Directory* for 1940 tells a very different story. The *Blue Book* enumerates 53 clothing factories, but the *Directory* gives names and addresses for at least 900. The *Blue Book* has 35 businesses in engineering and shipbuilding; the *Directory* has 200 names and addresses for firms in mechanical engineering alone, and another 27 in shipbuilding. The figures for metal products (miscellaneous) are 40 in the *Blue Book*, but 350 in the *Directory*. Weaving is the only important industry for which the *Blue Book* and *Directory* figures are almost identical. For knitting, a very modest case, the *Directory* figure is 25 per cent higher than that in the *Blue Book*. It is clear that before the war, as since, small factories not subject to registration employed in aggregate a similar number of workers to the total employed by registered factories. To judge from the *Directory*, there were in all about 7,500 factories and manufacturing workshops in Hong Kong in 1940, probably employing at least 60,000 people.

It is important to recognize that very much of this industry in the last years before the Pacific war was by no means of a traditional craft kind, but belonged to categories which are the foundations of modern manufacturing, especially in engineering.

To some extent, the myth of pre-war Hong Kong as a city practically without industry appears to have depended on misconceptions about industry as well as misconceptions about Hong Kong; there were few factory chimneys. The early Victorians saw more clearly. Sir John Davis, the first governor, wrote in 1846, 'A large number of Chinese are employed in their respective shops and houses in the exercise of industrial trades and manufactures, and there are scarcely any ordinary wants of the inhabitants which do not meet with a ready supply within the Town'.[11] In 1846, 29 per cent of Chinese properties in Victoria were in industrial use, by tailors, cabinet-makers, bakers, and so forth.[12] The implication of this evidence is that by 1846 Hong Kong had already reached that stage in the development of industry which is sometimes thought to have represented its achievement by 1946. It is probable that Hong Kong is more dependent on imported manufactures now than at any time in its previous history, due to the widening of the spectrum of demand.

TYPES OF LOCALITY AND LOCALITY STRUCTURE[13]

Hong Kong, a city which is physically bisected performs the double function of a great international seaport and a great Chinese manufacturing city. It is not surprising that it has several central or sub-central business districts.

Central District, the original British town, remains the central business heart of the whole city. Central District has the head offices of the banks, the big shipping companies, the big Western enterprises, and the property and financial interests. There are two stock exchanges, many of the best shops, some important restaurants and two of the best hotels. English is in fairly general use, and hawking and other kinds of street congestion are reduced to Western levels.

The other parts of urban Hong Kong which have central quality represent interests complementary to those of Central District, rather than functioning as detached fragments of it or competitors with it. There are four other areas which in various ways act as central districts for the whole city or a great part of it.

One of these is Sheung Wan (chapter III), which since the earliest days has been the main centre of Chinese business. This includes specialist trades like those which deal in Chinese medicines and Chinese groceries, and the big and predominantly Chinese rice importing business. As might be expected, Sheung Wan is conservative and stable in function, and its residential areas have tended to fall into advanced decay. Parts of it are now experiencing intensive activity by property redevelopers.

Causeway Bay (chapter V), which also has central functions, is a small, highly concentrated district lying about a mile to the east of Central District. It was a quiet, mixed suburban and warehousing area before the post-war expansions. It is now the chief Chinese entertainment, nightclub, hotel and restaurant area in Victoria, and also has some of the biggest and best shops. Some of this business represents new growth; some has been attracted from Central District and Sheung Wan, both of which are now relatively quiet in the evenings.

The other two secondary centres are in Kowloon. One is Tsimshatsui, which occupies the tip of the Kowloon peninsula. After the Pacific war, from quiet beginnings as a residential suburb, Tsimshatsui experienced rapid transformation into a big and professional tourist centre, based on a hotel, restaurant, bar and shopping area geared to the needs of Western customers. In terms of restaurants and shops, Tsimshatsui also has central functions within the city itself. The fourth of these central districts is Mongkok. Mongkok like Tsimshatsui lies on Nathan Road, about $1\frac{1}{2}$ miles to the north, and is the principal Chinese entertainment, restaurant, nightclub and shopping centre for Kowloon, increasingly a business and office centre, and the most extravagantly busy area in the whole city. It has changed out of all recognition since 1945, through ceaseless investment on the one hand, and the gradual crystallizing of the locality structure of the new and radically enlarged Kowloon on the other. Mongkok is now the business heart of this new city of 2 million people.

The growth of Tsimshatsui and Mongkok may be regarded as aspects of the growth of Nathan Road. Nathan Road has been the central thoroughfare of Kowloon since the first decade of the present century, but it waited until the post-war expansion for business development commensurate with its physical scale. Nathan Road is the heart of modern Kowloon and, perhaps, of modern Hong Kong itself. Nathan Road and Mongkok are both in a sense successors to Yaumati, the old Chinese town of British Kowloon (chapter IV), now a crowded and intensely mixed business, residential and industrial area.

Something remains to be said about the vast areas of the city which do not claim central or sub-central status.

In Victoria, there are five major areas beyond the three which have already been discussed. Between Central District and Causeway Bay lies the big and varied district called Wanchai, in part an industrial and commercial working-class area, in part a bar district for Western seamen.

Beyond Causeway Bay, to the north-east, lies North Point, redeveloped out of recognition since the Pacific war, originally by Shanghai-speaking immigrants. Beyond North Point with its housing, commercial and entertainment developments and its remnant industrial peripheries lies the old fishing village of Shaukiwan, now unmistakably a part of the city itself, and filled with the city's characteristic landscapes; beyond that again lies Chai Wan, a new suburb with reclamations in the bay, resettlement estates and factories.

On the other side of Central District and Sheung Wan, at the west end of Victoria, lies the industrial and mixed suburb of Kennedy Town, with abattoirs and wholesale markets, factories and warehouses, and a big working-class residential community. The trams run from Kennedy Town to Shaukiwan, slow but sure, along virtually the whole north shore of the island. To the south of the close-built city which lines the sea's edge and climbs to a standard height which does not generally exceed the Victorian level of 300 feet, a big suburban area of villas and apartment blocks occupies the steep hillsides and misty hilltops, ranging from the old-established and picturesque to the new and very smart.

The texture of Kowloon is generally looser than that of Victoria, and at the same time there is more diversity among localities.

On the west coast lies Yaumati, the old Chinese town of British Kowloon (chapter IV), and on the same coast to the north-west lies Taikoktsui, a dense industrial district (chapter VI). Beyond Taikoktsui lies the big industrial and mixed group of districts which includes Cheungshawan, Shumshuipo and Shek Kip Mei. This group of areas perhaps more than any other represents the ill-documented and incontinent but immensely important growth which took place at working-class level during the 1940s and 1950s based on beginnings extending back for a generation before the war. These areas are all related to the Nathan Road group of grid layouts, and constitute part of the mass of dense building lying between Nathan Road-Taipo Road and the west coast of the peninsula, which is the first fundamental of the city geography of Kowloon.

The centre of the Kowloon peninsula, loosely called Homantin, is occupied by almost a square mile of former hill, gully, garden and cemetery land, which has been brought within the practical ambit of city uses only since about 1965. This block of dead land formerly separated the tightly related communities of the west coast from the looser, more mixed and more industrial districts to the east, and separated both from the middle-class villas and apartment buildings of Prince Edward Road, Boundary Street and Kowloon Tong to the north; to a great degree it still does so.

Northwards again lies north-east Kowloon, which is dominated by three situations—widespread occupation of land by squatters beginning soon after or even before the Pacific war (chapter IX), the resettlement estates, some with populations upwards of 100,000, which rehouse former squatters; and the airport whose extension under the Japanese involved considerable loss of built-up areas, and whose partial removal to new reclaimed land in the bay in 1958–61 freed land first for the important new industrial area of Sanpokong, and later for the rationalization of the road approaches to the eastern side of the bay. The bay itself is now in the last stages of disappearance as a result of continued reclamation. Close to the airport lies the main pre-British Chinese settlement of the area, the former walled Kowloon City (chapter VIII).

Beyond the airport lie the resettlement and low-cost housing blocks of Ngautaukok, facing the runway across the new reclamations and the arm of water which is all that remains of Kowloon Bay. Further to the south-east beyond Ngautaukok lies the new industrial town of Kwuntong, begun only in 1954 and now, together with its own satellites to the south and inland, furnishing housing for some 500,000 people, and jobs for over 100,000 (chapter VII).

THE HONG KONG COMMUNITY

Hong Kong has tended to be neglected by sinologists because it lacks culture, because its spoken language is not standard Chinese but Cantonese, and because its official institutions are not Chinese but colonial. This neglect is founded partly on attitudes among Chinese intellectuals, but it is fundamentally misconceived. Generation by generation, individual localities in China have expanded their society and economy, have generated their own communities, and have made their contribution to humanity measured in centuries of time and millions of people. Hong Kong is one of the latest of these; here the root-stock of the Chinese people has once again burst into luxuriant growth, exceptional in drawing nourishment and stability from the world outside China, and individual in preserving and developing many features of the older civilization of working-class people in southern China—in this respect true to its historic inheritance. Hong Kong is not rich in Chinese culture, but it is rich in Chinese civilization. For this reason alone—the demonstration that a Chinese community can attain greatness without dependence on the historic impedimenta of Chinese culture—the study of Hong Kong ought to commend itself to sinologists with special force. Material civilization in Hong Kong today, especially in terms of density, diversity and organization, and above all in the restaurants, of whatever social class, is what is repeatedly brought to mind by the detail recorded of the imperial capital, Hangchow, towards the end of the thirteenth century.[14]

The achievements of Hong Kong since 1945 have been remarkable. Since 1945 she has absorbed a million immigrants, preserved administrative efficiency and civil peace, and maintained a practical liberalism which includes freedom of speech and the press and tolerance of people of all races. She has generated economic growth with the force of a pressure-cooker. She has built a big-scale, modern industrial economy with a speed, thoroughness and effectiveness which parallel and rival the bigger, but in some ways easier, achievement of Meiji Japan. On this basis, she has created steadily rising real incomes among the mass of the people, and has brought living standards in the city to within striking distance of those of Japan and Europe. The government has continued to interfere remarkably little with the day-to-day economic and social life of the people, but it has engaged in physical construction—in housing and in reclamation and the creation of new land—on a scale exceptional by any standards.

All this reflects the highest credit on the people and government of the city. No other city has achieved more since 1945 than has Hong Kong; indeed, where in these years Hong Kong has risen to greatness, some other great cities as far apart in space and spirit as Calcutta and New York have fallen into sickness which may well be mortal. Achievements once made are surprisingly easy to take for granted, especially by people who did not share the tremendous burden of work which created them, as some facile Western criticisms of Hong Kong show. In Hong Kong itself, in all parts of the community, the scale of the city's achievements is the foundation of a healthy self-respect. Even among the many other remarkable achievements of Chinese people since the Pacific war, contemporary Hong Kong takes an honourable place—perhaps a distinguished one.

To be sure, Hong Kong has faults. Western critics particularly identify the lack of democratic participation in public affairs,[15] the unequal distribution of wealth, the slow pace of improvement of social welfare provision for the poor and weak, the inadequacies of the school system and the slow growth and poor performance of trade unions in industry. They might add, from a Western standpoint, philistinism and the characteristic emptiness of the use of leisure.

The list of Hong Kong's faults as seen by the Chinese community is surprisingly different from this. Crime stands at the head of it. Robbery with more or less violence, in the street, in lifts or at home, is common and is believed to be extremely common; very probably as much as half of such crime goes unreported to the police because the police enjoy little trust among the people. Gangs of young hoodlums form black societies,[16] different from the older protection societies and with much less predictable behaviour. Corruption, especially small-scale and local corruption in relations between the police and the public, now occupies second place on the list, rather than first, because it is generally believed that at the institution of the new Independent Commission against Corruption, which invites anonymous accusations, has already reduced its extent significantly. Corruption continues to be greatly resented. People also resent the protection societies, and many bitterly criticize the whole system of dealing through personal relationships. Many people criticize materialism in the community; many criticize the failure to practise Confucian virtue (or any other kind of virtue); many deplore the lack of Chinese culture (or any other sort of culture); many criticize the dirt, litter and bad language in the streets and the intensity of physical congestion. Chinese people's criticisms are often criticisms of the community, as much as or more than they are criticisms of the institutions. The most usual ground of criticism of the institutions among ordinary Chinese people is the belief that the government invests surplus revenue in London to the advantage of Britain.

An obvious rationale for the marked differences between characteristic views of Western spectators and Chinese actors in the Hong Kong drama is that in the present phase of rapid physical transition in the city, accompanied by rather less rapid social and intellectual change, Hong Kong is still too much East Asian in style, socially still too much based on analogies with the family, to escape strong Western criticism for that reason, whilst at the same time it is too free from old-style (or new-style) Chinese obligation, too atomized and too Western, to satisfy Chinese people.

But Chinese people's disenchantment with Hong Kong goes deeper than this. For many of them, there is a sad and incurable sickness at the heart of the community. At one level this sickness is represented by the corruption, dirt and other visible faults of the city; but its ultimate causes are otherwise. Hong Kong is a Chinese city which is not within China. The sickness arises from the existence of the frontier which separates the Chinese people of the city from the world to which they belong, the limitless reality of China.

The relevance of this in real terms is both much deeper, and much less immediate and political, than is usually thought in the West. Not many Hong Kong people would like to live in mainland China at present, because life there is hard, material standards of living are low and material rewards for enterprise scanty, and there is far too much politics. Few people in the city hope for a speedy reunion with China, even though there is general respect for the achievements of the People's Government in physical construction and in making China peaceful, stable and powerful again, after a century of incompetence and impotence. Neither of these kinds of pragmatic consideration has much to do with the sense of alienation from China. Realistically, Hong Kong people recognize that they get a better deal as individuals, members of families and citizens from Hong Kong than from any likely Chinese government, but they cannot suppress a sense of alienation from, and disloyalty towards, the whole community of Chinese people in mainland China. The people do not shake off, or even wish to shake off, the commitment of loyalty to China—loyalty not primarily or mainly to the Chinese government, but to the mainland community. All this means that the commitment of loyalty would survive much worse governments than that at present in power in Peking, and much better social systems than that at present operating in Hong Kong. But it also means that before the commitment of loyalty begins to nourish a practical demand for reunion with China, conditions for working people in China will have to be very much better than they are at present, or conditions in Hong Kong very much worse.

By northern, metropolitan Chinese standards, which judge Chekiang and Canton strange, Hong Kong is the most unorthodox corner of an unorthodox province, a city founded by foreigners dealing with boat-people and émigrés—in the jargon of modern Hong Kong, from top to bottom no more than a tolerated structure. But by the standards of more distant overseas Chinese communities, with their loose grasp of Chinese habit and their adoption of foreign languages, Hong Kong, with its tremendous consumption of printed Chinese, its commitment to Chinese custom, and its vast recent influx of mainland-born people from all parts of China, is profoundly, almost unbearably, Chinese. However, the people do not easily accept this view. There is a widespread popular idea in the city that Hong Kong people have become un-Chinese through association with foreigners and using foreign innovations—this in spite of the fact that the overwhelming majority of the people never speak to a foreigner and seldom see one. To some extent this notion depends on a romantic anti-modern idea of what is Chinese, so that a paddy-farmer is thought *ipso facto* more Chinese than a bus-driver. But in this respect as in others, what is really at issue is less the adoption of non-traditional habits and jobs, which is commonplace in mainland China itself, than the sense that outside China a Chinese person cannot be complete.

1 A full 'Table of Shipping, Migration and Population' for 1841–1930 was published in *Historical and Statistical Abstracts of the Colony of Hong Kong, 1841–1930* (Hong Kong, 1932). It is reprinted in G.B. Endacott, *An eastern entrepot* (London, HMSO, Overseas research publication No. 4, 1964), document 26, pp. 132–4.

2 Census and Statistics Department, *Hong Kong Statistics, 1947–1967* (Hong Kong, 1969), Table 2.3, p. 15.

3 E. Szczepanik, *The economic growth of Hong Kong* (London, 1958), p. 25.

4 *Housing Board Report,* 1970. Chart and map, pp. 40–1.

5 The best short account of the Hong Kong economy is a paper by E.H. Phelps Brown, 'The Hong Kong economy; achievements and prospects', in Keith Hopkins (ed.), *Hong Kong: the industrial colony* (Hong Kong, 1971). A number of other valuable papers in the same volume relate to aspects of the Hong Kong economy—e.g. D. Podmore, 'The population of Hong Kong', and N.C. Owen, 'Economic policy'.

6 *Hong Kong 1974. Report for the year 1973* (Hong Kong, 1974), Appendix 4, pp. 220–2. The same relationships obtained in 1971 and 1972.

7 Labour Department, 'Number of employees in non-industrial establishments by districts', unpublished tables, May 1971. This imbalance is slowly correcting itself—in 1974 the percentage figures were 25 per cent and 75 per cent—ibid., May 1974.

8 E. Szczepanik, op. cit., pp. 142–3, cf. pp. 133–43 and Tables 42 and 43 on pp. 177–8.

9 Until the 1960s, it was usual in official publications to under-represent the industrial economy to an acute degree, partly no doubt because these were primarily reports on the activities of the government. But many writers have followed the official lead in this respect.

10 T'ang Chien-Hsün in *Tsui-hsin Hsiang-Kang chin-nan (Latest Hong Kong Guide),* (Hong Kong, 1950), p. 31, credits Hong Kong industry with a 'flying leap' after 1937. Among Western writers. G.C. Allen (*Cambridge economic history of Europe*, Vol. vi, p. 907) is exceptional in recognizing the force of this expansion after 1937. More detail on these and related points may be found in the author's paper, 'The earlier industrialisation of Hong Kong', in *Modern Asian studies*, 9 (3), (1975).

11 *Blue Book*, 1846. London, Public Record Office, C.O. 133/3. These remarks were repeated in subsequent years.

12 Ibid., pp. 139–41. This would not preclude people from living in these properties.

13 The best brief survey of the urban geography of Hong Kong is D.J. Dwyer: 'Problems

of urbanisation. The example of Hong Kong', in Institute of British Geographers, *Special publication no. 1, Sir Dudley Stamp memorial volume,* 1958, Chapter 12.

14 The best study of the remarkable contemporary Chinese accounts of Hangchow as the capital of the southern Sung is E. Balazs, 'Marco Polo in the capital of China', in his *Chinese civilisation and bureaucracy* (New Haven, 1964).

15 Cf. John Rear, 'One brand of politics', in Keith Hopkins (ed.), op. cit.

16 'Black societies' exactly translates the local term for these organizations. 'Secret societies' are regarded as more public and political in purpose. Similar criminal and semi-criminal organizations exist in Japanese cities.

2 The Buildings of the City

THE COMMUNITY AND THE BUILDINGS

HONG KONG's political and social position is so exceptional, and its economic and social history has been so individual, that it is not surprising to find the city full of its own peculiar institutions. Among these institutions is the corpus of Hong Kong building tradition and practice—neither Western nor Chinese, but rich in elements taken from both China and the West.

Hong Kong has seven main kinds of urban building. These are: the tenements, of various ages and styles (of which both halves of the city apart from Central District almost wholly consisted in 1955); the mixed commercial-residential blocks which were their characteristic replacement, especially after 1955; the various kinds of government housing built from 1954 onwards; the factory buildings, also of many kinds, mostly private enterprises but supplemented by government building; the office or combined office and shop buildings of Central District and in recent years of other districts too; the residential apartment blocks, old and new, with or without ground-floor service businesses, which are typical of the good residential sections; and various kinds of temporary structures such as squatter hutments and factories.

Building has been incessant since the Pacific war, but growth ever since the war has been so rapid and on so great a scale that the demand for new property has been insatiable. At the same time, changes in style, use and scale of the buildings are so rapid that buildings are obsolete within a generation, or in extreme cases within a decade, whilst use of property is so intensive, and maintenance often so lax, that buildings are in any case worn out within the same space of time. There is no attempt to preserve old buildings for their own sake, apart from a few official and temple buildings.

In these conditions, the present physical form of the buildings represents, primarily, a stage in the vast programme of rebuilding, intensification of use, and physical expansion of the built-up area, which has been, with immigration and industrialization, the central experience of the city during the past generation.

The limited range of kinds of buildings to be seen in the Hong Kong streets arises partly from the shortness of the local time-scale and the narrowness of the local building tradition. But most of all it arises from the pressure of government control. The fundamental instrument of this control has been since 1856 the Buildings Ordinance of the time. The present Ordinance is the 1966 revision of the Ordinance of 1955, a stout volume of some 260 pages all told. In recent years, moreover, the Buildings Ordinances have been increasingly supplemented in practice by various limitations imposed on development at the time of lease of the sites. In areas where official zoning plans have been finalized, these limitations reflect the zoning proposed in the plan. These phases of government activity have imposed important successive changes on the urban landscape. For instance, many lots leased in the inter-war years carried a condition limiting the height of building to 35 feet.[1] The Ordinance of 1955 allowed a much greater volume of building on a site: 'most of the changes are dictated by the advance of the science of building since the last Buildings Ordinance'.[2] But in 1963, 'these new regulations (of 1962, fully operative in 1966) will control development from a plot ratio and site coverage aspect rather than the existing concept of volume, which has led to over-development in some cases'.[3] It is this Ordinance which is now in force.

It is hard to over-estimate the extent of physical control exercised by the government in the appearance and layout of the streets and buildings. All land (apart from some church and temple sites) is owned by the government. Since the early days of the colony, land has been obtained from the government by private people by the purchase of leases. Public auctions of both new and expired leases now take place at intervals, at sales in which all the proceedings are conducted in both English and Cantonese.

A lessee must pay a crown rent assessed according to the district of the city, and he must accept the conditions on which his lease is granted. Some early leases were for 999 years, but leases are now generally granted either for the remaining part of the lease of the New Territories from China (in New Kowloon) or for 75 years (in Old Kowloon and on the island). The depths, widths, ground cover ratios, safety conditions and heights of permanent buildings are all strictly controlled by the government, and have been so, generally speaking, throughout this century.[4] These regulations apply to buildings in general. Conditions of lease imposed by the government in respect of an individual site may include specification of a relatively short period of time during which a building must be constructed (this kind of condition has a long history), specification of a minimum value and maximum height for the building, specification of conditions of access related to the site, and specification of kind of use. All these specifications are binding upon the lessee, and of course all are advertised at the time of the auction.

All these conditions of building are aspects of the formidable legal authority which the Hong Kong government can and does exercise in the management of the form of the city. This is one side of a central paradox. At the same time, the city is crammed with anomalous and often illegal activities and situations which the government does not usually challenge, many of them involving land use. Land surrounding the government's resettlement buildings is commonly packed with hawkers, sometimes to the extent that the roofs of hawkers' stalls form a complete cover between the blocks (Plate 28). Some streets, especially in Yaumati and Mongkok, are virtually blocked by hawkers. Most of the cooked-food-stall restaurants encroach illegally on street space. This is the other side of the paradox. In principle, Hong Kong is a planners' dream: a dense community with abundant public transport, much of it by water, an outdoor climate, rising standards and a strong and stable government with virtually total control over land and property, and a formidable amount of experience in both major engineering projects and public housing. But in practice, planning, apart from building and engineering, is weak. This is partly because of old leases and old buildings, the size of the physical inheritance of unplanned makeshift arrangements from the years of most acute crowding in the 1950s and earlier, physical congestion generally, and the density and diversity of the people's use of both buildings and streets, even in many new areas. It is also partly because thirty years of physical growth, much of it the direct responsibility of the government, has stretched government resources to the limit over long periods of time, and because the people neither welcome, nor perhaps need, much bureaucratic interference with their daily lives.

Yet a reform principle, as well as a construction principle, can be detected in administrative action by the government in recent years, though it has not been propounded in general terms. It might be called the principle of the separation of uses. It aims at a patient piecemeal unravelling of the tangled tight skein of property and street uses in the city. New leases are granted under limitations relating to property use, such as limitation to office or industrial uses only. Hawkers are removed from streets and forecourts to new bazaars. Control of uses in government housing and all new property is increasingly strict. Dirty and space-consuming industries are removed from the city to distant sites. Policies of this kind have a long history in western cities. In Hong Kong they are relatively new, and on the local scale particularly they lead away from the style of land use and property use preferred up to now by the people. The 'natural' human landscape in Hong Kong is diverse, small in scale, mixed and varied in function and style; it seeks to unite diversity with specialization in one spot; it minimizes travelling and maximizes the versatility of the individual locality; it scorns no economic opportunity, whatever its shape, size, content and implications; multiplicity of uses is central to it; its hallways are shops or kitchens, its staircases stores, its alleys sculleries; its kitchens are passageways and its flats factories; its factories double as sleeping and eating places, its shops as dining-rooms, and its pavements as shops or workshops. It is a landscape based fairly and squarely upon personal relationships, good and bad, among the people; a landscape of human symbiosis. All this has yet to be harmonized with the orderliness, hygiene and expense of the separation of uses.

The government makes haste slowly in these matters. Where the hawkers and squatters are concerned, it insists that illegal uses, though in many cases expressly tolerated, and in many others tolerated without comment, are strictly temporary. Uses will be regularized on a proper and humane basis, the argument runs, when the government has the resources to act in a given case. In privately owned buildings, little by little, incompatible uses (such as knitting factories or bean-curd factories in crowded residential blocks) are suppressed, as leases fall in and specific administrative actions are taken. In the hawker streets and public housing estates, hawkers are removed to planned bazaar areas. At the same time, rising standards are likely to generate demand for tidiness and to weaken the economic arguments for excessive densities and incongruities of use. At present, except in Central District, to some extent the sub-centres such as Sheung Wan, and the most western-style suburbs, there is very little present sign or future prospect of much genuine separation of uses, or any significant relaxation of densities except to some extent within flats. No attempt is made, or could realistically be made, to predict how far these policies might go in the future in an old working-class district like Yaumati, or how fast, except in sectors like the markets which fall under direct government control. On these points, the future must be allowed to speak for itself.

THE BUILDING TRADITION

Until the middle 1960s, the typical building in Hong Kong was the three-floor or four-floor tenement. These are the buildings with which Hong Kong grew up and came to maturity; they are those which bore the brunt of the staggering housing shortage of the 1950s, and they are those in which the first steps were taken in the transformation of the city into a mature manufacturing community. In some parts of the city, especially Sheung Wan, tenements in the style of the turn of the century still constitute a substantial minority of the buildings. (Plates 1, 5.)[5]

H.R. Butters wrote in 1935:

> The old-fashioned, but still the most common type of Chinese tenement house is of three or four storeys, often with a shop on the ground floor. The length (i.e. the depth) is about 43′ 6″ and the breadth (i.e. the frontage), which is determined by the length of the China fir pole, about 13′6″. The height of the flats might be 13′ but this is frequently utilized to erect a cockloft over part of the floor. Such a flat might be likened to a pigeon hole with an open verandah, windows between the verandah and the flat proper and the other end blocked by a kitchen but with a window in the corner over a covered yard. It is frequently let to a principal tenant who occupies a portion of the flat and sub-lets the remainder in cubicles to as many individuals or families as he or she can crowd in. A flat in normal times may have as many as twenty-five adults stowed away in cubicles, bedspaces and cocklofts, and the population is at present swollen with an addition of twenty-five to fifty per cent, (that is, of refugees), accommodated in existing houses.[6]

These tenements represent the physical, social and intellectual foundation of contemporary housing in Hong Kong. They are also still a significant part of the housing stock, though fast diminishing in numbers.

The essence of the tenement tradition was and is three-fold: first, that the standard property-managing unit was the individual floor of a building, reached by a common stair; second, that each floor could be divided up by party walls which were not part of the structure of the building;—this is the fundamental of *t'ang-lou* building, and it will be discussed at greater length in due course; and third, that the resultant cubicles could be let separately to individuals, family groups or even business users, who would have the use of the common stair, kitchen and (later) lavatory. The standard form of the tenement floor was in the first decades of this century, and on thousands of tenement floors up to the present in Hong Kong still is, of one of the kinds which are illustrated in this context in the *Report of the Housing Commission* of 1935 (Figure 3). As the *Report* shows, the style of tenement floors changed considerably for the better after 1902 as a result of the provisions of the Buildings Ordinance of that year; but from the standpoint of the present discussion the difference between the two styles is not marked.[7] Nor is there very much difference, in this context, between these two types of tenement and those brought in during the 1930s, with essentially the same kind of layout, but with improved staircase and kitchen, with improved access and ventilation at the rear, and a lavatory on each floor.[8]

From both social and hygienic standpoints, the tenement type of building has little to commend it, except where the whole floor, or the whole flat, is occupied as a unit. Cubicle partitions are made of wood, and occupy 8 or 9 feet of the 10 or 12 feet between floor and ceiling. Wire mesh, to prevent theft, may be fixed above the partition walls. No cubicles except those at the front receive any direct light or ventilation; and light and ventilation are in direct competition with domestic privacy. Nothing is ever painted, and there is little or no fundamental cleaning. The oldest tenements, which are also those which are most subdivided, have open joists and boards for ceilings, and the top ceiling is simply the roof. Cubicles are often furnished with bunk beds of two or three tiers, which add to the level of crowding resulting from the system. Cocklofts (as shown in the plan) may be fixed to any part of the whole structure, usually providing single bed-spaces. Tenants of cubicles cook their food in the common kitchen where each family has a charcoal stove, and they eat in the cubicles. To escape vermin, food may be stored in a small meat-safe hanging from the ceiling, but many Hong Kong people shop separately for food for each meal. Life in cubicles is one factor which drives Hong Kong people to live in public, in the streets and in restaurants. The cost of eating in restaurants and sharing the life of the streets is equally a factor which predisposes people not to spend more on housing.

Privacy for the individual family, cleanliness, the proper management of children, and the self-respect of the household, are all made difficult to attain and sometimes impossible of attainment in these conditions, although hundreds of thousands of solid, self-respecting Chinese people have been brought up through childhood in such cubicles in Hong Kong—and in China. The magnitude of the achievement of the public housing

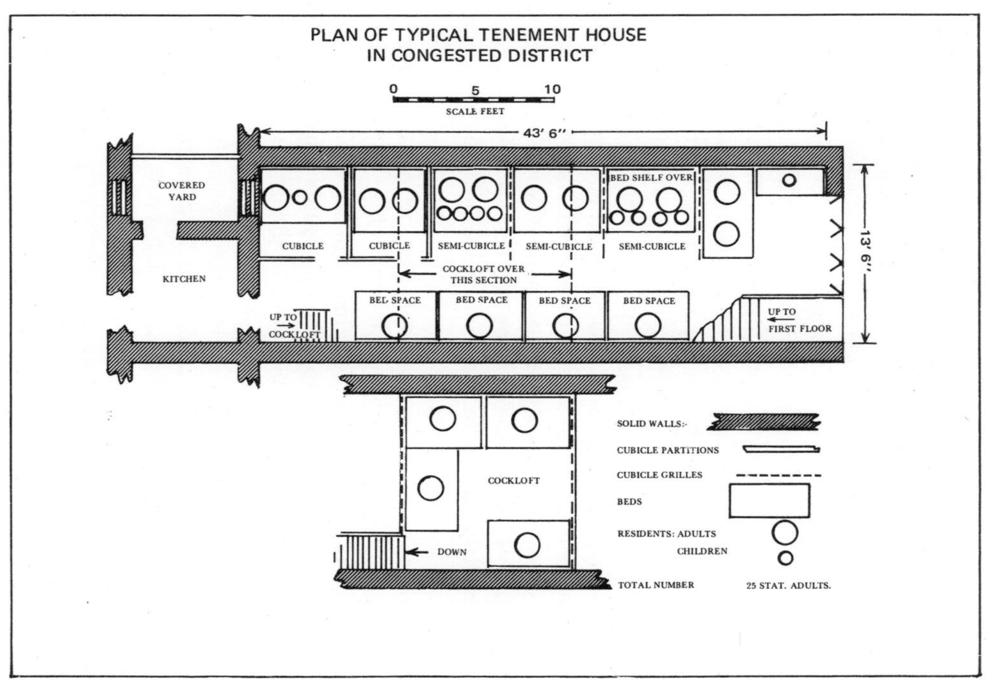

FIGURE 3

PLAN OF A TYPICAL TENEMENT HOUSE IN CONGESTED DISTRICT (1935, BUILT BEFORE 1903)

Source: Reproduced from the *Report of the Housing Commission*, 1935.

programme in the city has to be assessed in the dim light of the average tenement cubicle.

After the Pacific war, tenements were still built, sometimes with shoddy materials and poor workmanship, dodging the official regulations in the disturbed conditions of the times. When the new Buildings Ordinance was brought in in 1955, more ambitious building became feasible. (Figure 4, Plate 18.) The new buildings usually occupied the sites of four or more of the old tenements, and the property-owning and property-managing unit became not the floor, but the individual flat, usually of area roughly equal to that of the tenement floor which it replaced. Access now was by corridors, rather than stairs at each address. Load-bearing brick walls and wooden floors finally gave place about this time to reinforced concrete construction, and wooden window-frames to metal. The new technical capacity, and new legal freedom to build very big blocks, coupled with an acute state of overcrowding in all kinds of accommodation and a tradition of high rents and high densities of use, led to abuses which were convincingly described in a government paper of 1963:[9]

> Conditions in the speculatively built modern tenement blocks are often as bad or worse than those in pre-war tenement slums or many squatter shacks. Faced with an initial heavy outlay of key money and with maximum rents, and encouraged by the mounting demand by others for accommodation, the new occupant of premises designed to comply only with the minimum Buildings Regulations requirements partitions off these premises, if the landlord has not already done so, into cubicles with even less light and ventilation than they had to start with. Or he may not put up partitions: it is not unknown for 60 to 70 persons to be living in a three-room flat.

Blocks of this kind became a special and characteristic feature of parts of Togwawan, Cheungshawan and Hunghom, all industrial districts, and also of the tourist centre of Tsimshatsui. Under the 1955 Ordinance, a building with less than ten floors was not required to have a lift, and many big blocks were built with nine floors. Many buildings were built still in basic tenement form with a common stair for each address and usually a back stair as well, also for common use. Others were built with access to each address through a corridor, often open on one side, on each floor. This last arrangement is fundamentally akin to that of the government Mark I resettlement blocks of the same vintage.

The phase of building representing the 1955 Ordinance lasted for a decade. The new regulations of 1966, which came into force in stages from 1963 to 1966, are represented by buildings which are either high or dense, but not both, and are in consequence much better ventilated, which are better provided with lifts, and which if high are generally arranged on a kind of hallway principle, with flats opening from a central cluster of lift-shafts and stairways, rather than a corridor principle. (Figure 5, Plate 4.) Building on square or nearly square sites, rather than on the old deep, narrow sites of the tenements, has had much to do with this change.[10] During the later 1960s, the government also increasingly brought in conditions limiting the kinds of use to be permitted in buildings for which leases were granted, though they do not (apart from factory and related legislation) control density of use in private flats. These bodies of law and administrative practice are what limit the builders and developers today. Building under them has already added its quota to the city's inheritance of physical construction and administrative and technical experience. Rising standards in the community have contributed to improvements in finish and style in new building. The Multi-Storey Buildings (Owners' Incorporation) Ordinance of 1970 enables owners in multi-storey buildings to form organizations for managing the common parts of buildings, and to require all owners to contribute to the costs.[11] This ordinance has contributed very much to increased cleanliness.

Buildings of all the kinds which have been discussed are generally *t'ang-lou,* Chinese-style buildings. The essential feature of *t'ang-lou,* as opposed to *yang-lou,* foreign-style buildings, is that the internal partition walls of the building unit are not part of the original fabric. The old-style tenements constitute one standard kind of *t'ang-lou,* and formerly almost the only kind. The *t'ang-lou* tradition has displayed great vitality in the city, and so has the system of renting out house-room in cubicle form. Each has drawn sustenance from the other. *T'ang-lou* building, for better or worse, is one of the foundations of Hong Kong life for the working people, both in physical and in social terms. It is also one of the principal ways in which the city displays direct continuity with the past before the Pacific war.

T'ang-lou building and building use has enabled generations of Hong Kong people to make money out of their houses; it has stood to perpetuate the high rents which have always been typical of Hong Kong, and at the same time the high densities of all kinds of land use and property use. Until the 1960s, the public housing of the decade of the 1950s alone offered to working-class people of the city a kind of accommodation in which a family was freed from the necessity of choice between being either exploiting tenant or exploited sub-tenant.

The system of commercial exploitation of house-property is very old. The valuations of property which are recorded in the earlier registers of rateable values shows that a high proportion of properties in working-class streets, occupied by 'chair coolies', 'washermen' and the like, were valued at figures of the order of $150, that is, one-third, or even one-half, of the figures for shop properties with good addresses.[12] Valuations below $50 occurred only in the physical peripheries, to east and west. Rents of the kind which underlie these high valuations for working-class property could only be paid through letting to lodgers. It is clear that not only the rich were profiting from this system of exploitation; it went right through the community, as it does at the present time. At bottom, what it subserved was Hong Kong as a community of transients, making money and getting out. It is one of the things which tends to make contemporary Hong Kong a community of *rentiers*, making money and staying put.

Up to the 1960s, the complex of uses and relationships represented by *t'ang-lou* building and the renting of cubicles preserved every mark of

FIGURE 4

APARTMENT FLOOR, CORRIDOR PLAN

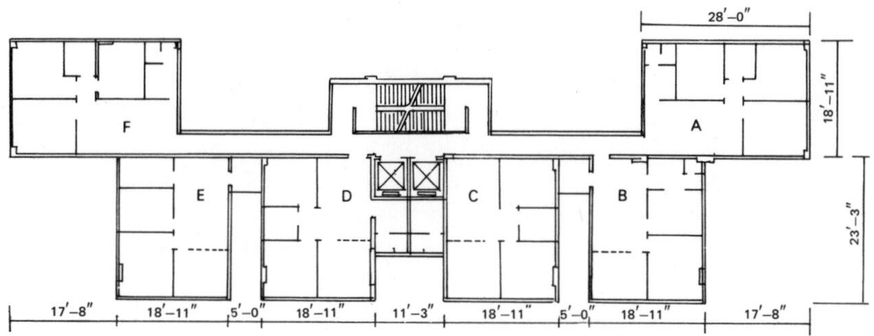

FIGURE 5

APARTMENT FLOOR, HALLWAY PLAN

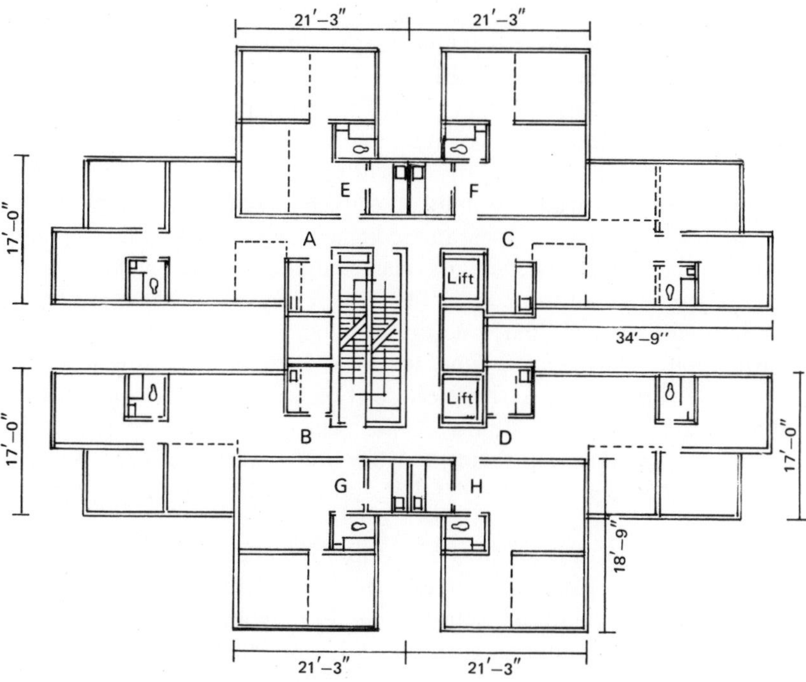

Note: Plans of apartment floors taken from recent advertisements of flats for sale. These blocks have been built under the present Buildings Ordinance. The corridor plan (Fig. 4) resembles some plans which were used under the 1955 Ordinance, though usually for much bigger buildings. The hallway plan (Fig. 5) is representative of those most used today. Both plans give indications of interior walls which are left for the first owner or tenant to build, on *t'ang-lou* principles.

social viability. To a great extent it does so up to the present, though it has now at last begun to crumble. The system readily fits the needs of the man who changes his job and would like to minimize the journey to work; of the man who spends little time at home and likes to live as cheaply as possible in a busy district with many restaurants and plenty of social life; and of many kinds of business where according to circumstances employees, especially unmarried men, are allowed space at work to live in. Earlier, the system was adapted to the needs of the immigrant looking for lodgings to rent. The arrangement could be adapted to accommodate offices and hotels.[13] It clearly suited those who profited from the high rents. It enabled sub-tenants, living close to the centre of a great city with a high-rent system, to occupy minimal accommodation at rents which although high, could be reckoned within their means, as complete flats certainly could not; and this remarkable achievement of the system is the main source of its vitality to the present. The subdivision principle tended to nourish itself, since dense crowding in family cubicles encouraged unmarried sons to move to bed-spaces close to their jobs, and the availability of cubicles within the family flat enabled married sons to remain at home. The system represents versatility, as well as high densities and low standards.

During the 1960s, the older tenement tradition began to give way to a style of building which was still usually *t'ang-lou* in the sense that the inner walls of the unit were not part of the structure, but was otherwise radically new. Buildings were coming into use which were tall, often with more than ten floors; which always had lifts; and which were often roughly square in plan, arranged internally on neither staircases nor corridors but on a hallway plan. Their appearance coincided with a new willingness and ability on the part of lower-middle-class people to buy their flats, usually with the help of a loan from one of the Chinese banks, and at the same time to adopt the principle that one family ought to occupy one complete housing unit.[14] At the same time, there has been an increasing tendency for new flats to be built in the Western style, with fixed interior walls. In 1965–71, an average of almost 70 per cent of new private residential building was in *t'ang-lou* form, and the rest in Western style; but this figure fell to 50 per cent in 1970–1,[15] and has since certainly continued to fall.

There are important features of continuity between *t'ang-lou* flats on the newer hallway plans, and the old tenements. Many people still build cubicles and let them on a business basis. The layout of the newer flats is less conducive to an internal corridor plan for cubicles than were the old tenement floors, but some owners and tenants nevertheless contrive to cram cubicles into their flats. Many people whose uses are purely domestic also have need of many rooms. In these circumstances, forms of partition of the newer kind of *t'ang-lou* are numberless: and the proportion of them in which the main living-room has unimpeded access to a window is perhaps not more than half. It is common to erect partitions, solid, partly louvred, or partly made of glass, cutting off extra rooms until the main room used for eating, sitting, watching television and playing mah-jong is no more than a 10-feet square space surrounded by various special rooms. Flats of this kind are called in newspaper advertisements *yang-shih t'ang-lou*, foreign-style Chinese buildings. They form a continuum with the 'completely independent small flats', not least because flats in the newer Western style, with fixed interior walls, may also be further sub-divided like *t'ang-lou* as need arises.

It is also still quite common for an owner or tenant in this kind of block to open a small factory. A flat occupied by a factory or a group of sub-tenants pays no more rent or rates than one occupied by a family; apart from personal pressure by neighbours, and the unlikely event of interference by the Fire Department, there is nothing to stop anyone from running an unregistered factory in any place, at least until it attracts the attention of the Labour Department.

Even if the flat is not being fitted with cubicles, it still remains for the first occupant in the new-style *t'ang-lou* to have the interior walls built. This is in many ways a very sensible and convenient arrangement, though it can lead to all kinds of structural oddities. Subsequent owners or tenants can alter the internal arrangements of the flat if they so wish and if they have the money to spend.[16]

Two factors united in the 1960s to take some of the pressure off the tenements. One was the ever-growing stock of public housing; the other, the increasing willingness and ability of families, especially the younger generation of parents, to pay for a self-contained flat without lodgers. The extreme congestion of the 1950s has gone; the joke about eight-people-to-one-bed has at last become laughable. Figures higher than Butter's of 30 to 40 adults living on a tenement floor can still be found on big floors in Western District, where 50 people to a floor is said to be the maximum.[17] They can also be found in tenements where bed-spaces are let to single men, but figures of this kind are increasingly becoming exceptional. The usual number of people living on a standard tenement floor or in a sub-tenanted flat of equivalent size is now about 12 or 15—rarely less than 8 or 10; rarely more than about 22. In fact, in housing as in other respects, Hong Kong has survived the hardest times and has now begun to relax. People who have flats with cubicles are beginning to take down some of the partitions, to give up lodgers, and to occupy the space themselves. Even in the tenements, standards of housing have begun to rise, however slowly.

But if the big problems are solved or approaching solution, for many ordinary people, the smaller ones remain. Newspaper articles[18] give realistic advice to purchasers of flats, especially people who purchase flats before they are finished, or even before they are started. They are advised to satisfy themselves about the conditions of the lease of the site and about many characteristic details including the conditions for the use of public space such as the roof (often used for drying washing), whether business owners are allowed to erect neon signs or to pile merchandise on the stairs, and whether the sanitary water comes from a well (wells often dry up in the winter) or from the sea. As one author points out, if a building deteriorates, the value of the individual properties falls.

Articles of this kind may well be pointers to fundamental changes going on in the public mind on the whole subject of property use. If so, the government's attitude to the separation of uses during recent years will be handsomely vindicated.

INVESTMENT AND BUILDING

A developer purchases a lease either at auction from the Crown (that is, from the Hong Kong government) or from an earlier leaseholder, borrows and builds, and sells the units which he has built. The typical source of capital for a developer is one of the Chinese banks. In contemporary Hong Kong, a developer can reasonably expect to take his profit and get his capital back within three or four years if all goes well; certainly within much less than ten years. The properties are finally bought as residences, business places or investments, mainly by Hong Kong people of all kinds. For some years, better returns on capital have been had from commercial and residential buildings than from industrial.

A small property which is ripe for redevelopment is usually put by the lessee into the hands of a property broker, whose business is to find a purchaser for the building and the lease. Sometimes the construction company which buys such a lease pays for it in the form of a proportion—10, 20, 30 or more per cent—of the new flats. Bigger owners may well redevelop for themselves, but small owners lack capital and expertise, and are usually glad to sell out, particularly if their properties fall within the government's rent control regulations on pre-war residential property.

The following are hypothetical figures for typical development situations of moderate size and customary conditions.[19]

A COMMERCIAL/RESIDENTIAL BUILDING

This is envisaged as a standard building in an old developed area such as Mongkok.

Building:-			$ thou.
	Land	5,000 sq. ft. at $400 per sq. ft.[20]	2,000
	Building	Ten floors; five units of 450 sq. ft. per floor on the upper floors,[21] ground floor as shops.[22]	
		Ground floor: 5,000 sq. ft. × 14½ ft. high.	
		Gives 72,500 cu. ft.	
		Upper floors 9 floors at 2,600 (52 % proportion) sq. ft. × 9½ ft. high, this gives 222,300 cu. ft.	
		In all, 294,800 cu. ft.	
		say 300,000 cu. ft., at $3.60 per cu. ft.	1,080
	Piling		170
	Lifts		150
	Bank Interest (on half the capital)		300
	Incidentals		100
		Total Investment	$ 3,800

Selling:- A flat of the kind envisaged here, in an area such as Mongkok, sells for about $45,000.

		$ thou.
There are 45 flats, selling for		2,025
The shops are worth (say)		2,700
	Total	$ 4,725

The developer makes $925,000, on the basis of these figures. The whole work, from the time of lease of the land, may well take no more than two years. In these conditions there is little incentive to the developer to rent the finished buildings, especially since in present conditions there is no sign of any slackening of demand for flats to buy, and abundant evidence that purchase of flats as investments is both expanding in general and becoming increasingly common among working-class people. The cost of the site represents about half of the cost of the building—a high proportion.

A FACTORY BUILDING

Building:-

		$ thou.
Land	10,000 sq. ft. at $100 per sq. ft.	1,000
Building	A typical building of 10 floors,[23] cover of 8,500 sq. ft. 8,500 sq. ft. × 120 ft. high is 1,020,000 cu. ft. At $2.2 per cu. ft., this is	2,244
Piling		270
Lifts		200
Interest		300
Incidentals		100
	Total Investment	$ 4,114

Selling:-

		$ thou.
The 9 upper floors comprise 76,500 sq. ft. The standard price is (say) $52 per sq. ft. Hence		3,980
The ground floor has 8,500 sq. ft. sold at (say) $100 per sq. ft.		850
	Total	$ 4,830

Hence, the developer makes $716,000.

Figures for the development of 'garden lots'—high-class residential property on suburban sites—are much bigger in aggregate than these, and the rates of return are also much higher. This is partly because costs per square foot of built space are lower in garden lot development, and partly because selling prices per square foot are higher. Suburban property at present represents the main thrust in the development business.

Apart from the selling price of the lease and the crown rent—a kind of ground rent—the government may make one further charge on the lessee of a site. This is a charge raised when old expired leases are re-granted, sometimes but not always on improved conditions such as the lifting of the pre-war 35-feet height restriction. This regrant premium is in effect a development charge. Until 1973 it was assessed as half the increased value which the site had on regrant, a capital sum which could be paid in instalments; but in that year the regrant premium became an annual charge of 3 per cent of the rateable value of the property.[24]

RECLAMATION, SITE FORMATION AND THE SUPPLY OF LAND

It is natural to ask, what is the process by which land progresses from the 'raw' state—open hillside, or the sea bed—to the status of a building site? The process is generally simple. Lessees of hillside land who intend to build have to do their own job of levelling and providing access since the government provides only drainage facilities and access within the framework of its own engineering programme. The extent of levelling and other engineering work which has to be done by the builder is reflected in the price which the land fetches at auction, and so is its general location. Reclaimed land at the sea's edge is normally formed by both private and government dumping of rocks and builders' refuse, behind a sea-wall constructed by the government for the purpose of the reclamation; it must be remembered that the Hong Kong sea is usually perfectly calm. The reclaimed land is new crown land, and is either used by the government for its own purposes (like the site of the City Hall) or leased to developers in the usual way. Building on reclaimed land necessitates piling down into the sea-bed, which involves prior consideration of which parts of the area must be kept free of fill containing boulders.

Costs for the formation of building land on hillsides or by reclamation vary a good deal from place to place, but are not consistently higher for one kind of land than another. In either case, costs range from about $90,000 per acre to about $420,000, with global average figures for 1969–70 of $136,000 per acre expanded for works then completed, and $239,000 per acre estimated for works then planned.[25] The figure suggested by officials of the Crown Lands in 1971 was $6 per sq. ft., or $260,000 per acre, and for drains and roads, an additional cost of at least $6 per sq. ft. or $260,000 per acre. Hence, cost for the formation of land which is ready for lessees to prepare for building amount to upwards of $500,000 per acre, or at least $12 per sq. ft. A figure of $14 per sq. ft. was 'assumed' for the cost of land for resettlement building until 1970, when the figure was raised to $17 per sq. ft.[26] Costs in conditions of maximum difficulty are considerably more than this, but there is no evidence that they would reach more than about double these figures.

These figures bear little relation to the prices which sites fetched at auction in 1971. Standard former hillside land in the Kowloon suburbs rarely fell below $180 per sq. ft. ($7,840,000 per acre); the official upset price on such land at auction might be $100 per sq. ft. ($4,356,000 per acre). Inferior sites zoned for factory use, especially in peripheral areas like Kwuntong and Tsuen Wan, were cheaper, but not very much cheaper ($80, or as low as $50, per sq. ft., $3,485,000 or $2,178,000 per acre). The very best land—and some of that which is newly created comes into that category because of its central location—fetched prices upwards of $1,500 per sq. ft. ($65 million per acre) and usually of the order of $2,000 per sq. ft. Standard old developed land in congested districts like Sheung Wan and Yaumati usually carried an upset price, when old leases came up for re-sale, of about $250 per sq. ft. This figuring suggests that standard urban sites are leased by the government at prices which are never less than double the cost of creating them, and are usually ten or more times greater than cost—sometimes much more.

It is quite clear from these figures that although the physical creation and preparation of land constitutes a continuum of processes, the valuation of the same land in money terms displays continuity less with the engineering works than with the spectrum of uses.

The creation of land is a relatively cheap process. A wide gap yawns between the cost of land and its selling price. It is sometimes said that the government (which creates fresh land and offers any kind of fresh land for lease only at its own pace) restricts the supply of land so as to keep up prices at auction. The essence of the reply to this criticism has three points: first, that land can be made ready for leasing (in terms of access, planning and major engineering works) only at a limited speed; second, that if land were released at a rate sufficiently fast to bring down prices for a time, there is every reason to think that those who purchased the leases would have big profits to pocket, at the expense of subsequent would-be purchasers and the community; and third, that where all land is public property, all the income from sales of leases and other charges on land goes into the purse of the community, which has created the high values. All this applies with particular force to Victoria and Kowloon. It is true that in considering very big new developments like the new towns programme, the government has usually shown a degree of caution which, however reasonable at the time, has turned out to be excessive. Except in Kwuntong, Kwaichung and the big housing developments—and these are all big exceptions—the government has tended to follow public need in the provision of land, rather than anticipating it, and too much development has been encouraged in older areas, especially northern Kowloon. The government is moving, through the new towns programme, towards rectifying this weakness.

THE ECONOMICS OF THE TENEMENT FLOORS

In a post-war building in contemporary Kowloon, the owner of a flat pays about $800 per month in mortgage repayments and interest, plus rates (17 per cent of assessed rental) and electricity, water and probably telephone charges—in all, about $1,050. He lets three rooms, worth in all

$850, and keeps the main living-room and one bedroom for himself. He makes no profit in cash, but pays only $200 (the lowest rent for a cubicle if he were a sub-tenant) for the use of two good rooms, control of the whole flat including the right to invite his friends as he chooses, social position both inside the flat and in the building, the payment of his mortgage interest, and the rising capital value of the whole flat. In order to live and pay his share of the cost of the flat, this man must have a job or some other income from outside the flat.

If this man, or the tenant-in-chief of a similar flat, is living alone and is prepared to sleep in a bed-space or the smallest cubicle, he can let the remaining space for an additional $400, enabling the flat to pay for itself and giving him an income of $200 per month, sufficient to maintain one person completely.

Broadly speaking, relationships in roughly these proportions between necessary expenditure and income or potential income are those which operate throughout the world of sub-tenancies in the city. It is usually possible at any social level to sub-let cubicles or rooms in a flat at a differential sufficient to maintain one person who is not occupying a good room; but this is not the form which the system usually takes. Generally speaking, the most that the tenant-in-chief gets is his own accommodation rent-free, plus the social convenience and status of that position.[27] His advantage is not that he can show a profit at the end of the month, but that the alternative to letting rooms as tenant-in-chief is renting a room, at the same cost, as sub-tenant.

Rents paid by tenants-in-chief are normally fixed by contract for a short term of years: in the whole universe of tenement floors, fresh contracts are always being made, which reflect the behaviour and expected behaviour of sub-rents at the time, among other things. Much of the buoyancy in the system depends on tenants' exploitation of the differential between rises in rents, which are relatively slow, and rises in sub-rents, which are faster. This differential exists partly because sub-tenants come and go much more rapidly than tenants, and partly because tenants profit from rent control which in practice does not greatly affect sub-rents, although it is supposed to do so. Viewed charitably, the tenement system enables many people to increase their incomes by providing more or less centrally situated accommodation at rents which are by Hong Kong standards if not low, then at least practicable. Viewed less charitably, the system operates by creating and perpetuating vested interests in very low physical standards in housing. It contributes to the acutely high residential densities which are characteristic of the city, and also to the high levels of total congestion. Standard residential densities in working-class private accommodation have continued at about the same levels as those in public housing at high densities: in both, densities range from about 16 sq.ft. to about 35 sq.ft. per person, but private tenants pay much higher rents, not only per square foot, but also per liveable room. A family of five in a cubicle pays at least $250 per month (more probably $300–$350) for minimum accommodation, probably quite well situated.

The same family in a middle-vintage resettlement block would pay $28.50 to $34 per month for a room nearly twice the size, though with bus-fares and the trouble of daily travel to consider. The great strength of the cubicles, broadly speaking, is their central location. For the same reason, people tolerate the most acute overcrowding rather than leave the best-situated of the public estates such as Shek Kip Mei.[28]

Some additional examples will illustrate the diversity which the tenement system nourishes, though they add little to the principles by which it operates.[29]

A big tenement floor in a post-war corridor block in Taikoktsui is about 900 sq.ft. in area. There are six cubicles, housing about 25 people: in 1971 sub-rents amounted to about $700 per month. The tenant-in-chief then paid $320 in rent, plus $55 in rates, plus water, electricity and telephone charges—in all, about $500, leaving him about $200 in pocket, but very poorly housed. In the 1970s, rents and sub-rents have been rising rapidly. In the conditions of 1974, sub-rents for these cubicles are not less than $1,500 per month, and rent for the flat not less than $1,100—more probably $2,000 in sub-rents and $1,400 in rent for the flat, plus $300 in rates and other expenses. Obviously in these unstable conditions, the personal position of the tenant depends critically upon the maintenance of favourable differentials between sub-rents on the one hand, and rents and other costs on the other. In a good location in a good district, like King's Road in North Point, the tenant-in-chief of a post-war flat might pay $1,200 per month in 1974, with rents and services in addition—up to $1,600 in all. He can rent four rooms at about $400 per month each, accommodating 15–20 people, and live in a fifth rent-free. In a good district like Argyle Street, a tenant draws $880 in sub-rents, but pays $1,320 in rent, rates and other charges. In this case, he is in effect paying $440 for two big rooms and control over the whole flat; but the rent for the whole flat is now out of date, and may shortly rise dramatically.

In respect of post-war domestic premises, a limited degree of rent control was introduced by the government in 1970.[30] Rents for pre-war premises have been strictly controlled since 1945.[31] This legislation is supposed to protect sub-tenants as well as tenants, but is usually found to be ineffective in doing so. Recent rapid rises in all rents except those which are strictly controlled have greatly increased the amounts which can be made from sub-letting in pre-war properties. Big tenement floors in Sheung Wan may well house as many as 40 people. The lowest rent is $40 per person, giving an income to the tenant-in-chief of the order of $1,600 per month, against controlled rent of about $100 per month.[32] Pre-war flats of this kind have long changed hands among owners and tenants-in-chief with the help of tea-money. They are mostly of the kind represented in Figure 3, and they are now, of course, very old-fashioned and usually rather squalid. Many of them, however, are extremely well located, especially those in Sheung Wan and Yaumati, and for this reason they are still easy to let, and still fetch standard rents. Sub-rents in a property per unit of physical space are a function of demand, and the most potent differentiating force within demand is the nearness of the property to the centres of business and social activity. Now at last, as a result of continual redevelopment, properties of this kind are becoming scarce, even in Sheung Wan.

Bed-spaces are a special case but not a radically different one. Some people, especially in factory districts, let out accommodation to individuals in the form of a bunk bed and a place to hang clothing and store personal gear. The usual customers of such businesses are young working men. Physically, bed-space businesses do not differ much from the dormitories maintained by some small factories and some department stores and restaurants, notably left-wing ones. According to Higuchi, in the industrial districts in the early 1960s, a flat with four rooms accommodated 50 or 60 beds, each at $17 per month rent. Hence the manager would draw between $850 and $1,000 per month, against his own rent of $500 or $600—plus rates at 17 per cent and water and electricity charges, in all say $620 to $740.[33] These figures relate to a big bed-space enterprise of a kind which was probably commoner at that time than now. Bed-space businesses very often occupy ordinary tenements, and rank with the cubicled tenements with which they form a continuum. In 1974, bed-spaces rented from $30 to $70 per month, according to amenity, location, and whether lower, middle or upper bunk.

Some limited documentation can be found for the essentials of this system in the past. In the 1950s, at the height of the housing shortage, the tenant-in-chief's rent for a good pre-war tenement would still be about $80, and he would let his space out as 6 or 7 cubicles at $30 each. In another situation in 1950, a tenant-in-chief, himself paying $31 per month in controlled rent, might let his tenement as six cubicles, plus bed-spaces, at $19 for a cubicle and $16 for a bed-space, producing a total sub-rental of about $200.[34] A working man's wage at that time was about $150 per month.

Key-money was also an important feature of those years, though it is little documented, partly no doubt because it was illegal. At a level accessible to educated and probably rather middle-class people, it was likely to start at about $2,000 per floor, and it could rise to $20,000 or even $30,000 per floor, according to a guide to Hong Kong life intended for Shanghai immigrants, published in 1950.[35] According to this account, profit from sub-letting was in principle limited to 20 per cent. Hence a flat renting at $200, supplied with water and electricity and divided into four cubicles, three of them sub-rented, ought to bring in an income of $216 from these three cubicles. But, the author adds, cubicles as cheap as this were not to be had.

The historic record enables the essentials and even some of the details of the system to be recognized back into the nineteenth century. In Simpson's report of 1903 on the plague[36] and Chadwick's sanitary report of 1882,[37] the cubicle system was obviously the central feature of working-class housing in the city. Simpson gives details of a number of lettings and sub-lettings of tenement floors in Sheung Wan. No profit was made by the tenant-in-chief in any of these cases, and most of them, according to Simpson's account and theirs, lived cheaply but not rent-free.[38] This suggests that the basic rationale of the system was the same then as now.

THE RATIONALE OF CONGESTION

To a visitor who comes to Hong Kong from the West, the most conspicuous feature—indeed the overriding dominant—of urban life in Hong Kong is congestion. Everywhere, except in the best suburbs, various impoverished backwaters, and to some extent Central District, congestion exists at problem level, and in most working-class and most business districts, it is all-pervading, apparently limitless, and impenetrable. Moreover, in the mind of the common people, congestion is one of the central characteristics of their city, and its great physical fault.

It is clear that in Hong Kong human life is lived at densities which are exceptional. This is true not only in simple terms of people resident per unit of physical space; it is true also of people in jobs, people circulating, businesses operating, and production taking place. The city is full of the physical evidence of these high densities, such as physical crowding at home and at work, private encroachment on public and private circulation space, physical congestion in the streets, and multiple uses everywhere. It is natural to ask, what are the densities which yield these visible evidences of physical crowding? And furthermore, what are the causes of these high densities, and how is the system of acutely high densities maintained?

The highest residential density for a big area recorded in the 1971 census was 401,000 persons to the square mile in Mongkok.[39] This is about 155,000 to the square kilometre, or 625 to the acre. Gross densities of population in the old resettlement estates rise to about 2,500 per acre, and to about 2,000 per acre in the new low-cost housing estates. Net densities of course rise to much higher figures: in resettlement and in some big private developments such as those at the seaward end of Jordan Road in Yaumati, to 5,000 per acre or even more. Moreover, it has been shown that in working-class Hong Kong, space in houses works out typically at figures between 16 sq.ft. and 35 sq.ft. per person.

These densities are high. English figures for conditions in public housing have ranged between 125 and 180 sq.ft. of floor area per person since 1918. Housing densities in East Asia are, however, typically high. In suburban or city conditions in contemporary Japan, a typical family of four has a six-mat room, plus a two-mat kitchen, giving 36 sq.ft. per person. Information about housing densities in mainland China is of course scarce, but densities are certainly high, at or approaching Hong Kong levels in the cities. 'For 1957, the average housing space per capita in 175 cities was 3.5 (square) metres, varying from 4.9 in small cities to 2.2 in big cities.[40] Figures in the official *Ten Great Years* suggest that the rate of provision of additional workers' housing in China during the fairly stable conditions of 1952–7 was about 11.2 sq.m. (120 sq.ft.) for each additional male worker, and by implication for each additional family.[41] These figures obviously relate closely to those in Hong Kong.

The standard superficial rationalization about the high residential and other densities of Hong Kong is that they were a direct response to the constricted mountainous nature of the island site. But this explanation is not satisfactory. Kowloon is not so characteristically constricted—before 1941 it was certainly not so; and moreover, land can be and has long been created by reclamation, though within limits. The figures for density of occupation of residential building which have been quoted for cities in China also go to counter claims that Hong Kong is exceptional because of its site.

In Hong Kong, the supply of land for building is mainly an aspect of government policy, but demand for land is mainly an aspect of Chinese social habit and economic activity. Land prices and rents are high, and have long been so, in relation to unit area; but they are not high in relation to levels of use. Are we then to think of high rents as enforcing high densities of use, or of high densities of use as nourishing a high rent system? And even if we accept realistically that in this generation the system nourishes itself, with high prices for property leading to dense use in order to share costs, and dense use justifying and tending to perpetuate high prices and rents—still, where do the root causes of the system lie, and how is it maintained?

More sophisticated answers to these questions are broadly of two opposing kinds: those which point to poverty among the mass of the Chinese people as the root cause (so that high rents enforce high densities), and those which treat Chinese social custom as the root cause (so that high densities invite high rents). Neither of these arguments is as easy to dismiss as the protagonists of each tends to imagine of the other.

The poverty argument is based fairly and squarely, as to documentation, on the forceful and well-founded observations of the *Report of the Housing Commission* of 1935.

> Overcrowding arises almost entirely from poverty which in Hong Kong is so dire that many families cannot afford any rent at all, and that, of the remainder, the majority can afford so little rent that a normal interest rate on capital outlay for housing cannot be obtained. . . . For a great number of the population the rents which can be afforded vary from nothing to a maximum of about $7.50 per month per family.[42]

There is some evidence that the root cause of this situation was the migrant and transient habits of the working-class Chinese community of the city during the nineteenth century. In 1844 there were 4,786 Chinese men in Victoria, against only 253 married women.[43] As late as 1911, in the whole colony, there were 296,000 males against 161,000 females.[44] There were said to be 20,000 labourers without lodgings in the city in 1909 or 1910.[45] The essence of all these facts is that Hong Kong was a migrants' city in which from the very start a workman's wife and children remained in China, maintained within the village or small town economy hopefully with the help of his remittances. Hong Kong did not provide either in building terms or in economic terms for a man to maintain his family in the city.[46] Not the least of Hong Kong's achievements during the twentieth century has been its success in lifting itself from a community of migrant workers in which working men were not supposed to be maintaining families at all, to a community of families with rising amenities and expectations.

It is happily not the case today that a significant number of Hong Kong people are too poor to pay any rent at all. The essence of the poverty side of Chinese housing conditions in Hong Kong in the present generation is the high cost of all housing outside the government sector, and the steep climb of rents up the rocky economic slopes which lead to better conditions.

Resettlement accommodation is available only to cleared squatters and a few other categories of families including those removed from dangerous buildings. Rents in resettlement are now, in new blocks, high-built but with lifts, relatively sophisticated in design and with standard density of 35 sq.ft. per person, $38 per month per standard unit of 140 sq.ft.[47] This comes to $0.27 per sq.ft.

The only tenancies in buildings of this kind which are easy to come by, even for people with entitlement, are those on the peripheries of the city, involving the much-resented inconvenience and cost of daily travel. Rents in the old blocks are still only $18 per standard unit of 120 sq.ft., or $0.15 per sq.ft.; standard allotment of space can be low as the original resettlement figure of 24 sq.ft. per person, and in Shek Kip Mei where conditions were and are exceptional, 80 per cent of the people lived below this level of space provision in 1970.[48] The resettlement department does not necessarily enforce action on over-crowding until density reaches 16 sq.ft. per person.[49] Group A public housing provides accommodation for people of limited incomes at standard rents of from $35 to $53 per unit accommodating four people. These flats allow 35 sq.ft. of space per person, at between $0.25 and $0.55 per sq.ft.[50]

Government tenancies represent the most advantageous conditions of cost and crowding which are generally available to working-class people looking for accommodation in Hong Kong. Accommodation at the social and economic lower end of the private sector, that is in effect accommodation in cubicles, is generally much more expensive, and usually offers similar conditions of crowding and similar or inferior conditions of amenity. Cubicles have only two kinds of merit. They are usually nearer the city centres than the government estates, and they offer the individual much better choice of a place to live than the government system. But they are not cheap. A cubicle of 60 to 120 sq.ft. rented at between $2.00 and $4.00 per sq.ft. per month in 1974, varying according to district and other factors. Moreover, the cubicle system represents crowding. In a cubicle, 20 to 30 sq.ft. per person is usual—that is, the same space per person as the official allowance in the more crowded resettlement estates like Shek Kip Mei.

The private sector can provide whole flats only at rentals of at least $400 per month, and these can be of standard size about 240 sq.ft.[51] These are the 'completely independent small flats' mentioned earlier. Crowding takes place within them, very often, until the rent *per person* is brought down to between $40 and $100 per month, which brings us back to the cubicle and bed-space system. Those people at the upper end of the working-class family incomes spectrum (for instance, where there are two wages in the family), who also care more than the average for housing comfort and privacy, can and do purchase or rent small flats for their own exclusive use, and such people can also take a lodger to help with the repayments or the rent without going to the length of building cubicles.

The crude essence of the argument from inclination is that Chinese people like congestion, and feel uneasy without it. In this crude form, applied to crowding *inside* domestic premises, the argument does not have many friends, though some people use it. As overcrowding cases from Shek Kip Mei show, in the oldest and shabbiest of the resettlement estates, but one of the best situated, there are still families who remain in overcrowded cheap accommodation even where they are paying in rent less than 2 per cent of the family income.[52] The Housing Commissioners of 1935 also pointed to such anomalies in the 'poverty' argument. 'In Hong Kong there are many people occupying flats in the congested areas, who could well afford to . . . pay rents for much better houses than they now occupy. . . . In Hong Kong it is true that there is a tendency to overcrowd, even when more commodious accommodation can be afforded'.[53] It is not likely that the people in these cases enjoy living in the overcrowded conditions, but it is evident that they tolerate acute degrees of overcrowding rather than change their address, whether by reason of economy or of convenience. Only Richthofen says roundly, 'Chinese like crowding, the tighter the better'.[54]

Where the argument from inclination does have real substance, is in the context of street congestion; and the recognition of this may bring us closer to recognition of the fundamentals of congestion in Hong Kong in general. At the turn of the century, 'La rue, à Péking, c'est l'image de l'anarchie triomphante'.[55] On vit beaucoup sur le trottoir le jour, mais pas la nuit comme à Calcutta',[56]—this of contemporary Shanghai. 'The wider the street the more the uses to which it can be put, so that travel in the broad streets of Peking is often as difficult as that in the narrow alleys of Canton.'[57] Abundant documentation of street congestion in contemporary Hong Kong is given in other chapters, together with evidence that congestion here is based on encroachment and multiple use, as it was at Peking seventy-five years ago.[58] But this is a different question from the origins of *residential* crowding.

The truth of the matter is that congestion in Hong Kong usually means either or both of two things which are related but different, residential crowding, and total congestion. The latter is an experience not of rooms or flats, but of buildings, streets and whole localities (Plate 10). Total congestion in an ordinary street begins with dense residential and business occupation in not less than four floors, with a normal quota of traffic and passers-by, deliveries and building-works, and adds various kinds of hawking and the extension of shops, domestic life and workshop life on to the pavements, and in many cases cooking and eating as well. Within a standard building total congention means not only residential crowding to an acute degree, but a range of money-making activities in addition, with odd corners of space occupied by business uses (Plate 21), and storage blocking the stairs and landings. This, it has been shown, is one normal state of localities in Hong Kong which are not directly protected from it. Residential crowding is still acute in some areas. But by itself, it cannot create total congestion, as is shown by the experience of some depressed areas, for instance Saiyingpoon and Kowloon City, where residential crowding is acute but street congestion very slight. Where residential crowding coexists with total congestion, as in Yaumati, it is in itself no more than one part of the main underlying condition for total congestion. Moreover, residential crowding is at last beginning to diminish in most of the areas where it is intense, but total congestion is not. In scale and in type, residential crowding has only limited relevance to the vast congestions which are now created by industry and business, for instance in Taikoktsui and other industrial areas. Business lies at the heart of the whole system.

With the argument from residential crowding must go the argument from poverty. Poverty still leads to residential crowding as it has always done; but poverty cannot be made to account for total congestion, which is not primarily residential, which shuns poverty, and which is related to prosperity and economic opportunity.

Congestion arises because each patch of land is used to an intense degree for making money, or for saving it in a business context.[59] Hawkers often bring total congestion to a climax, because they are attracted to congested streets, and forthwith greatly increase congestion in them. Working a circular saw, storing sheet steel, conducting a circulating library, cleaning fowls, cutting hair, respraying vans, and a hundred other street, pavement and alley activities share with hawking the responsibility for setting up obstacles to public circulation, and creating total congestion; and so does the cooking of food for sale in the street at many different levels. The essence of congestion of this kind is either encroachment or multiple use, or both, all in the line of business. Many restaurants keep a scullery in the alley behind their premises. The business has expanded to a size beyond that which its premises can well house. Rather than take bigger and more expensive premises, the restauranteur helps himself to an unauthorized subsidy from the public in the form of getting his scullery work performed in the alley. The businessman in a factory or mixed block who stores hundreds of cardboard boxes on the common stair is following precisely the same rationale, and so is the painter and decorator who stores his complete equipment and his stocks of paint on the stairs in a residential block. This is the encroachment side. The man who starts a small factory in his residential flat does not hurry to rent a second flat either to put his family into, or to put his business into, even when the business is well-established and the crowding in the household has become acute. High rents and the habit of business instability no doubt do nothing to encourage such a move. The practice of single men sleeping in business premises, in surgeries, garages and small factories, instead of renting bed-spaces or living at home, is another aspect of the same situation. The entrepreneur who contracts from his kitchen—on a pavement, on vacant land or in a mixed block—to deliver cooked meals to factory workers at lunch-time—all these and many others belong to the multiple-use side of the argument.

The Multi-Storey Buildings (Owners' Incorporation) Ordinance of 1970 has had a considerable effect in reducing encroachment and hence congestion inside mixed buildings—storage on public stairs is now visibly less than it was in 1970. Encroachment and multiple use in the street, on the other hand, has increased, particularly in areas like Yaumati where it was already intense. The physical separation of uses is still far distant from the thinking of ordinary people in the city, especially when it is applied to business uses. In busy working-class districts, where there has been long accumulation and the government is tolerant, congestion resulting from encroachment and multiple use may be pressed virtually to the physical limits of what is possible in the space which exists—a state of 'saturation'. The 'saturated' landscape is that which furnishes the essential Hong Kong stereotype to the people of the city: an urban landscape dense, versatile, cellular, predictable, repetitious, intensely human; a landscape charged with opportunity, tension, familiarity and risk.

1 *Annual Report,* 1963, 'Review—Land', p. 16. This review chapter is a valuable general survey of the history of land and building and of policy related to them.

2 *Annual Report,* 1955, p. 134.

3 *Annual Report,* 1963, p. 181.

4 For example: 'a wall fronting but not abutting on a street shall not project through a line drawn at an angle of 76° with the horizontal from the centre line of the street'—except in a number of specified alternative but equivalent situations. This is a typical and fundamental regulation. *Laws of Hong Kong, Buildings Ordinance,* chapter 173, (1966). *Building (Planning) Regulations,* 16, (1) (b), p. F8.

5 As photographs of Hong Kong streets of a century ago show, there was little change in the physical style of tenement buildings, as seen from outside, from then until they were given up in the 1950s (Plate 1). Tenements in essentially the same tradition as those of Hong Kong, though usually only of two or three floors and called shophouses, are characteristic of the 'Chinatown' area of Singapore. Barrington Kaye in his *Upper Nankin Street, Singapore* (Singapore, 1960) has made a sociological study of one such tenement area.

6 *Report by the Labour Officer, Mr. H.R. Butters, on Labour and Labour Conditions in Hong Kong,* 1939, Para. 171, pp. 149–50. The words in brackets have been added. Butter's account does not differ in essentials from that given by Osbert Chadwick nearly 60 years earlier. (O. Chadwick, *Report on the sanitary condition of Hong Kong,* London, Colonial Office, Eastern No. 38, 1882, p. 11). Among other things Chadwick recorded the closing of shop-fronts at night by upright wooden bars fitting into sockets in thresholds and lintels—a system which still survived in places in Sheung Wan in 1971.

A cockloft (Cantonese, *gok-lau*) is a kind of half-upper-floor built into an existing room.

7 The Buildings Ordinance of 1902 (*Hong Kong Government Gazette*, 11 July 1902, pp. 1253–342), which was in part a response to the plague of 1894, laid down the first minimum standards for the steepness of staircases, required floorboards to be tongued and grooved, and prohibited the building of cubicles without windows in buildings erected after that time. It also reaffirmed many important provisions on such points as heights of buildings and of storeys, building of cocklofts, thickness of walls, concreting of ground surfaces, and many others, from earlier Ordinances.

8 It is natural to ask, to what extent were these conditions parallel to those in other Chinese cities? Evidence is not as plentiful as might be expected, even for building form. W.H. Owen, the author of the Appendix to the *Report of the Housing Commission* (Hong Kong, 1935) thought (Para. 12, p. 11) that 'the standard tenement has followed the traditional lines of the village house, but with an increased number of floors'. Tenements are also much deeper, between front and back, than village houses. In Shanghai, the evidence is that the basic building style was based on Chinese traditions, both as to layout in alleys and long courts rather than streets, and as to external structure (*Shih-li yang-ch'ang hua Shanghai, (Reminiscences of Shanghai)*, (Hong Kong, 1970), part ii, p. 5). Eleanor Hinder (*Life and labour in Shanghai* (New York, 1944), p. 83) agrees, but also shows that the internal arrangements developed the same features as those common in tenement Hong Kong—'one house itself originally contains a single front room downstairs, and a kitchen behind, with two rooms above. By the construction of horizontal and vertical partitions, however, spaces are provided for additional families'. These buildings generally had two storeys. These features can also be found in contemporary Taipei, where cubicles are very common. When the centre of Canton was rebuilt during the 1920s, tenements like those of Hong Kong were introduced, but this was in imitation of the Hong Kong style. Old Canton was built in the form of alleys. The buildings generally had one floor only, and a windowless cockloft, sometimes with rooms adjoining, was usual. (M. Yuan, *Canton, un coin du céleste empire*, Paris, 1867.) Buildings of this kind are still commonplace in the older Canton away from the main thoroughfares, and in contemporary Macao. They are also the normal type of house in Tai O, in south-west Lantao, by common consent the most traditional-style town in Hong Kong.

9 Hong Kong. *Report of the 1963 Working Party on government policies and practices with regard to squatters, resettlement and government low cost housing,* Para. 13, pp. 7–8.

10 In the West and Hong Kong alike, reformers have long pointed out the wastefulness of tenement sites. A number of intelligent proposals for improvement, made by various authorities, are quoted in the *Report* (to the Colonial Secretary) *on the question of the housing of the population of Hong Kong* (Hong Kong, 1902). Most of these would however have produced very dense buildings, rather like those of the 1955 phase. There are interesting parallels with suggestions in Ernest Flagg, 'The New York tenement house and its cure', in K.A. Woods and others, *The poor in great cities* (London, 1896), pp. 370–92.

11 *Annual Report,* 1970, pp. 8–9.

12 *Valuation Table for Victoria, Hong Kong,* 1871. Tables for other years during the nineteenth century reveal the same situation.

13 Until 1972 or 1973, examples of both of these forms could still be found in Connaught Road, on the western waterfront. *T'ang-lou* tenements were adapted for use as offices by partitioning the standard tenement floor exactly as for residential cubicles. These offices of course lacked both light and privacy; and in fact, they were quite often shared as well. An old office block in Central District itself, called China Building, is arranged in essentially the same way internally. It was built about 1922.

In 1971, an old-fashioned but still respectable hotel in Connaught Road Central occupied a single tenement floor, also arranged on *t'ang-lou* principles, the office at the front, with half-a-dozen cubicles each 60 to 80 sq.ft. comprising the hotel accommodation. This was one of a number of hotels whose location on the waterfront reflected the old traffic by boat to Canton. All of them, or nearly all, have now disappeared.

14 A parallel trend was visible in the physical form of new government housing. By 1964 resettlement blocks were being designed with an internal corridor and private balconies,

and from 1965 blocks with sixteen floors and lifts were introduced—though these blocks are still on a corridor plan, which there can be little prospect of giving up, in view of the size of the blocks.

15 *HKCCNC*, 1972, part i, p. 212.

16 Well-off people may spend very freely in this respect, without apparently taking account of factors which in a Western community would be thought cardinal. A family may spend tens of thousands of dollars on redecorating and refitting a fairly new flat in a crowded district like Yaumati, in spite of the presence of a small unregistered factory on the same floor, and two much-advertised brothels in the same building.

17 Harold Ingrams's *Hong Kong* (in the semi-official Corona series, HMSO, London, 1952) records conditions in 1950, close to the height of the physical crowding of the pre-war city in the post-war transformations. The tenement floors which he describes usually had no more than 30 people resident, though he quotes one from hearsay (p. 73) as having 23 families.

18 e.g., *Sing Pao (Daily News)*, 15 May 1972, p. 7.

19 These figures were suggested in September 1971 by Mr. Cho Shiu-Chung, M.B.E., Chairman of the Mongkok Kaifong Association and managing director of a number of property companies, to whom the author expresses warm thanks. Prices have since risen generally, and some have become much less stable.

20 Bought from a previous lessee, the price for the same land might be $300 per sq.ft. Compensation to tenants is at present at the rate of about $33 per sq.ft., for a shop, and $18 per sq.ft., for a domestic tenant. Compensation at this rate will work out (averaged over 5,000 sq.ft.) at about $55 per sq.ft. for a building with a ground floor shop and two upper floors in residence.

21 A composite commercial and domestic building is envisaged. Government regulations limit the proportion of building which is permitted on a site. (*Laws of Hong Kong. Chapter 123, Buildings Ordinance*, (1966).) Building (Planning) Regulations, First Schedule. (Subsidiary, F 28). The figures given here relate to a typical building 100 ft. high on a class B site (corner site but not one with access to three streets). In this case, the builder may cover 52 per cent of the site area, and (subject to a group of detailed regulations, Building (Planning) Regulations, Part III) may also cover the whole site area for the ground floor, which is normally designed for commerical use.

22 Five units of 450 sq.ft. each per floor are envisaged here. This comes to 2,250 sq.ft. per floor, leaving 350 sq.ft. per floor for corridors, lifts, stairs, etc.

23 The building which is envisaged has 10 floors and is 120 ft. high. It occupies a 3-street or island site; hence 85 per cent cover of the site is permitted for a non-domestic building.

24 *Hong Kong 1974. Report for the year 1973*, pp. 88–89.

25 Hong Kong. Director of Public Works, *Annual Departmental Report, 1969–70*, Appendix Q, p. 157.

26 Commissioner for Resettlement, *Annual departmental report*, 1972–73, Paras. 81, 83, p. 20. This figure is intended to include site formation, piling and engineering costs, and represents the capital cost of the land made ready to build.

27 Investigation in Taipei indicates that essentially the same rationale applies to sub-let cubicled properties in that city as that which is outlined here for Hong Kong.

28 The allowance of space in resettlement, when the programme was started in 1954, was 24 sq. ft. per adult. Rent in resettlement accommodation was then about half the rental of comparable private cubicles; it is now one quarter or less. The lowest figure of $19 per month (including water) in the oldest blocks is now about 2 per cent of a working man's wage. It is not without interest that in the name of adaptation to circumstances, the resettlement authorities adopted *t'ang-lou* principles and permitted internal subdivision from the start. Hence, some rooms in resettlement estates now have cubicles exactly like those in the old private tenements. According to the regulations, resettlement tenants may not take lodgers, though some people do. But here as elsewhere cubicle arrange-

ments are not a certain sign of lettings for profit. They may be built as part of the arrangements within a family.

29 The figures given above and below are based on information from a variety of sources, including personal knowledge and discussion with Chinese people who have personal knowledge.

30 Rent increases in post-war domestic premises may be agreed between landlord and tenant, but must receive the endorsement of the Commissioner of Rating and Valuation.

31 Rent increases for pre-war premises are restricted by law to 55 per cent of pre-war rents for domestic premises, and 150 per cent for business premises. *Hong Kong 1974, Report for the year 1973,* pp. 95–96.

32 W.F. Maunders in his detailed study of rents in Victoria made in 1963 (*Hong Kong urban rents and housing* (Hong Kong, 1969), p. 139), found that consistently higher returns from sub-letting were enjoyed by tenants of controlled property than of uncontrolled; but of course at that time the differentials were much less.

33 M. Higuchi, *Honkon Chūgoku Jin (Hong Kong Chinese),* (Tokyo, 1964), pp. 83–4.

34 These figures for sub-rents come from Harold Ingrams, *Hong Kong* (1952), p. 72. The property was in Shantung Street, Mongkok. Controlled rents in typical Shantung Street property were then about $31.

35 T'ang Chien-Hsün, *Tsui-hsin Hsiang-Kang chih-nan (Latest Hong Kong Guide),* (Hong Kong, 1950), pp. 142–5.

36 W.J. Simpson, *Report on the causes and continuance of plague in Hong Kong* (London, 1903).

37 O. Chadwick, *Report on the sanitary condition of Hong Kong* (London, 1882). Chadwick unfortunately does not give any figures for sub-rents.

38 Simpson, op. cit. Appendix K, pp. 120 ff. Of particular interest among the cases reported by Simpson are several flats rented *in common* by working men—'each man pays 25/21 of a dollar as his share of the rent' (ibid. p. 125).

39 It is remarkable that the highest density figure recorded in the 1961 census, 616,000 per sq. mile in Sheung Wan, had fallen by 1971 to 255,000 per sq. mile. The figure for Mongkok rose slightly between 1961 and 1971. (*Hong Kong population and housing census, 1971* (Hong Kong, 1972), Table 4, p. 28.)

40 C.M. Li, *Economic development of communist China* (Berkeley and Los Angeles, 1959), p. 215, quoted by L.F. Goodstadt in 'Urban housing in Hong Kong', in I.C. Jarvie and J. Agassi, *Hong Kong, a society in transition* (London, 1969), p. 260 (3.5 square metres is 37.5 square feet).

41 China, State Statistical Bureau, *Ten Great Years* (Peking, 1960), pp. 180, 182 and 217.

Figures derived from specialized Chinese sources have the same implications. Residential accommodation was occupied in or around 1956 at a rate of 3.51 sq.m. per person in Canton, 2.54 in Harbin, and 2.26 in Shanghai—that is, from 38 sq.ft. down to 24 sq.ft. per person. (C. Howe, 'The supply and administration of urban housing in mainland China; the case of Shanghai', *China Quarterly,* 33 (January–March 1968), pp. 79, 90, 92, 94.) Some new industrial centres apparently had only 1.8 sq.m. (19 sq.ft.) per person.

In a recent article describing new and obviously prestigious building in Hsüchow, Kiangsu, 18–20 sq. metres is reckoned to be the right space for an average family of 4.5 persons, giving 4½ sq. metres (41–49 sq. ft.) per person. (*Chien-chu hsüeh-pao (Architectural Journal),* Peking, 1973 (2), p. 1.)

Hong Kong people who have lived in mainland China since the Liberation say that many families who live in old buildings do so in windowless cubicles like those of the old Hong Kong, and cook in the street.

42 *Report,* Para 14 (i) and (ii), p. 4, and Appendix, Paras. 19–23, pp. 12–13.

43 *Blue Book*, 1844, p. 101.

44 Hong Kong, Census and Statistics Department, *Hong Kong Statistics, 1947–1967*, p. 13.

45 J.S. Thomson, *The Chinese* (London, n.d., about 1910), p. 39. n.d. =no date.

46 In some degree, this was true of all Chinese cities in the nineteenth and earlier centuries. In contemporary Taipei, it is uncommon for a whole family to live in a cubicle—a cubicle is thought adequate accommodation for one or two people. Sub-tenants do not usually have cooking facilities. In this respect, present custom in Taipei may be a pointer to earlier custom in Hong Kong.

47 Commissioner for Resettlement, *Annual Departmental Report, 1972–73*, Para. 34, p. 10.

48 Hong Kong, *Housing Board Report*, 1970, Para. 52, p. 16.

49 Commissioner for Resettlement, *Annual Departmental Report, 1968–69*, Para. 78, p. 29. This figure is not given explicitly in the *Report* for 1972–3, but the figures for decantation in Appendix 7 on p. 32 show that conditions have not significantly changed in this respect.

50 *Hong Kong 1974, Report for the year 1973*, p. 99.

51 Commissioner of Rating and Valuation, *Annual Departmental Report, 1972–73*, Table xiii, p. 66.

52 In Keith Hopkins (ed.): *Hong Kong, The Industrial Colony* (Hong Kong, 1971), the Editor's chapter, 'Housing the poor', pp. 305–14, five case studies reported by Margaret Wong. These cases happen to be documented, but there is no reason to think them exceptional. Nearly 6,000 families—apparently almost half the total number—were housed at below 24 sq.ft. per person in Shek Kip Mei in 1973. (Commissioner for Resettlement, *Annual Departmental Report, 1972–73*, Appendix 7, p. 32.) A similar proportion of tenants lived in the same degree of overcrowding at Hung Hom. Personal enquiry among tenants at Hung Hom showed clearly that whilst they dislike the dirt and overcrowding, people are very unwilling to consider moving to anywhere less well situated.

53 Hong, Kong, *Report of the Housing Commission, 1935*, Appendix, Paras. 33 and 35, p.15.

54 *Baron Richtofen's Letters*, 2nd ed. (Shanghai, 1903), p. 165.

55 M. Monner, *L'Empire du Milieu* (Paris, 1899).

56 R. Dumont, *Chine surpeuplée* (Paris, 1965), p. 181.

57 A.H. Smith, *Village life in China* (New York, 1899), p. 35.

58 Or in Ch'ang-An, the imperial capital, 1,200 years ago. In 767 the Emperor proclaimed an ordinance against physical encroachment in the streets, and required the people to clear away encumbrances, on pain of punishment. *T'ang Hui-yao (Laws of T'ang)*, 86.

59 All the examples which follow are taken from particular cases.

3 Sheung Wan

DOMINANTS IN SHEUNG WAN

SHEUNG WAN is the original Chinese town of Hong Kong. From the earliest days until well after 1945, it remained the unchallenged centre of Chinese Hong Kong, with its Chinese wholesaling trades, its traffic by sea to and from Canton, its restaurants and tea-houses, and until the expansion of Kowloon in the late 1930s, its overwhelming preponderance in investment, prestige and activity over all other areas of the city except Central District. Now, in some specialized respects such as Chinese wholesaling, it retains primacy, but since the Pacific war it has lost some of its individuality and much of its former function in housing and entertainment. In the 1960s the area was static by Hong Kong standards, partly because of the extreme conditions brought in by the emergencies of the 1940s and 1950s, but since about 1970 private capital has once more entered the property market on a big scale, and redevelopment has grown from a trickle to a flood, so that demolition and rebuilding are now one of the characteristic features of the whole district, especially on the old reclaimed land close to the waterfront. At the same time, a public programme of urban renewal has been started in the hillside streets to the south.

Sheung Wan still preserves essentially the structure of localities which it had seventy or even a hundred years ago—and if the experience of other parts of the city is a reliable guide, it will preserve this structure even through extensive redevelopment. The district is characterized by a number of separate situations, each in its own way central to the area as it has developed. One is the continued location here of the chief Chinese business district. Another is the harbour frontage and the status of the area as a part of the port—formerly, the greater part of it. Another has been the successive reclamations of the sea-front, which added critically to the space available in the level and more accessible business half of the Chinese town, and accommodated the growth of the main business clusters of the area up to modern times. Four or five of these clusters, together with many minor ones, dominate the economic landscape on the reclaimed land between Queen's Road and the harbour. Another dominant feature has been the relatively slow pace of change during the present century; there has been development and some change in the business area since the Pacific war, but little growth; and in the hillside streets there has been long-protracted decay. Property in Sheung Wan is very mixed indeed; the greater part of that which is now being pulled down, even in the main business streets, is half-a-century old and more, and relatively low-built—characteristically, with only four floors in all.

These are the situations, some of them arising in the present and some essentially inheritances from the past, which taken together dominate Sheung Wan as it now is. Fundamentally, the Sheung Wan which emerges from these situations is cellular in structure. It comprises an agglomeration of agglomerations; a place of endless complexity and numberless contingent relationships, but almost lacking a hierarchy of localities. In the business streets on the reclaimed land, its characteristic feature is old-established and close-knit complexes of related businesses which are closely tied to the localities which they occupy.

The layout of Sheung Wan is simple in essence, though complex in detail (Figure 6). Its morphological spine is Queen's Road, the original beach-head main road of the whole city. Immediately to the south rises the steep flank of Victoria Peak, a formidable hillside which must originally have been rocky, irregular and broken by deep boulder-strewn gullies filled at intervals by raging torrents. This hillside is now occupied by a dirty, undistinguished working-class and mixed tenement area which may be called the Taipingshan town. During the nineteenth century, this area was the main working-class section of the city, provided with shops, workshops and entertainments as well as tenement housing. Immediately to the north of Queen's Road lies the slope of the original beach, and beyond that the flat land, usually about 500 feet wide in the Sheung Wan area, which has been created by reclamation from the harbour. The first Chinese bazaar was situated at the top of the beach in what was later Jervois Street. This bazaar was the forerunner of the main Chinese business area of the whole city, which now occupies most of the reclaimed land lying between Queen's Road and the sea.

THE *NAM-PAK-HONG* BUSINESSES

The heart of the Chinese business area in Sheung Wan is a complex of features partly topographical and partly commercial, namely the Chinese wholesaling businesses and the specialist localities in which they are conducted. The businesses involved may be grouped in various ways, but among those which are prominent are rice, Chinese medicines, salt fish, cotton and silk textiles, and Chinese dry groceries. Each of these trades occupies a customary location or group of locations, and it is the sum total of these and many other related trades and localities which comprises the fabric of the business half of Sheung Wan.

A number of these trades may be considered to fall within the *nam-pak-hong* group. It is this complex of trades which lies at the topographical heart of Sheung Wan, and which is the most characteristic of the business groupings of the area. It is intended to discuss a number of these trades

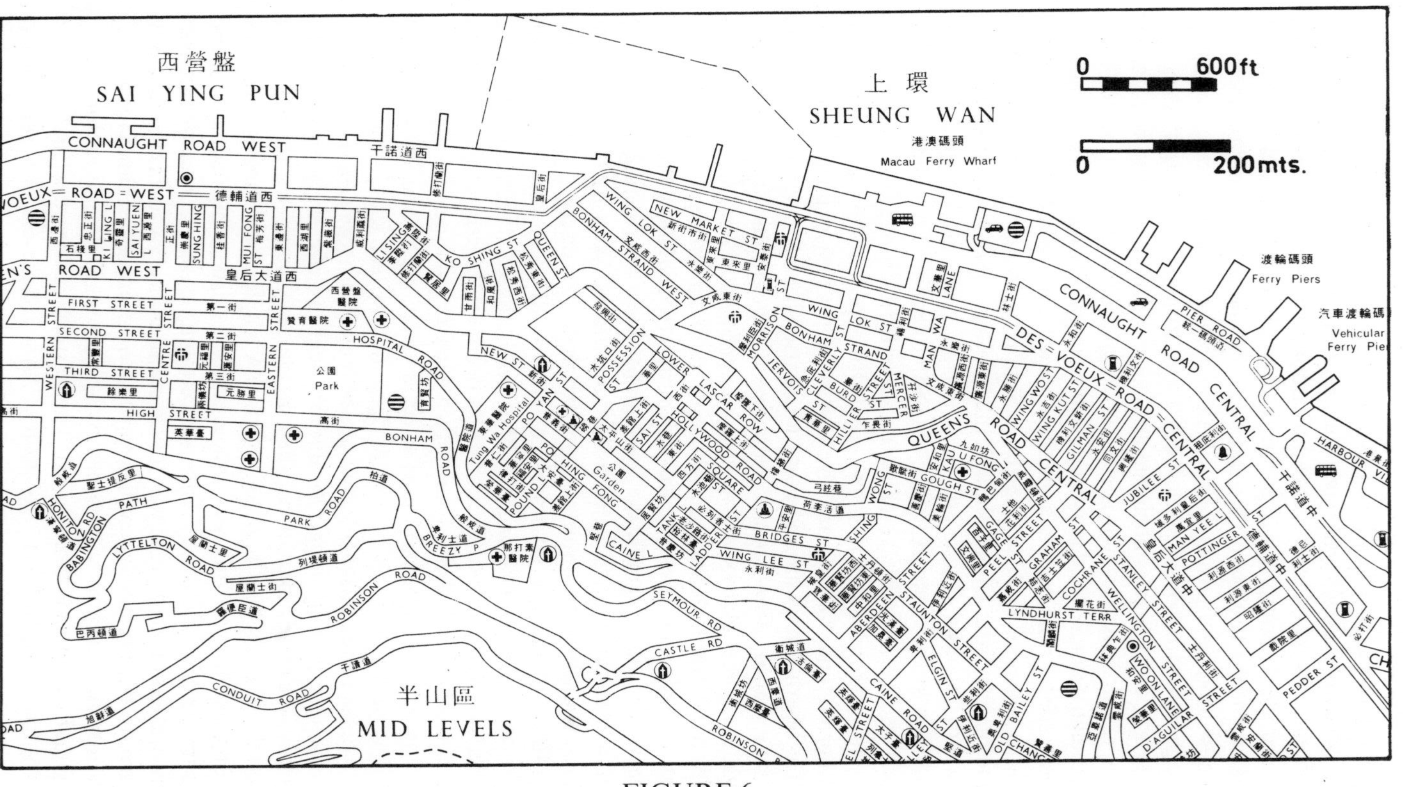

FIGURE 6

STREET PLAN FOR SHEUNG WAN AND ITS PERIPHERIES (1974)

Scale: 8 inches to 1 mile.

and the localities which they occupy, and to use the *nam-pak-hong* group as a prototype.

Nam-pak-hong means businesses trading between north and south.[1] The world of the *nam-pak-hong* businesses is not a particularly big one. Defined narrowly, it comprises only about a hundred businesses. But it is complex. It comprises a group of related specialisms with no determinate end or beginning. Essentially, it is the wholesaling of specialist Chinese food products. Generously defined, these include preserved fruits, rice, grains, edible oils, noodles, dried fish, tinned foods, sugar, some raw materials, and Chinese medicines and wines—and the list can be extended further.[2] More narrowly it is centred on specialist groceries, which comprise such items as dried mushrooms of various kinds, dried fruits, pepper, melon seeds, nuts and fruit kernels, dried and salted vegetables, and various kinds of flour and grains.[3] Supplies of these commodities still come mainly from China, though the term *nam-pak-hong* (dealers acting between northern China and South-East Asia), no longer covers the situations in the trade, if it ever did. Some commodities such as ginseng now come from Korea as well as from northern China; dried mushrooms are imported from Japan. Many goods for export come from central and southern China. Canada and the United States are significant markets as well as South-East Asia, and Hong Kong itself has become a major market in these trades. *Nam-pak-hong* also has a topographic significance. The name itself may be used to mean Bonham Strand West. Bonham Strand West and Wing Lok Street have almost identical interests. Together with parts of adjacent streets, they constitute the *nam-pak-hong* group of streets. The street landscape created by these interesting trades is a relatively subdued one (Plate 2). Bonham Strand West itself is a straight street lined almost completely with wholesale businesses, except where rebuilding is actually taking place. Nearly all these businesses belong either to the *nam-pak-hong* complex or to the related rice or Chinese medicine groups. Typically, a business occupies the ground floor and one or more others in either a four-floor tenement building or a recent taller building with a shop-front to the street; in Bonham Strand West a typical old tenement plot is 50 or 60 feet deep and 14 feet wide, and some are much deeper than this. Most businesses keep their stocks on the premises, but some, especially bigger businesses such as rice importers, do not. Broadly speaking, as will be shown, the rice trade lies further west, especially the physical handling of rice. A single-floor business occupies ten or more men; a business with a staff of thirty is big. Some of these men may well live on the premises, occupying parts of the dark interior. Until well after the Pacific war it was common for the owner and family to live on the premises as well. Upper floor premises in Bonham Strand West are now generally occupied by shipping agents and so forth.

Wing Lok Street is more mixed. The western half, parallel and adjacent to Bonham Strand West, has ground floor businesses in a very varied range of trades, formed by the assembling of related specialisms by each business, from a range which includes dried fruit, various kinds of beans and grains, rice, edible oils, flour, sugar and various specialities such as nuts or beeswax. The rest of the street, beyond the complex crossing at the Western Market, with its congestion and piles of refuse, is still occupied mainly in wholesaling, but of shoes, fancy goods and Western pharmaceutical products. These assemblages do not arise not out of traditional specialist Chinese trades, but represent Chinese businesses occupied in wholesaling of other kinds. The same is true of the remarkably mixed wholesaling trades (electrical machinery, piece-goods, frozen foods, plastic colorants) and other specialists (navigation lamps) of Hillier Street.

Bonham Strand (East) itself also runs eastward from the crossing by the Western Market, but its scale is smaller and its style a little more old-fashioned. Businesses at the western end are mostly wholesalers, generally in the *nam-pak-hong* group and related trades such as Chinese medicines, but also including baskets and matting, string and paper. From Cleverly Street eastward, the street has a character of its own, based on gold dealers and Chinese banks. Bonham Strand is an example of the tendency of the 'cells' of this 'cellular' city to interpenetrate. They do so partly through time. In both Bonham Strand and Wing Lok Street, the tendency has been for mixed wholesale business to migrate westward. The *nam-pak-hong* group of businesses had displayed a parallel tendency to move westward, with rice also moving westward ahead of it. Chinese medicine wholesaling has also done the same, moving in part from Bonham Strand West to Koshing Street. But this has not been a rapid or a drastic tendency. Except for rice, the distances involved have been of the order of 1,000 feet, and the time-period involved has been up to a century.

Nam-pak-hong has one additional meaning. The expression is also the name of a Chinese merchants' association, founded in 1868[4] but now with strong Maoist sympathies, and membership mainly in the grocery trades. It is also the name of a new office building in Bonham Strand West owned by this association, which houses a number of firms which display mainland propaganda material, including offices of some mainland banks. The mainland China connexion is fundamental to the *nam-pak-hong* businesses. Quite apart from the origins of the whole complex in a time when travel to and from China was virtually unrestricted, most of the present business interests of the complex involve dealing with mainland China. There is a spectrum of degrees of dependence. Rice and cloth are not really dependent, though a great deal of business is done with China. In grains other than rice, beans, preserved vegetables and dried fish, there is more dependence; and in tea, Chinese medicines and specialist groceries authentic commodities are very hard to find except from China, let alone at mainland China prices. Business with mainland China is done through a series of specialist agencies, all ultimately responsible to the China Resources Corporation with headquarters at the Bank of China. Some of these agencies have headquarters within Sheung Wan, usually in recent high-built properties partly let to other Communist firms, like the *nam-pak-hong* building in Bonham Strand West: this is the case with the Teck Soon Hong which occupies a building of this kind not far from Bonham Strand West, on the waterfront. Others, like the Ng Fung Hong, have their offices in the Bank of China building in Central District. A few, like the business which handles the wholesaling of musical instruments from China, have their offices in tenement shops or other small properties. Apart from the banks and the departmental stores, mainland China business interests are sharply concentrated in Western and Central Districts.

Firms which deal in mainland China commodities tend through a series of related mechanisms to be sympathetic to Peking, or at least to appear to be so. For one thing, businessmen who greatly dislike the Communists, either from the time of the Liberation in 1949 or from the Hong Kong riots of 1967, refrain from dealing with the mainland agencies altogether, and hence have given up dealing in mainland China produce. For another, the importing agencies put pressure of various sorts on firms which do depend on mainland China produce. They did so especially during the Cultural Revolution in China—pressures to display propaganda, to subscribe to left-wing causes, and so forth. The Chinese medicine business appears to be that in which political pressure reaches its maximum. People who know the trade say that money is secure and not hard to make in this business, but there is an element of unpredictability, and sometimes blackmail, of a political kind. It is not clear to what extent these pressures are reinforced by left-wing groundswells, whether based on hostility to British imperial rule or on labour solidarity; the most usual opinion is that the communism of mainland business contact is essentially an external pressure, to which people accommodate as best they can, and which picks up its allies where it finds them. Its degree of activity at any time appears to be related not primarily to tensions in Hong Kong or high-level decisions in Peking but mainly to the level of political agitation in China generally and Kwangtung particularly.

By Hong Kong standards, the *nam-pak-hong* group of businesses is old as well as distinguished. In the Directory for 1877, among the 'principal Chinese Hongs, dealing with foreigners', under the heading 'general Chinese Merchants', of the 77 businesses listed, only 16 were not located in Bonham Strand, Bonham Strand West, or Wing Lok Fong (i.e. Wing Lok Street), and of these all but a handful were in Praya West—that is on the waterfront, which at that time (before the Connaught Road reclamations early in the present century) was des Voeux Road. 'General commission agents' were also characteristically in Wing Lok Fong. The flour merchants, medicine dealers, and rice merchants occupied the same group of streets. Eleven of the sixteen gold merchants named had their businesses in Bonham Strand, and most of the rest in Wing Lok Fong. Mat and bag sellers were mostly in Bonham Strand, as they are still. Businesses of these kinds then occupied what are called here the *nam-pak-hong* group of streets, and have stayed there ever since. Most people in the area agree that the most prosperous phase in the history of the complex was the last years before the Pacific war.

It might be expected that continuity in locality terms would be a direct outcome of continuity of individual businesses, but this is not so. Turnover of businesses is surprisingly rapid, and apparently has always been so. Of the 77 'general Chinese Merchants' of 1877, presumably all substantial firms if they were listed as dealing with foreigners, only one is still in existence. Of the 30 *nam-pak-hong* businesses listed in a Japanese study of 1919,[5] only five survive to the present. Parallel results emerge from examination of lists of firms in other kinds of business. The marked degree of business continuity in this locality does not arise from longevity and continuity of individual firms. It arises rather from continuity of a business cluster within which the fortunes of individual firms are comparatively unimportant.

CLUSTERS OF BUSINESSES

The businesses in the *nam-pak-hong* complex are typically family ones. Most businesses belong to, and are managed by, partnerships among groups of relatives. Overseas contacts are usually based on uncles and cousins living overseas. Business contacts are friends, and virtually all business is based on personal contact.[6]

When a number of businesses in the same trade or closely related trades occupy a specific locality, and depend heavily on personal relationships in business, it is reasonable to speak of the clustering of businesses, and of business clusters. Clustering of businesses is not restricted to the *nam-pak-hong* business community, as many examples show; but it is most marked in the wholesaling side of specifically Chinese trades. It has been shown that whilst firms come and go with surprising rapidity, trades as a whole and the localities they occupy remain remarkably stable.

The stability of the clusters arises out of the conditions in which business is done, especially the fact that business depends in theory and practice upon personal contacts among individuals. These individuals find it convenient and natural to do business in a part of the city to which they belong, which they know and in which they are known, and which has the relevant business repute. If a firm goes bankrupt, another firm will buy its assets, and will usually change its name. New firms virtually cannot be started except by people already in the trade—usually a foreman or chief clerk, who has saved money and assembled potential customers, possibly attracting them from his former employer's clientele, but also possibly encouraged and helped to set up in business by his former employer. Considered in terms of practical dealing, the system is thought to be a convenience both for the businessmen who share the specialism, because they can exchange specialist help when needed, and for the customers, who know where to go for specialist goods and services, and can shop around in the locality for their particular needs. A specialist locality is in reality less a collection of related businesses than a network of personal contacts. New businesses are almost always born within this network; hence the network is self-perpetuating, and the perpetuation of the network of relationships carries with it the perpetuation of the physical cluster of businesses. High death-rates among businesses may be an outcome of high birth-rates, or vice versa, but neither is directly related to continuity of the locality, which is the outcome of continuity within the network.

From a Western standpoint, this rationale has one obvious weakness: it makes no allowance for competition among the businessmen who together constitute the cluster, and who (occupying premises in close proximity) cannot fail to be aware of one another's weaknesses and strengths. The essence of the businessmen's rejoinder to this is that proximity does not create problems of competition, because prices do not vary from firm to firm, and because practical competition among firms is a matter of business contacts and personal relationships and very little else. Dealing is characteristically restrictive. Undercutting is practically unknown because people would lose friends (and business) very rapidly by it, and because (the argument runs) nobody in the trade would gain by it in the end. Quality and reliability of merchandise is the only regular way in which a customer may get a better deal from one firm than another, and in modern conditions, with wholesale business increasingly done on the telephone, even this has tended to be based increasingly on personal trust. Sometimes, personal loyalty and business interest do come into direct conflict. In such a case, those involved will usually look for a compromise. Failing that, people make their own decisions, but a man will not necessarily be expected to come down on the side of loyalty rather than profit.[7]

This optimistic rejoinder comes from businessmen whose firms have survived. It makes little allowance for the high death-rates which afflict businesses in clusters. These high death-rates among firms are not usually thought to have any special explanation beyond the general volatility of business in Hong Kong, and the inadequate capitalization and too limited range of business contacts which are common causes of failures of firms in all parts of the economy—and in the second generation, sons who have official jobs or who for other reasons do not carry on the business. However it may be thought that clustering itself creates special problems of survival for businesses in a cluster. What seems to be involved is the problem of competition in another guise: how does the business cluster limit its own size? The Hong Kong businessman unhesitatingly follows precedent in locating his business, and when new businesses all arise within a network, they naturally arise within the physical cluster as well. When new ginseng businesses arise out of the network of older ginseng businesses, they naturally do so in or close to Bonham Strand West. Bookshops go to Nelson Street in Mongkok, bars to Tsimshatsui, wholesale textiles to Jervois Street or Cheungshawan, pickled vegetables to des Voeux Road West, fashion clothing to Nathan Road. 'If you start a fashion business in Nathan Road' (rather than in, say, an industrial district), says one business-woman, 'the mark-up is much better and the custom can be relied on—everyone comes to look round, and buy what suits them.' Hence the self-perpetuating cluster, from the customer's point of view based on repute; from the businessman's based on the habits of the customers as well as on the business network.

Until a viable business cluster has become established, and even after unless some kind of restrictive policy towards newcomers is adopted, clustering itself must create conditions in which the risk of failure of some or all of the businesses is high. Once a cluster has become established, its attractiveness to newcomers must be increased, but the more business accretion takes place, the more must be the risk of the cluster's growing beyond the power of its custom to support it. In this system, everyone is trying to climb on to everyone else's back. This reasoning suggests a degree of competition beyond the practice of the *nam-pak-hong* businesses, but may also suggest the underlying rationale of the restrictionist side of attitudes among *nam-pak-hong* business people, and of the system as a whole. Clustering provides the conditions for high death-rates of businesses, and the businesses most prone to failure are those with inadequate resources or weak business backing or both. In obviously unstable situations, like the tourist shopping trade in Tsimshatsui during the past decade, businesses proliferate visibly in good times and fail in bad, on a short time-scale. In Victorian Sheung Wan, much the same state of affairs seems to have prevailed. It appears to be essentially the same scheme which regulates the death-rates of firms even in mature and stable situations, like *nam-pak-hong* and others of its kind today.

Ideally, then, the business cluster is essentially a community. Its practical function is the joint one of attracting customers to shop around among the member businesses, with a reasonable degree of assurance that (since there is nowhere else to go) they will buy from one or another; and of exercising general supervision over prices, particularly to prevent their being lowered to levels which could be considered competitive. In the last analysis, the business community is a merchants' protection organization. But the community which takes such trouble to provide business security for its members is at perpetual risk of growing beyond a viable size. Self-interest among the established businessmen may cause them to try to limit the opening of new businesses, but the basic reality which faces newcomers is the problem of building up adequate business contacts with other firms and of getting commitments from them. Hence the inevitably limited size of the total business done within the cluster (that is, within the trade) forces people back into competitive situations and necessarily squeezes some people out.

The system of business clusters has a long history in Sheung Wan. Moreover, the *nam-pak-hong* group of businesses is explicitly considered by business people to be essentially the same in form and function as the same kinds of business grouping were in old China. Among these people, the *nam-pak-hong* world is not thought to have changed much, except in respect of relations with suppliers in China, since the Pacific war, nor to have changed radically since its establishment a century ago or more. There is abundant evidence to support this view in the literature on

Chinese towns before 1949. With the important exception of the whole field of relationships with the officials of the government, there seems no reason to dispute that the Hong Kong clusters are closely akin to those of pre-Communist China.

Moreover the clustering of businesses, both shops and market stalls, in specialist localities, and the conduct of business through communities are rooted in traditional Chinese town organization.[8] In Hong Kong, the system is usually called *ch'eng hang ch'eng shih*. Katō shows that in T'ang and Sung times, *hang* and *shih* both meant a street or block occupied by merchants dealing in a particular specialism.[9] *Hang* also means an association of merchants with common interests. *Shih* could also mean a business district in general, and a fair where stalls were arranged according to their kinds of business. Katō thought that recognition of the essentials of this system could be pushed back to Han times and earlier.[10] A specialist market might be held in a street specializing in the same trade;[11] and *hang* streets could have shops for trades other than the specialism[12]—the range of variation was considerable. Katō does not add that the Chinese expression *hang shih* means, in the words used by one Hong Kong businessman in discussing this point, 'making a price'—that is, the settling of a standard price by the group of merchants in a trade.

The system which has been outlined depends wholly on personal relationships. These relationships are in principle rooted in either family ties or friendship, but of course relationships of both kinds vary in degrees of sincerity. In practice, an individual operating within a business group may find people playing him false, for instance by offering bad business deals, or trying to use him, for instance by accepting payment for making an introduction. The system loses through the exploitation of personal relationships in a bad sense some of what it gains from reliance on them in a good sense. At business levels less stable and less illustrious than the *nam-pak-hong*, the civilization of trust and personal relationships in the city forms a continuum with a civilization of personal relationships and gossip. Most Hong Kong people get their jobs through personal contact, but this system does not guarantee either a decent job or a worthwhile employee; inferior jobs and poor workers are not less common than in other communities. By the same token, the normal way to get a supplier or a client is also through personal recommendation, but this method cannot guarantee good suppliers or reliable clients, although the implication of the system is that it can. Failure of an introduction may well result in a souring of relationships with the person who was responsible for it, though either or both of the persons introduced may have no better alternative. Hence in day-to-day dealings of all kinds, personal relationships turn out to be as exploitable as other kinds of relationships. In this situation, hostility and confrontation are rather scarce, but recrimination and resentment rather common.

Western authorities often discuss Hong Kong in language which takes for granted that the city is essentially Western, though exceptional, and that naked economic force reigns supreme. In a number of ways it is clear that these simple assumptions are mistaken. Sheung Wan business practice is essentially Chinese, as has been shown, and at the same time essentially anti-competitive. Similarly, a number of non-Western principles underlie labour relations in the city.[13] Further study is likely to reveal that Hong Kong is much less a special case in Western than in Chinese experience.

RICE AND SOME OTHER TRADES

The restrictive side of dealing within business clusters can best be illustrated from the special case of the rice business. Here there is an officially sanctioned scheme of restrictions in the importing and wholesaling parts of the trade, and a formal and officially sanctioned distinction among importers, wholesalers and retailers.[14]

Like the *nam-pak-hong* trades, the rice business in Hong Kong had its origin in the historic entrepot trade. Up to 1941 there was no government control, and the import of rice for consumption in the city was not a major part of the trade. Government control of the rice trade began in 1951, and took its present form in 1955. At present, thirty-eight firms are licensed by the government to import rice, according to quotas expressed in units of $\frac{1}{110}$ of quarterly demand; they must keep stocks on a certain minimum scale, and each is licensed to import only from certain producing areas. Rice from mainland China, which is generally of good quality and proportionately expensive, comprised 25 per cent of rice imports in 1970. Thailand furnished 55 per cent and most of the rest came, of course, from various parts of South-East Asia.[15]

'The object of the Scheme is to ensure regular and adequate supplies of rice to consumers, at reasonably stable prices, and to provide a reserve stock for emergency purposes.'[16] It is said that the rice control scheme serves to prevent the cornering of the rice market by a single supplier, such as mainland China. It is also said, rightly, that the scheme operates in a restrictive sense: that it creates and preserves a kind of privilege among licensed importers, who have to take the rough of prices with the smooth, but who nevertheless have in the rice control scheme a legally binding case of what is essentially a *hang* situation; prices are established by agreement among merchants.[17] 'The importers are traditionally accustomed to sell rice by auction exclusively to members of the wholesalers association (who are effectively 32 in number)...wholesalers in turn sell to retailers, usually but not invariably, at importers' auction price plus a standard mark-up....'[18] The scheme is clearly one which makes for stability in all phases of the trade, which now supplies about one thousand tons per day of rice to the city, through upwards of 3,000 retailers.[19]

A number of the licensed importers, including some which deal with mainland China, are European firms. Most of these have their offices in Central District. Most of the other rice importers have their offices either in the *nam-pak-hong* group of streets or in related streets to the west. In the Directory of 1875, most of the rice merchants had addresses in the *nam-pak-hong* streets, including some in Wing Lok Street for which an old popular name—*Mi Kai*, Rice Street—is still sometimes quoted.

In the *nam-pak-hong* streets, the rice trade is not conspicuous; rice is simply one more of the standard trades of the area. The contribution of the rice trade to the organization of the city is most visible westward of Sheung Wan, where in the bigger-scale warehousing district of Sai Wan, fronting the harbour, the importers keep most of their stores. The rice trade also contributes visibly to the street landscape in Connaught Road, westward of Wing Lok Wharf, where most of the registered wholesalers do business and where most of the businesses are rice dealers. Although in principle wholesalers sell on commission and do not handle rice, many of these businesses do carry considerable stocks, apparently because they have retail functions as well. Connaught Road west of the Wing Lok Street corner is lined on the inland side with rice wholesaling businesses, some in old 4-floor tenements, some in newly built taller buildings. It is edged on the seaward side with parked lorries and piles of refuse, and at the sea-wall a vast congregation of wooden junks used to unload the ships in the harbour.

Business clustering in Sheung Wan is represented by a number of other trades as well as rice and Chinese groceries. Some of these are big organizations which are conspicuous in the streets. For instance, the dried and salt fish and vegetable cluster in des Voeux Road has up to a hundred businesses, many quite big, its own internal specialisms such as sharks' fins, and its own local history at the west end of Sheung Wan (Plate 3). Another such cluster is the Chinese medicine business, which like rice overlaps with the *nam-pak-hong* trades in both commodity and locality terms, and which supports extensive packing businesses around Koshing Street, adjacent to the dried fish cluster in des Voeux Road. Some are conspicuous but small, like the card-printing cluster which occupies tiny stalls in Man Wa Lane. The cluster of tea businesses in and around des Voeux Road, many occupying premises on upper floors, is not particularly small but it is quite inconspicuous. Each cluster has its own business and locality history.

It is interesting to look finally at what may be called a 'failed' cluster—that is, one which in the changed conditions of the city since the Pacific war, and even in the last years before the war, has failed to maintain its grip on the location of the trade it represents.

The original home of the textile business was Jervois Street, the original location of the Sheung Wan business district (Plate 4). In 1871, Jervois Street had some 50 drapery businesses in the first hundred addresses. In 1877, it is clear that Jervois Street dominated the piece-goods trade, though it was also the centre of the opium business, which must have been an important part of Chinese merchandising at least up to the government monopoly of 1909. In 1870 Wing On Street, which later became a distinguished street for cotton textiles, was a common servicing lane with carpenters, barbers, blacksmiths and gambling houses.

The evidence of the directories is that throughout the twentieth century there has been a progressive loosening of the ties between Jervois Street and the wholesale and retail textile business, so that although Jervois Street, apart from its western end, is now still obviously and impressively a textile wholesaling street, it no longer dominates the textile business in the city as a whole.

The 1927 Directory names 71 silk merchants all told, 37 of them in Jervois Street, and most of the rest either nearby (including a number in Fat Hing Street, now a haberdashery street primarily) or elsewhere in the *nam-pak-hong* group of streets. A very few were located in Central District, and in Kowloon there were nine in Shanghai Street, but apparently none at all in Tsimshatsui, now an important centre.

In 1927, Jervois Street had a significant group of cotton textile businesses as well. But of the total of roughly 170 cotton piece-goods merchants of that time, only 26 were in Jervois Street against 40 in Wing On Street, which had already earned its alternative unofficial name *Fa-pu Kai*, Flowered Cottons Street. About 30 were in various parts of Kowloon, especially Yaumati.

The 1940 Directory names 92 silk merchants in the city, 28 of them in Jervois Street, five in Shanghai Street, and a dozen in Tsimshatsui, especially Nathan Road, foreshadowing the future. Most of the rest were either in the *nam-pak-hong* streets or in Central District. This directory names about 300 dealers in cotton piece-goods. Most of these were scattered about the main shopping centres of the city. Only 12 of them were in Jervois Street, but about 70 in Wing On Street, and many in Wing Kut Street which is close to it.

The Yellow Pages for 1971 show how this situation continued to develop. About 150 silk merchants are mentioned, only 8 of them in Jervois Street, but about half in Tsimshatsui or Nathan Road. Here the pressure of tourist spending has wholly overridden the historic location. Cotton cloth businesses are now impossible to separate from those dealing in other fabrics. There are about 680 businesses all told, about thirty of them in Jervois Street, and the same in Wing On Street and its neighbour Wing Kut Street; the largest group now is probably that in Cheungshawan, centred on Un Chak Street (about 70 businesses), obviously drawn by the clothing manufacturers of that area. The wide base of the trade naturally results in a wide distribution. Jervois Street remains an important centre for textile wholesaling, and according to people in the trade does considerable business with clothing manufacturers in areas like Cheungshawan, so that the trade remains prosperous. Nevertheless the main bulk of the business has clearly migrated, in a time of vast growth, to a series of fresh locations, drawn by new factors of at least two different kinds—tourist trade and the new factory locations. At the same time the clustering principle has to some extent been eroded in the old location, whilst exhibiting remarkable vitality in the new.

A parallel case is that of the egg wholesaling business. Wing Sing Street, a narrow lane without traffic access lying on the east side of Sheung Wan, housed 80 per cent or more of the wholesale egg businesses until the 1960s, but its proportion then fell sharply to about one-third. Part of the business migrated to the wholesale market at Kennedy Town to the west; part to the tall and gloomy tenements of Kam Lam Street in Mongkok, on the Kowloon side. Wing Sing Street, narrow and congested, proved unable to maintain its hold on the business. In 1974 it was in the full flood of rebuilding.

THE TAIPINGSHAN TOWN

Victorian Sheung Wan had two parts, which remain quite distinctive to the present. Between Queen's Road and the harbour lay the important business streets some of which have been discussed, with big sites, good access, and solid property. On the landward side of Queen's Road, rising up the flanks of the Peak, lay a predominantly working-class town of lodging-houses, workshops and small businesses of all kinds, with mixed and often small sites, access impeded by steep slopes and flights of steps, and property mixed and in many cases very poor. The latter area may be called the Taipingshan town.

During the past forty years, the growth of specialist business and entertainment areas elsewhere in the city has tended to narrow the range of social and business activity in the Taipingshan town. At the same time, various phases of slum clearance in the past, and some wartime bomb damage, have created gaps in the town's structure which have often been filled by enterprises and institutions (such as hospitals) which create blank walls where formerly people lived and worked. Population density in the area taken as a whole is no longer very high, though it remains high in individual buildings due to dense cubicle occupation which persists mainly because the area is very convenient for people who work in Central District.

These pressures have left their traces on the ground in the form of two typical landscapes. One of these is represented by the congested mixed streets centred on the hawker market in Possession Street, with ground floor workshops and businesses selling convenience goods, and upper-floor cubicles (Plate 7). In varying degrees, this kind of mixed townscape has occupied most of the streets in the group below the Hollywood Road level, though by 1974 a planners' blight was extending through the area, due to demolitions and expected demolitions for the urban renewal pilot scheme. The other kind of Taipingshan landscape occurs mainly above Hollywood Road. Here, street use is much less intensive, and (partly because of slum clearances in the past) much of the land is now in institutional use, for instance by schools. Consequently the streets are quiet and a little dreary. Square Street is typical. In 1870 Square Street had 78 addresses, 23 of them brothels and most of the rest in small business use.[20] In 1966 it had only 12 addresses, due to demolitions. By 1970 it was partly rebuilt, but in the new property the ground floor premises were mainly occupied by small factories. A good deal of the remaining older property was occupied by bed-spaces. A century ago Square Street was a working-class business and entertainment street. Now it has settled down to life as a commonplace, rather quiet workshop street with some working-class residence. This kind of change, together with the effective sterilization of sites by their use for schools, has been typical of the experience of most of the upper half of the Taipingshan town, in one form or another, during the twentieth century. As these examples show, the Taipingshan area now is essentially a small-scale, rather depressed, working-class town; business, while not wholly confined to the serving of local needs, is predominantly of a local shopping and servicing kind; in much of the area ground floor property is typically occupied by small workshops, engaged in such industries as printing, box-making, cabinet-making, and various kinds of small metal-working. This is one of the chief areas for all these industries in Victoria. Several newspapers, including the big *Wah Kiu Yat Po*, publish in the area.

A few Victorian mixed streets have remained relatively unchanged in this area to the present, but many others have been swept away in the present spate of clearances of slum property. One of the most interesting of these streets, and one which demonstrated the inexhaustible capacity of the city to create business community cells, was the Circular Pathway. This odd curved lane of about 40 addresses, with some very old terraced villas, lay perched on the hillside with access only by steps at either end (Plate 6). It was pulled down in 1970–1. It had a long association with the paper box manufacturing business. All the 'paper box makers stores' named in the Directory for 1915 were in the Circular Pathway. There was one business of this kind there in 1870, though at that time most of the lane was in family occupation or boarding houses. In 1927 there were 8 paper box businesses there, the only specialists in the city according to the directory. In 1940 there were 11, and by that time there were a few also in nearby Lascar Row, and many in Kowloon. In 1969, there were 7 paper or cardboard box businesses in the Circular Pathway. Freedom from traffic enabled the factories to dry paper boxes in the street. The Circular Pathway also had a slowly diminishing share in the jewellery business. In 1940 the street had 10 jewellers or goldsmiths; in 1927 there were 6; in 1951 only 4. These were probably always workshops rather than shops. In 1969, there were 3 small factories working for the jewellery trades.

On a general view in 1969, there were 6 trades in the Circular Pathway. There was a group of 5 pavement shacks, 4 of them accommodating wood-carvers. A few premises housed metal-work factories akin to those of the Lascar Rows to the west. A few had businesses preparing Chinese medicines, and there were a few printers, and the jewellery and paper box businesses which have been discussed. The rest of the property was in residence alone, most of it very dense with cubicles.

In the Taipingshan town, the curio business is of special interest. Under such names as 'Cat Street', 'Thieves' Market', and the like, the Lascar Rows have begun to appear in tourist promotion literature—none too soon, since systematic demolitions for urban renewal have already begun.

In the eastern halves of both streets, together with Ladder Street which gives access to both by steps from Queen's Road, more than half of the businesses are interested in tourist custom, in a spectrum which starts with second-hand junk and finishes with smart curios. The rest of the businesses are occupied mainly in servicing and second-hand sales of machinery such as fans and air conditioners, and this shades into metal-working. Most of these businesses make extensive use of street space. The Lascar Rows are also the site of an old-established cluster of leather wholesaling businesses. Tourists coming to look at the dirty and expensive junk, and the clean and expensive curios, displayed in this odd semi-industrial backwater, at once unlovely, untraditional and authentic, find the place both fascinating and repellent, like much else in Hong Kong.

'URBAN RENEWAL'

The government appointed a working party on slum clearance in 1964, and it reported in 1965.[21] They considered that 'in some areas nothing less than complete clearance and redevelopment' was necessary. They named an area comprising Sheung Wan and its western neighbour Saiyingpoon, both generously defined, as an Urban Renewal District. Broadly speaking, the Working Party proposed that residential densities should be increased per unit of land in residential use, but that the proportion of all land in private use (residential or commercial) should be reduced, to make way for greatly increased provision of public open space and schools.

They also proposed sweeping changes in land use, especially in the old business heart of Sheung Wan, where Bonham Strand West was apparently to become an urban motorway. These plans were wisely revised in the subsequent *Report* of 1970. The official *Outline Zoning Plan* for the area which was published in 1972 proposes relatively few changes in land use, and takes into account the extent to which private redevelopment has demonstrated capacity to create urban renewal in the area since the working party first reported in 1965; it recognizes that the northern half of the area concerned is neither a slum-district nor primarily residential, and it recognizes the reality of the 'commercial/residential' category of land use. The separation of divergent and potentially incompatible uses of property will be relegated to the level of individual leases, within the broad framework of the plan. Connaught Road, the present waterfront, will be the main traffic road, and (though this does not emerge from the outline zoning plan) there is to be further reclamation along the shore which will provide space to separate cargo handling from through traffic. These are all welcome proposals. Less welcome is the small provision for open spaces and gardens.

The working party proposed that work should start with a Pilot Scheme, which is to occupy the northern part of what is here called the Taipingshan town. Compulsory purchase, demolitions and the assembly of sites for the Pilot Scheme began in 1970, and has progressed slowly up to the present. There had already been some rebuilding in the area before the Scheme was started—more no doubt than was originally envisaged (Plate 5).

The area of the Pilot Scheme was reasonably promising ground for a policy of urban renewal in official terms and by comprehensive methods. Up to 1965, private enterprise had shown little capacity to bring the standards of property up to date.

> The degree of overcrowding in this Area (1 person per 25 sq. ft. of gross floor area or 1 person per 15 sq. ft. of net floor area) is even worse than the average for the District (1 person per 29 sq. ft. of gross floor area or 1 person per 18 sq. ft. of net floor area). There are virtually no public open space or educational facilities. A large proportion of the area is divided into very small lots which cannot be developed and a great many of the buildings are potentially dangerous.[22]

But in the upshot, even in the Pilot Scheme area where there was a good deal of residential slum property, government policy has settled down for the present to action on a rather less interventionist level than was at first contemplated. Present policy for the Pilot Scheme area is to reserve some amalgamated sites for community facilities and to lease others commercially.

One factor which must have influenced the government in making these decisions was surely the extent to which private redevelopment of sites has already taken place in Sheung Wan. If it is true that private redevelopment can and generally will create urban renewal, three kinds of situation still remain for government action. These are the acquisition of sites and construction of buildings (and provision of gardens and trees, squares and traffic-free areas of all kinds) for public use; the assembling of sites which are too small for private redevelopment, and where necessary the changing of street geography to exclude traffic or to permit rebuilding to realistic heights; and the purchase and clearance of slum property which for whatever reason has not been redeveloped by the owners or private redevelopers. Government planning for Yaumati is already based more or less on considerations of these kinds. There is abundant scope for all these kinds of activity throughout the older parts of both Victoria and Kowloon. All this means that in guiding the direction and extent of change in the city under private development, conditions of lease are likely to remain paramount.

Open space was a revealing oddity in the working party's report, and one which shows every sign of developing into a long-term problem. The Pilot Scheme would provide 1.35 acres of public open space. But the extent of open space at present in use by the people is roughly the same as that figure when the open space at Possession Point (which did not appear to be recorded by the working party) is added to that in the streets which are free or almost free from traffic, and freely used by the people as they choose, especially for working and eating. In realistic terms, when the likelihood of sharper police control after redevelopment is brought to mind, comprehensive redevelopment is likely to reduce, rather than enlarge, the amount of public open space which the people can use as they wish.

TOWARDS THE SEPARATION OF USES

Sheung Wan is both a residential district and a business centre. There is a deep-seated and increasing tendency for the two functions to separate out. On the street scale, this has to a large extent already happened. On the scale of the individual building, the separation of uses is still relatively limited, but there is certainly a tendency for it to increase. Even ten years ago, many prosperous businessmen still lived over their shops in Bonham Strand West. During the past decade they have moved out, to Happy Valley and elsewhere. They have done so partly in response to rebuilding. The gradual shift away from the older tenement tradition has been one result, and also one cause, of this change.[23]

In an increasing number of cases, conditions of lease which prescribe limitations on use are tending to separate out kinds of use. Typically, these forbid the introduction of either domestic or industrial uses into office buildings. Partly under the pressure of such conditions of lease, partly because of the supervisory mechanism introduced for buildings in multiple ownership in 1970, and partly because it is now being argued by purchasers of offices that a fall in the physical and amenity standard of the building is a fall in prestige and hence a fall in values, it now seems likely that office buildings where a deliberate attempt is made to keep out factory work and cooking will actually succeed in keeping these intrusive uses out. This kind of separation of uses is already common, though not universal, in Central District. It is now quite common in new buildings in Sheung Wan, and during the coming decade it seems certain to extend much further.

Typically, the older buildings have the more mixed uses. One commercial building of about 1935 on an excellent site in Queen's Road, which was demolished in 1972 or 1973, had nine shop premises, seven of them selling Chinese-style jewellery. The space upstairs (three floors, no lift) was arranged on the basis of central corridors, each lined with offices behind wooden partitions with space above, opening from the corridors by Chinese half-doors. In effect, each floor of this *t'ang-lou* building operated like a tenement floor. Privacy for business discussions in these offices could not be much greater than would be enjoyed in a tea-house—and in fact partitions of basically the same kind were standard fittings in the Chinese-style restaurants in the city 30 years ago. The use of the upstairs property in this block was originally commercial by intention (an ancient notice painted on a wall forbade cooking), and it remained basically commercial; but there was a great deal of domestic living in the building, and the top floor was wholly residential. The most important kind of business upstairs in this building was dentistry, but there were also various offices and small factories, some with residential cubicles and cockloft beds. The building fell to this undistinguished level in the hectic years after 1945. In the present phase of radical redevelopment in Sheung Wan, both private and official, buildings of this kind are becoming scarce.

A post-war building opposite this one brings the story up to date for premises of this kind. This building was finished about 1966. The Queen's Road frontage comprises eight shops in a mixed group of trades: two ivory businesses, tailors, food shops, and a patent medicine business. The Jervois Street frontage has textile businesses. There are four floors above ground level, each with four addresses on an open corridor overlooking Jervois Street, and there is a lift. The top floor is occupied by a Chinese locality association (*t'ung-hsiang-hui*); lower floors by factories making light metal goods such as jewellery,[24] a textile wholesaler, various trading offices, some flats with cubicles used as lodging-houses, and dentists' surgeries, apparently much smarter than those in the building last discussed.

Recent office buildings differ a good deal from those which have just been described. They do so in two ways: in physical layout, which is typically on the hallway plan, in tall buildings with lifts; and also in the intention to enforce the separation of uses, which so far appears effective. The new office buildings now going up in streets like Bonham Strand West are light and, so far at least, clean; the staircases are clean and almost free from stores of merchandise; and cooking, residence, and the use of office flats for manufacturing are prohibited, apparently successfully. The building of the owner's own partition walls, on *t'ang-lou* principles, is also prohibited. It remains to be seen whether the separation of uses in the new buildings will resist indefinitely the encroachment of tenants' stores, the domestic preoccupations of the caretakers, and odd adventitious arrangements which soon become necessary commitments.

Sheung Wan now has a number of buildings which have seen some years of service under the new principles. Evidence from these is mixed, though all are much cleaner than such buildings used to be, and there seems to be little or no cooking or manufacturing in such buildings. The best buildings do preserve the cleanliness and order of the new state very well, even after several years. In the less well-kept buildings, there is a good deal of variation from floor to floor; some landings are encumbered with merchandise and some offices are quite heavily sub-partitioned, whilst other parts of the same building have little sign of unorthodox use. Apparently the physical state of a building adapts to its socio-economic pretensions, and vice versa, in a continuum of cause and effect.

CONCLUSION

From what has been said about Sheung Wan and its various parts, and the characteristic processes of development which operate in the area, some generalizations can be drawn.

The first of these is the simplest: that Queen's Road divides Sheung Wan into two areas, one built on the hillsides and commercially weak, and the other built on reclaimed land and commercially much stronger. These two areas have little in common from any point of view, including planning for the future.

The second is related to the first: that in this elderly and complex area, localities based on various kinds of specialism—morphological, economic, social, institutional, historic—separate themselves out with remarkable effectiveness, whether it be rice businesses on the waterfront, salt fish in des Voeux Road and ginseng in Bonham Strand West, cubicles in the Taipingshan streets, various Western-based wholesaling trades in Wing Lok Street, or marketing of vegetables and other domestic trades like butchers' shops in the neighbourhood of the Western Market.

At the level of the big and stable wholesaling trades, such as rice, Chinese medicines and the *nam-pak-hong* group, it has been shown that stability of local clusters of businesses arises out of stability of business networks which are based on personal relationships among businessmen. It is not suggested that all locality clusters arise in contexts as stable as these, but most, perhaps all, are based on local continuity of repute, local precedent, local adaptations which have recognizable rationales, and local groups of individuals, including customers, suppliers and sub-contractors, who know one another. Instability of firms in these clusters is another story; it arises not only from individual inadequacies, but also from tension between the necessarily limited size of each trade as a whole, and the cluster's capacity for growth.

Together with local continuities deriving from such situations, goes far-reaching local change which may be rapid and total. The present phase of redevelopment on and behind the waterfront, replacing old tenements on four floors and with mixed uses by tall buildings subject to the separation of uses is one example. The disappearance of vitality from night-life in most of Sheung Wan since 1950 is another. The creation of the busy evening fair on the waterfront is a third. The removal of cargo handling and other waterfront uses from a great part of the Sheung Wan waterfront by fresh reclamation and in other ways since 1945 is a fourth. The urban renewal clearances are a fifth.

What these cross-currents create and tend to perpetuate is a Sheung Wan whose structure is in locality terms *cellular*. Particular localities, which may be no more than half a block in extent but which are often much bigger, emerge from the business or social or access or investment pressures of the preceding decade with specific dominant characteristics. They react in recognizable ways towards the pressures of the following decade, weakening and dissolving or strengthening and growing; and they exert their own pressures on their surroundings. Specialism, defined in terms which include everything which can create distinctiveness in a group of addresses, hence dominates the Sheung Wan landscapes. The evidence is that this scheme of things arises almost wholly out of Chinese social and economic custom.

1 *Nam-pak-hong (nan-pei-hang)* is not a specifically Hong Kong expression or institution. In Yoneda's general account of business institutions in China, obviously written as a practical business introduction, *nam-pak-hong* takes its place among about forty other trades. Yoneda regarded the trade as limited to specialist items of grocery such as dried fruits, together with sugar. Y. Yoneda, *Shina shōten to shōkanshū* (Tokyo, 1941).

2 This list is taken from *HKCCNC* (1971), part i, p. 143, where it is supplemented by another which ranges still more widely, including rubber, coffee-beans, tin and handicrafts.

3 *HKCCNC* (1971), part i, p. 124, has a list of specialities.

4 This date is reported by H. Ingrams, *Hong Kong* (HMSO, London, 1952), p. 147. In Ingrams's time, the association proclaimed moral principles and displayed a portrait of Sun Yat-Sen.

5 H. Maeda, *Honkon gaikan* (Tokyo, 1919), pp. 191–2.

6 All the generalizations about business practice in this section are based on a number of conversations with merchants and others who were kind enough to give me their time and to answer questions.

7 The topic of personal relationships as the foundation of business dealing in a Chinese community is a recurrent one in W.E. Willmott (ed.), *Economic organisation in Chinese society* (Stanford, 1972), especially in D.R. de Glopper's paper, 'Doing business in Lukang', and R.H. Silin's paper, 'Marketing and credit in a Hong Kong wholesale market', which deals with the organization and structure of business dealing in the Kennedy Town vegetable market to the west of Sheung Wan. These authors discuss what Willmott in the introduction to the book calls 'conscious particularisation of economic relationships' (p. 5), and the place of both trust and *rapport* in economic dealings. In Lukang (which is in Taiwan), a man can do business with whoever he likes, but 'one does not do business with people one does not know' (de Glopper, op. cit., pp. 302–3). In these terms, the typical Hong Kong situation as it has emerged in the present work is that a man only does business with friends, but that he by no means expects to do any kind of business with any sort of friend; within the circle of his friends he deals according to his own wishes and the needs of the moment.

8 And in Japanese town organization. T. Yazaki, *Social change and the city in Japan* (San Francisco, 1968), pp. 185ff, 150ff, 438ff. 'Chinatowns' exhibit similar features. Cf. J.C. Jackson, 'The Chinatowns of Southeast Asia', *Pacific Viewpoint*, 16 (1), 1975, pp. 45–77.

9 Shigesi Katō. 'On the *hang* or associations of merchants in China, with especial reference to the institution in the T'ang and Sung periods'. *Memoirs of the research department of the Tōyō Bunko*, 8 (1936), pp. 45–83.

10 Katō, op. cit., 79ff. According to Balazs, specialist trade or craft quarters were called *hang* from the seventh century, 'and contained the germ of the guild organisation'. E. Balazs, 'Fairs in China', in *Chinese civilisation and bureaucracy* (New Haven, 1964), p. 60.

11 Katō, op. cit., p. 54. This type of situation can be illustrated from the engineering trades in Canton Road, Yaumati (Chapter IV).

12 Ibid., p. 59.

13 As shown clearly by Joe England in his interesting paper, 'Industrial relations in Hong Kong' in Keith Hopkins (ed.), *Hong Kong: the Industrial Colony* (Hong Kong, 1971).

14 The account of these special features which follows is based on the government's publication, *Background information on the Hong Kong rice trade, together with a statement by the Hon. T.D. Sorby . . .* (Hong Kong, 1967). It is interesting to read that the rice trade in China in Sung times distinguished among merchants, brokers and retailers, and that brokers 'enjoyed a more or less monopolistic position buttressed by official support'. (Y. Shiba, *Commerce and Society in Sung China* (Tokyo, 1968), translated by Mark Elvin, Michigan series no. 2, 1970, pp. 73–80.)

15 *HKCCNC* (1971), part i, p. 111.

16 Sorby, *Background information...*, op. cit., p. 2.

17 In 1974 the Consumer Council proposed not a suppression of the scheme, but a widening of the franchise to import, using these arguments. *Sing Pao (Daily News)*, 30 August 1974, p. 4.

18 Sorby, op. cit., p. 4.

19 *HKCCNC* (1971), part i, p. 110.

20 Office of the Commissioner for Rating and Valuation, *Valuation Table for 1870*. Pound Lane is another case in point. It had 36 addresses in 1871, but has only 5 today.

21 *Report of the Working Party on slum clearance and the effects on urban redevelopment of the Buildings (Amendment) (No. 2) Ordinance 1964*, n.d. The working party was concerned not only with squalor in slum areas, but also with problems arising from demolition of old buildings and private redevelopment of the sites, where it was feared that neighbouring buildings might collapse.

22 Ibid., Para. 95, p. 18.

23 The former custom of living over the shop in Sheung Wan is vouched for by businessmen in the area at the present. It is documented in R.H. Hughes's record of 'the occupation of ten tenement houses, 1948', in des Voeux Road West ('Hong Kong, an urban study', in *Geographical Journal*, 117, i (1951), p. 19). One of the ten tenement houses was occupied by a money-changer's shop, his flat and his staff quarters. Another was partly occupied by a goldsmith's shop and his flat and staff quarters combined.

24 A factory in a block of this kind pays about $1,000 per month in rent. A rent of this kind for a flat where there may be 10 or 15 men employed—quite legitimately—in making jewellery, with a total output (value-added, including wages) of not less than $15,000–20,000 per month, is not a very important item. Here as elsewhere, rents in Hong Kong are high considered in relation to the property rented; but considered in relation to the use made of the property, they are less so.

4 Yaumati and Old Kowloon

ORIGINS AND GROWTH

THE Kowloon peninsula, south of Boundary Street, became part of the British colony in 1860. Given the steep slopes of the island, and the relatively flat and open topography of the peninsula less than a mile away across the harbour, it is not surprising that the Army hoped to keep the whole peninsula for military use,[1] and in the upshot the Army did keep the best site on the peninsula, the group of low hills close to the south-western corner, which until 1970 remained in Army use under the name of Whitfield Barracks. The sterilization of this site has been one of the dominating conditions of the physical growth of Old Kowloon, since (together with a small naval yard which occupied part of the adjacent coast until after the Pacific war) it has separated Tsimshatsui, the southern tip, from Yaumati and Mongkok on the western coast, and governed the line taken by Nathan Road.

There were two other factors of comparable general importance in the early physical growth of Yaumati. One was the layout of the streets. The whole area is laid out on grid plans, of which there are only two; most of the streets belong to a single grid layout. The other has been the history of foreshore reclamation. Much more than half of the area between Nathan Road and the sea shown in Figure 7 (cf. Plate 8) has been artificially created.

More than half of this work, particularly the northern part, was done in the phase 1887–1904, and most of the rest was completed by 1924 (Figure 2). The shape and size of the modern Yaumati and Mongkok west of Nathan Road are really the outcome of the extent of reclamation. Reclamation is a continuing factor in the development of Yaumati. Hong Kong is close to the technical limits of reclamation in the eastern part of the harbour where the main achievements of the past generation have been. For space for fresh schemes, the government is now necessarily turning to the western part of the harbour, including the Yaumati waterfront.

Piers for shipping were built on the west-facing coast of the peninsula, which had the calmer and deeper water. Both Yaumati and Tsimshatsui started life as dockside and suburban villages, serving the needs of shipping and sailor and soldier communities, but they did not develop in similar ways. By 1920, Yaumati had become a moderate-sized Chinese town, with its own town centre, markets, restaurants and other civilized central amenities, as well as grim wasteland and industrial peripheries. Tsimshatsui was more cosmopolitan, and retained more of the tone of a colonial town, though a quiet and backward one. Neither was very significant by the standards of Victoria on the island.

Yaumati grew slowly, and at first with little dignity. Groups of hovels, derelict boats, and workshops engaged in the shipping trades, fringed the little town in 1882.[2] At that time the town centre in Shanghai Street had tailors, barbers, silversmiths, chandlers, brothels and coffin businesses, but the fringes of the town, for instance in Reclamation Street which was then the waterfront, had little but maritime trades.[3]

The street grids were filled up decade by decade outwards from Shanghai Street. Jordan Road, now a major artery, was slow to develop. It had very few businesses in 1927, as the directory shows. By 1940 there were tea-houses there, but no big restaurants *(chiu-lou)*. The ferry at Jordan Road started passenger business (in common with the Mongkok ferry at Shantung Street and the Shumshuipo ferry at Pak Hoi Street) in 1924. The vehicular ferry service to Victoria started at Jordan Road in 1932. Land to the west of Canton Road in Mongkok, including some of that now occupied by parts of the engineering complex which will be discussed later, was not built up until after 1945; according to local people, the Japanese authorities stored coal there during the Pacific war. But the tools market in Canton Road existed even then. Clearly, the phase of rebuilding with high property in Shanghai Street and the phase of first building in Canton Road must have overlapped, or come close to doing so, in the 1950s. The phase of infilling is continuous in both time and place with the phase of overfilling; and the two may even coalesce, so that a street fills up to its physical limits as soon as it is built.

Yaumati is intensely varied—perhaps more intensely so than any other part of the city. It is at once metropolitan and suburban, industrial, commercial and residential, seafaring and land-based. Its densities, especially of street use, are exceptionally high. In style, as in history, it occupies some of the space which lies between the dense uses and established traditional trades and methods of Sheung Wan, and the vast scale factory industries and new interpretations of Chinese traditions of the great bulk of contemporary Kowloon. A group of characteristic features have been selected, and it is hoped through these to demonstrate the human richness of the area and its place in the spectrum of Hong Kong localities. These features are, Shanghai Street, the original main business street; some business clusters akin to those of Sheung Wan, including the important engineering group; and some very important street trades. It is intended to give an account of each of these in turn. Something will also be said about the realities of the rebuilding process, which has been central in Yaumati during the past generation. Finally, an attempt is made to put present-day Yaumati into its proper historic context, which is the contemporary growth of Nathan Road and Mongkok on a scale beyond the past or present experience of the old Yaumati.

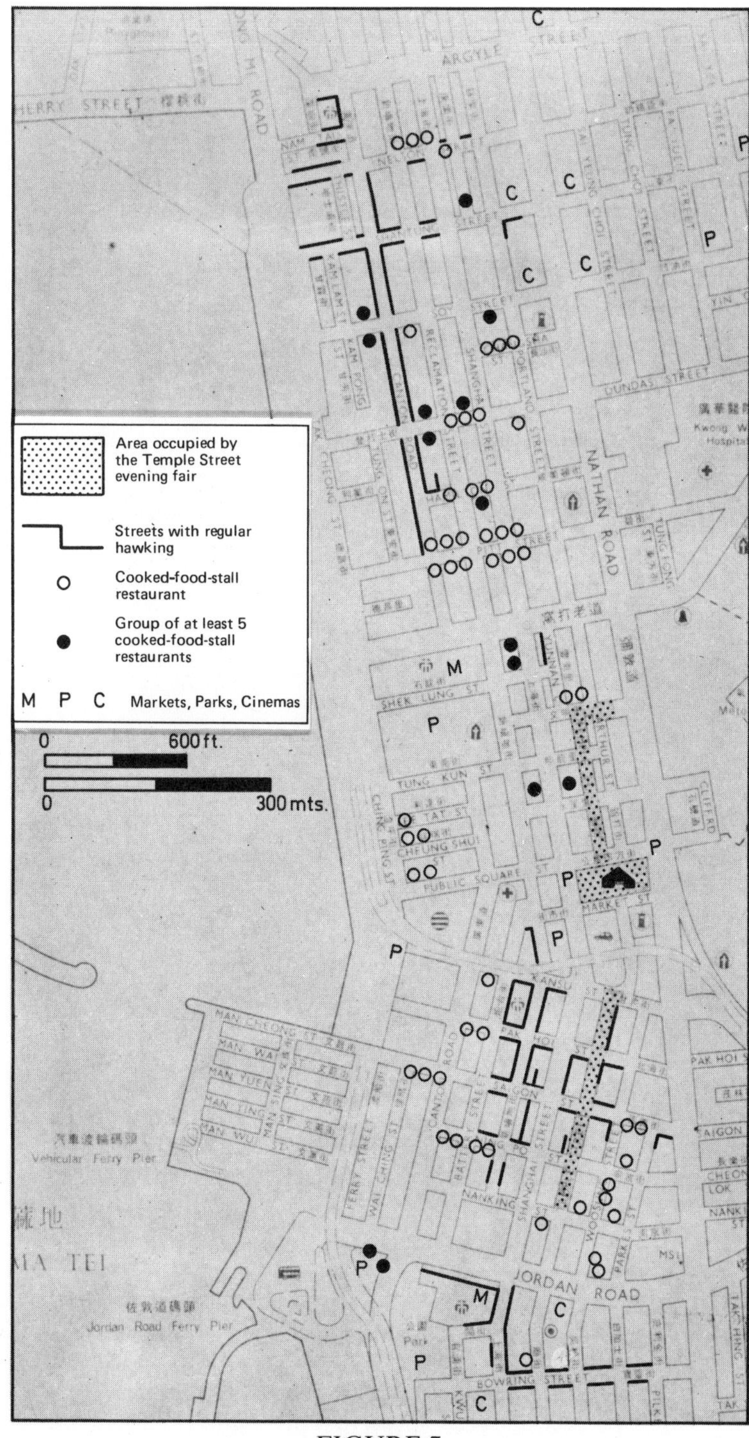

FIGURE 7

YAUMATI AND PART OF MONGKOK. STREET PLAN SHOWING MARKETS AND HAWKER STREETS (1974)

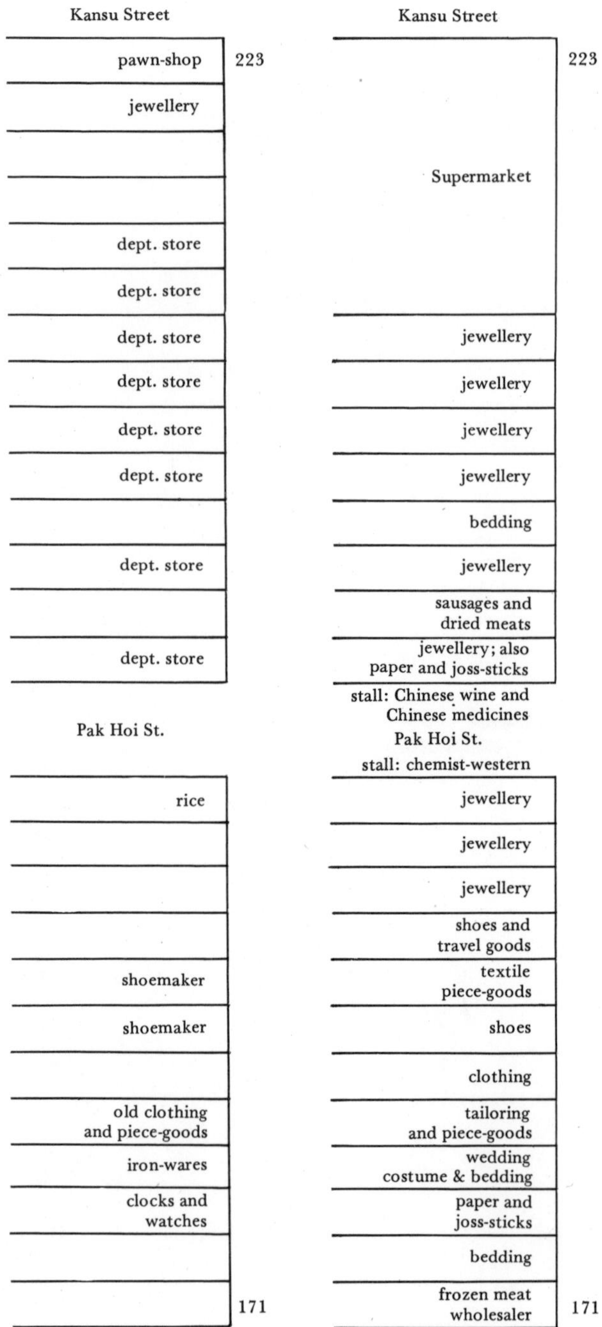

FIGURE 8

ASSEMBLAGES OF USES IN GROUND-FLOOR PROPERTY, 1927 AND 1974, AT 171–223 SHANGHAI STREET

Note: Both at the present time and in earlier generations, a 'departmental store' may be quite a modest business. For 1927, the term is used to translate *Su-hang yang-huo shang-tien,* a Soochow and foreign merchant.

SHANGHAI STREET—CHANGE AND CONTINUITY IN AN OLD BUSINESS STREET

Shanghai Street was originally the main street of Yaumati, and the principal street in Kowloon. It is still full of interest. An attempt will be made to illustrate the range of activities which go on there and their historic contexts, through some assemblages of property uses.

The assemblage shown in Figure 8 comes from the southern section, the part which has the longest history of dense development. The assemblage for 1927, reconstructed from the directory for that year, is also given for the sake of comparison.

At the present time, this is a typical good section of Shanghai Street, with many Chinese-style jewellers, cloth businesses and businesses specializing in Chinese wedding clothing together with bedding. Business, apart from the new supermarket at the northern end, is conservative in character, both in terms of kinds of specialism and in terms of recent changes—apart from the supermarket, there were no changes in 1970–4 which introduced new kinds of business into the assemblage. The supermarket is new since 1971. It occupies six addresses, and in terms of scale, kind of business and manner of dealing alike it marks a radical departure from the past in these otherwise traditional blocks.

The supermarket has occupied property in the best part of this section of the street, adjacent to Kansu Street and the vicinity of the old Tin Hau temple. This section was already the best, apparently, in 1927, when it was dominated by the mixed clothing and novelties 'departmental stores'.

It is clear that the bulk of the businesses recorded in this assemblage for 1974 belong to a class of shopping for special occasions which is somewhat more traditional than that which would figure in any corresponding assemblage for Nathan Road, with its electrical appliance businesses, camera and fashion shops, and jewellers also selling watches. The style of shop-fitting in Shanghai Street is also generally more traditional than in Nathan Road; various compromises are adopted between the old-fashioned open style, which is still usual in the food shops in Canton Road to the west, and the plate-glass-window style.

The property in these two blocks (Plate 9) varies in age between about 1970 and about 1960—except two old tenements which were probably built about 1925. None of the buildings has more than 9 floors, and there are no lifts. Upper-floor uses in this property in 1974 included, apart from residence (much of it in cubicles), a hotel, factories, a school, a dentist, a dispensary, a photographer, and a fortune-teller.

At a typical address, in post-war property with 6 floors, there is a flat on each side of the staircase on the five upper floors. Most of the flats have cubicles, and one is a dormitory with bed-spaces in two-tier bunks. A Chinese-style doctor has consulting rooms in a flat on the first floor.

Figure 9 shows the assemblage of property uses on the east side of Shanghai Street between Pitt Street and Hamilton Street, some blocks to the north. Information is also given for 1927. Comparison between these

1927

Hamilton Street

No.	Use
404	rice-dealer
	tea-house
	bamboo wares
	tobacco
	foreign goods; copper and ironware
	bamboo wares
	mirrors and glass
	tobacco
380	

Pitt Street

1974

Hamilton Street

No.	Use
404	chemist, Chinese and western
	restaurant
	Chinese wines
	departmental store (including groceries and rice)
	hairdressing, men and women
	hardware and builders' materials
	bank
	tools and builders' materials
	books and stationery
	chemist, Chinese and western
380	TV and electrical goods

Pitt Street

FIGURE 9

ASSEMBLAGES OF USES IN GROUND-FLOOR PROPERTY, 1927 AND 1974, AT 380–404 SHANGHAI STREET two assemblages may be thought to point as much to overall change in social and economic custom in the city, as to change in the status or function of Shanghai Street. Western chemists, banks and TV businesses have now entered streets like Shanghai Street. Bamboo wares, prominent in 1927, are now less common. However, no change of use took place in this block between 1970 and 1974.

Property in this block ranges between 7 and 12 floors, and in date between about 1957 and 1967. Apart from one clothing factory, there is little use of the upper floors except for residence, though many flats are heavily cubicled.

The assemblage shown in Figure 10 comes from the west side of Shanghai Street, between Nelson Street and Argyle Street, in Mongkok territory. The past record, for 1927, 1951 and (as far as it goes) 1940 is also given in Figure 10.

For 1927, less than half of the addresses were mentioned in the directory. Those which were named were very mixed. A dealer in electrical appliances at that time occupied a property facing this block. It seems clear that in 1927 this block of property lay at the northern fringes of business Yaumati. At present, of course, this block of property is very strong and prosperous.

The assemblage of 1951, with some additions for 1940, incomplete as it is for both years, must furnish a link between these two, though it does not greatly resemble either. By 1951, not far from the height of the hectic post-war expansion, this had plainly become a good shopping block, with a cluster of a goldsmiths and 'departmental stores' (mixed clothing, shoes and related accessories businesses, not necessarily big shops). It is clear that by 1951 much more money was being spent in this part of Shanghai Street than a generation earlier, and this in turn suggests that by 1951 the Yaumati side of the new Mongkok was already very well developed. The two goldsmiths and four 'departmental stores' of 1940 seem to furnish evidence of the beginning of this process. In both 1940 and 1951, there is evidence of the sharing of shop premises, which was done (and is done still, though less commonly) by means of any one of a wide variety of degrees of physical separation, ranging from fully partitioned premises to facing but unrelated counters.

A study of the upper floor uses adds to the understanding of this property block in 1974. It comes in four physical parts (Figure 11). Property use above the ground floor in this group of buildings appears to depend in some degree upon the physical style of the property itself. Possession of a lift raises both the general commercial viability of a building, and (more sharply) the commercial viability of the upper floors. Secondly, in a negative sense, pre-war tenement buildings attract very little commercial use apart from lodgings. This must be in part because residential tenants are protected by rent control, and in part because these properties are not very suitable physically for commercial use, because of poor stair access and lack of interior light. Thirdly, the building on the Argyle Street corner evidently has some advantage of accessibility.

	1927	1951	1974
	Argyle Street	Argyle Street	Argyle Street
599			grocery stores wines
		goldsmith, tea-house	jewellery
		goldsmith (also in 1940)	Chinese doctor
			jewellery
			chemist-Chinese and western
		goldsmith	brassieres; wedding costume and bedding
	wooden clogs maker		textile wholesaler
	money-changer	dept. store (also in 1940)	chemist-Chinese
	machine-made clothing factory	chemist-western	wedding costume and bedding
		dept. store (also in 1940)	wedding costume and bedding
			textile piece-goods
	dept. store		clothing (men)
	Chinese prepared drugs	dept. store in 1940	textile piece-goods
		goldsmith & dept. store (also 1940)	tools and machinery
	ground-nuts dealer	goldsmith	jewellery
	sign-board maker	goldsmith	textile piece-goods
		dept. store	clothing (men) and bedding
565	Chinese prepared drugs	western chemist in 1940; goldsmith in 1940	chemist-Chinese and western
			stall: textiles
	Nelson Street	Nelson Street	Nelson Street

FIGURE 10

ASSEMBLAGES OF USES IN GROUND-FLOOR PROPERTY AT VARIOUS DATES AT 565–599 SHANGHAI STREET

Argyle Street extends the busy, prestigious crossing with Nathan Road as far as this corner.

It is clear from the assemblages of contemporary uses in these three places that Shanghai Street varies rather less, in its considerable length, than might be expected. From a study of the assemblages for 1927 it also emerges, less clearly but still convincingly, that Shanghai Street has changed its functions less, during the past forty or more years, than might be expected—particularly when it is borne in mind that most of the property has been rebuilt since that time. Shanghai Street has not changed very much; that is its chief weakness. Nathan Road is the new Shanghai Street. Local opinion agrees with the visible evidence: Shanghai Street has been in slow relative decline for the past twenty-five years.

It is true that Shanghai Street itself has not been stagnant. Relative decline must not be taken (as it may in parts of Sheung Wan) for absolute decline. The old-clothes businesses for which it once formed a focus have gone, and so have some of the ironmongers and most of the rattan dealers. Banks have moved in, and there are dealers in television sets and refrigerators. Businesses have become more specialized. There are still good restaurants and tea-houses, though few fashionable ones. Even so, the transformation of the Nathan Road frontage community from a discontinuous jumble of peripheries—which is what it amounted to in 1945—into a great shopping street which dominates all of Old Kowloon, has left little room for effective competition by the small scale, relative crowding, slower rates of adaptation, working-class tone and old-fashioned style of Shanghai Street—except through lower prices and more polite shopkeepers, and in some degree through specialist goods and services.

CANTON ROAD—THE CLUSTER OF SPECIALIST ENGINEERING BUSINESSES

One most remarkable feature of the area under discussion is the engineering complex of Canton Road and some half-dozen adjacent streets (Plate 12). This group of businesses is so varied and ramifying that definition of it would be difficult, but so much interdigitated in its parts that it cannot but be treated as a whole. It comprises businesses dealing in a range of goods which includes hand tools and small machine tools of all kinds, mechanical and electrical equipment such as fans, pumps, compressors and motors, machinery parts such as ball-races, accessories such as cables, pulleys and rubber wheels, and second-hand machinery and machinery parts. There is also a wide variety of servicing and repair facilities for small machines. Most of these businesses do both retailing and wholesaling; many deal in both new and second-hand machinery and parts; many do servicing as well as selling. Most of the businesses specialize in some way, and some specialize quite narrowly, for instance in ball-bearings or springs, driving belts or chains. Some of the businesses approximate to workshops in appearance, especially those with a strong

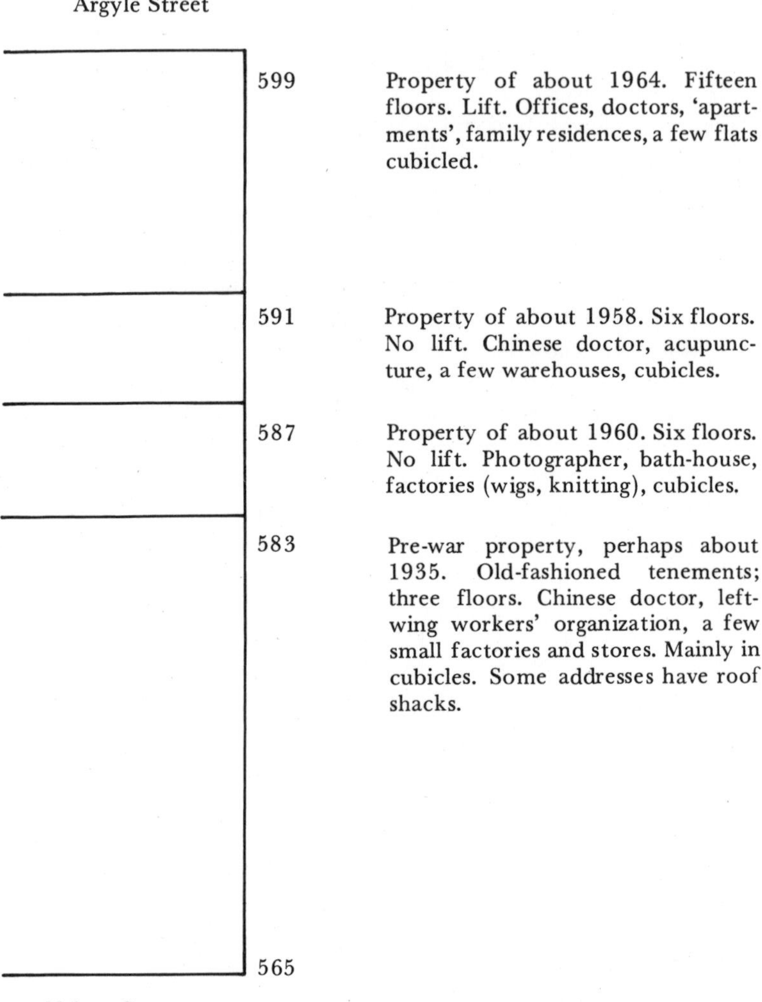

FIGURE 11

CONTEMPORARY PROPERTY TYPES AND UPPER-FLOOR USES AT 565–599 SHANGHAI STREET

second-hand element; others are big places, showrooms rather than shops, selling machinery to small factories.[4] Figure 12 gives an indication of the specialisms in the heart of the complex, Canton Road between Soy Street and Dundas Street. In this section of Canton Road, there is also a regular assemblage of hawkers' stalls dealing in small parts and tools of all kinds; and these are an integral part of the whole complex. Trade in new articles here includes hand tools, trolleys, jacks, fire-extinguishers and sugar-cane crushers. Second-hand trade includes radio and other electrical equipment and parts, pipes, wheels, gears, pulleys and hand tools.

This engineering complex has a variety of tributary business interests, and—what is perhaps the same thing—it shades off at the edges in a number of directions, in both a physical and a business sense. One of these is motor vehicle engineering and repairs. Another is manufacture of metal components, electroplating and so forth, and some manufacture of machinery. Another is the sheet and bar iron and steel business and other metal stockholding. Another is the servicing of machinery for factories. Most work of this kind is done by firms in north-eastern and north-western Kowloon, where the bulk of the manufacturing machinery is installed and where the bulk of the machinery-building industry of Hong Kong is located, but they buy parts in this area, and may have work done here. Some work of this kind is also done for the building industry, and the area still has a shipping side, based originally, according to local people, on the fitting of ships for smuggling in the years before the Pacific war. Businessmen agree that there is everywhere a high degree of interdependence among firms.

This cluster of businesses is still growing in terms of both physical extent and density. Canton Road in the area of the hawkers' stalls is still recognized as its centre, but business has tended in the past twenty years to expand increasingly into adjoining streets. Firms are said to be specialized, generally highly capitalized, to depend strongly on personal contacts in business, and to make high profits to set against high risks.[5]

During the past few years, the evidence is that within the engineering group miscellaneous and second-hand parts businesses have tended to give way to more businesses selling machinery, and small businesses to big. In the streets occupied by the complex, there are also some signs of the few non-engineering businesses giving place to businesses within the engineering field. It seems clear that the engineering complex is becoming denser, more modern and more highly capitalized, as well as continuing to grow in size.

This business cluster seems to have taken its present form during the past twenty-five years, and possibly even during the past fifteen. Here as elsewhere in Hong Kong, complex organizations of profoundly stable appearance turn out to have astonishingly short histories. Yaumati was one of the original homes of the metal industry, much of which migrated after the war to cheaper property in Taikoktsui. The pre-war directories show that there were some engineering businesses in this part of Canton Road and adjoining streets such as Tung On Street back into the 1920s;

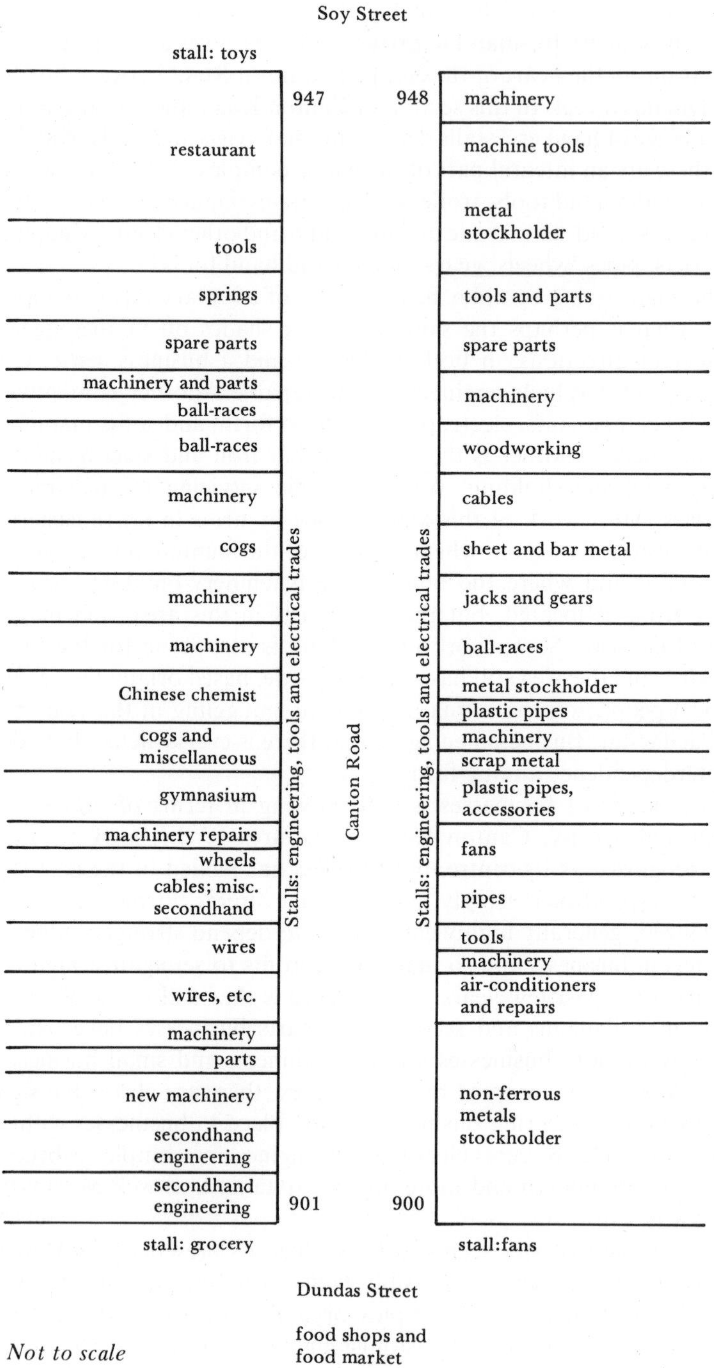

Soy Street

stall: toys			stall: toys
947			948
restaurant			machinery
tools			machine tools
springs			metal stockholder
spare parts			tools and parts
machinery and parts			spare parts
ball-races			machinery
ball-races			woodworking
machinery			cables
cogs			sheet and bar metal
machinery			jacks and gears
machinery			ball-races
Chinese chemist			metal stockholder
cogs and miscellaneous			plastic pipes
gymnasium			machinery
machinery repairs			scrap metal
wheels			plastic pipes, accessories
cables; misc. secondhand			fans
wires			pipes
wires, etc.			tools
machinery			machinery
parts			air-conditioners and repairs
new machinery			non-ferrous metals stockholder
secondhand engineering			
secondhand engineering			
901			900
stall: grocery			stall: fans

Stalls: engineering, tools and electrical trades — Canton Road — Stalls: engineering, tools and electrical trades

Dundas Street

food shops and food market

Not to scale

FIGURE 12

ASSEMBLAGE OF GROUND-FLOOR USES AT 901–947 AND 900–948 CANTON ROAD, 1974 and the early motor-car firms and transport companies in Kowloon were clustered at that time in and around the corresponding section of Nathan Road. But up to 1940 at least, engineering works in this part of Kowloon were mostly in Portland Street or Reclamation Street. The complex does not seem to owe much to the expansions of the late 1930s. The seaward side of this part of Canton Road was not built up at all until the 1950s. The second-hand tools bazaar in Canton Road is another matter. It makes no appearance in the directories, but it is said by local people to be at least fifty years old. Many people claim that it dates from the turn of the century, probably rightly.

It is tempting to suppose that the tools bazaar may be the origin of the whole tools, machinery and engineering complex in this part of Canton Road, and some local people say explicitly that this is so. It is generally said by people in the trade that the characteristic way in which new businesses were—and still are—started is by artisans who save money; and that some of these people started business as street stallholders.

Excluding street stalls, there are now about 250 businesses in this whole cluster, of very mixed sizes and kinds. Most of them lie within a radius of some 1,000 feet from the section of Canton Road between Soy Street and Dundas Street, which is the heart of the area. The locality serves customers from every part of Hong Kong, and it is said by some people to have significant status in the tools and light engineering trades even overseas in South-East Asia.

Many writers have used a 'dual economy' notion of urban economy in Third World cities. McGee, following Franklin, Santos and others, has adopted the notion of an 'upper circuit' and 'lower circuit' of the urban economy in his study of Hong Kong hawkers.[6] Geertz introduced the expressions 'bazaar-type economy' and 'firm-type economy', and showed that in 'Modjokuto' some businessmen were trying to create 'firm-type' businesses within the 'bazaar-type' business world of a small town in Java. In Hong Kong there is no lack of situations which approximate to the two halves of the stereotype (the departmental stores and international businesses in Central District and the big garment manufacturers on the one hand; the hawkers, boat people and small shopkeepers on the other); but there is also an abundance of situations which will not fit neatly into either half. The engineering district which has been described is a case in point. There is a visible continuum, which is vouched for by people in the trade, in the same or related kinds of business and the same streets, from small workshops, street stalls and family shops, members surely of the bazaar economy, through bigger but hardly less domestic workshop or retailing arrangements, through retailers with a wholesaling side or bigger workshops doing sub-contract work for export manufacturers, to big wholesale/retail suppliers of factory machinery with sophisticated catalogues and extensive contacts, surely to be reckoned as belonging to the 'firm-centred economy', or to manufacturing businesses which have risen within a generation from 'bazaar' workshop level to clear 'firm' status.[8] It is not surprising to find that in Hong Kong the movement towards 'firms' is already far advanced, even though the 'bazaar-type economy' retains many characteristics of both prosperity and social utility.

BUSINESS USES IN THE STREETS. THE COOKED-FOOD-STALL RESTAURANTS AND OTHER HAWKING

The cross streets like Ningpo Street towards the southern end of Yaumati have their own character. Apart from Kansu Street and Jordan Road, all in varying degrees furnish fixed sites for hawkers, who more or less dominate the streets. Traffic takes second place. In particular, there are many fixed-pitch cooked-food stalls—or, as they might more realistically be called—cooked-food-stall restaurants. (Figure 7.)

In Hong Kong, hawking of any kind requires a government licence. A fixed-pitch hawking licence costs $20 for a year, and a pedlar's licence $10. The cost of a fixed-pitch cooked-food-stall licence is $250 per year. None of these sums is large, judged by the scale of the business which most hawkers do. The problem is not the cost of the licence, but the obtaining of a site. This is all particularly true for the cooked-food-stall restaurants. 'In a good site stalls can get business all day and all night.'[9] These establishments flourish especially in the older parts of the two cities. Each establishment has its own specialism—for instance, noodle dishes, fritters, tripe; and some sell full meals, with very competent cooking. The fundamental fixture is the same for every stall. It is a solid roofed hut with open sides, which stands freely at the side of the street and forms the kitchen (Plate 13). In principle the customers sit at the stall fixture on benches, but in practice the majority of these stalls also operate several tables which occupy parts of the public pavement or premises rented for the purpose.

A big and successful cooked-food-stall restaurant may have not only the original tent-like kitchen, now used only for cooking rice and serving roast meats and as a larder, but a big gas stove beside it, where most of the cooking is done; a kind of scullery installation for chopping meat and cleaning fish and vegetables; one or two big refrigerators, a number of electric fans in the summer and about a dozen tables and upwards of sixty seats. The urban council's experiment of 1957 showed that 'however large an area for seating accommodation was allowed it was filled up'. Such a place employs two cooks with two assistants, four waiters and a woman to wash crockery, and it may be worked in two shifts. Most Hong Kong people believe that this illegal use of street space is often a source of local police corruption, on a scale proportionate to the business which is being done.[10]

The cooked-food-stall restaurants dominate the cross streets which lie between Kansu Street and Jordan Road and contribute to the appearance of antiquity and long-established tradition which the streets have.[11] But the stalls have occupied sites in these streets for much less time than appearances would suggest. Until about 1965, most or all of these cooked-food-stall restaurants occupied sites in the 'Public Square' in front of the Tin Hau temple, and formed a continuum with other kinds of activity such as the Temple Street evening fair, and gambling around and even inside the temple. Uses have been separated here too. The Public Square has been renovated, with some new trees to supplement the old, grass heavily protected by railings, and new concrete seats. Limited as it is, it represents a new dimension in these crowded tenement streets.

In Yaumati, quite apart from the cooked-food-stall restaurants, there are also many hawkers' stalls of other kinds, especially occupying the sites where the ends of the building blocks abut on to the pavements. These stalls may be in any of a wide variety of businesses—various kinds of repairs, such as shoes or electrical equipment; barbers', tinsmiths', grocery 'stores' with drinks; tailoring; sale of shoes or goldfish. Twenty years ago, businesses akin to these were much more usually itinerant, with portable equipment, like the cooking businesses still earlier. Shops in the regular fixed street property may also occupy street space. There is clearly abundant practical difference between the structure of a building itself, which rarely breaks the law, and the addition of accretions, which commonly do so, by using the public street for private purposes. It is usually thought that the local police may levy blackmail on a store which (for example) stores crates of bottles on the pavement, unless the store owner has friends in the police department—though here too the payment of such money has recently become more nearly optional.

Hawking of all kinds is a surprisingly important feature of the Hong Kong scene.[12] Attention is drawn later (chapter IX) to its relationship with squatting and other kinds of irregular use of public space; here something must be said about its practical consequences, especially in the streets of old tenement areas like Yaumati and the forecourts of the resettlement estates, which are the places where it is most densely developed.

Hawking creates litter, dirt, noise and a degree of congestion which in case of fire might be disastrous. Much of the hawking which goes on is illegal in one respect or another, and consequently hawking is one of the foundations of small-scale blackmail and corruption in the community. Hawking also supplies social needs. Most of the community's fruit and vegetables are sold by hawkers (Plate 14). Hawkers also sell many other kinds of food, including cooked snacks of all kinds. Hawking provides a livelihood for some tens of thousands of working people. In the resettlement estates, it is the hawker markets, however unsightly, which recreate an environment on the human scale, especially among the new high blocks (Plate 27).

It is this complex of social utility combined with social disorderliness which is called the hawker problem. The government's approach to the hawker problem is another phase of the policy of the separation of uses. The government is building, and intends to go on building, fixed bazaars to accommodate licensed hawkers. In these bazaars, hopefully, the litter created by hawking can be contained and the corruption suppressed, and the congestion will not arise. However, so far the bazaar policy has met with only limited success. Customers tend to be scarce in the bazaars. The evidence is that potential customers are those who find hawkers lining the pedestrian routes which they are taking. Hawker bazaars only become 'pedestrian routes' in this sense if they are big and special. They may do so more readily, once other hawking in the locality is suppressed; this policy of hawker bazaars can expect to be cumulatively more successful as it is put into practice. Meanwhile, the people in working-class districts treat the streets as their property, which perhaps is what they are.

In the short term at least, the government is also coming to grips with this situation. Hawker permitted streets are now to be designated, where hawking will be allowed; and to this end all fixed pitches have now been surveyed.[13] The people have also not been idle. During the past few years, the tendency in all the streets under discussion has been to expand hawking, cooking and eating in the street. Regular sites have been extended and occasional sites have become regular—and the same seems to be broadly true of hawker markets elsewhere in the city.

It is one characteristic of the problem of litter and dirt that it forms a continuum with the hawker problem. Both belong characteristically to the old working-class tenements and streets. Both have been reinvigorated in the resettlement estates, and neither has really been solved in the rebuilt tenement areas. The problem of litter and dirt is centred in the habitual indifference of the public to litter, even very dirty litter in such places as their own stretches of pavement or their own ventilation wells. It is wider than the hawker problem, but perhaps a little less intractable. The campaign for a cleaner Hong Kong which was opened in 1972 has had visible effects in many kinds of areas including the dirtiest; but continued effort will be needed throughout the foreseeable future if progress is to be maintained.

TEMPLE STREET—THE EVENING FAIR

Another remarkable feature of Yaumati is the evening hawkers' and pedlars' fair held in Temple Street (Plate 11). Every evening, almost the whole length of Temple Street—about one-third of a mile—is occupied by an assemblage of hawkers' and pedlars' stalls. The great majority of those who come either as customers, or simply to walk about, are working-class men. This is reflected in the types of merchandise sold—men's clothing of all kinds (including suits and shirts which can be had made-to-measure); records; watches; novelties like toys; revitalizers; books including cheap reprints of the Chinese classics; clothing accessories like belts; shoes and pens. Prices are low. Some of the goods are factory rejects; some may be stolen from factories or warehouses; some are imported; much simply represents cheap Hong Kong production. There are cooked-food sellers, with portable equipment, generally at the street intersections. Towards its northern end, Temple Street opens out into the open space at the Tin Hau temple which gives the street its name. In the evenings the fair occupies the Public Square as well as the northern extension of Temple Street which is detached from the rest by the temple site. In the northern extension, there are more and bigger cooked-food stalls, many with tables and benches, many selling cooked seafood. The Public Square has more performers of all kinds, including several singers all of whom use electronic amplifiers, together with fortune-tellers, palmists and quack doctors.

On a relatively quiet night, there may be about 1,500 people in Temple Street at any one time; at busy times, about 2,500. On a busy night, there are about 450 merchandise stalls and about 70 cooked-food stalls in the whole fair. Upwards of 20,000 people may pass through the fair on a busy evening. Naturally, the fixed property uses include many restaurants, mah-jong houses and so forth; these in a sense form part of the night fair. There are also shops, many of which remain open until late in the evening at least at some times of the year—furniture businesses are a case in point. The fair is noisy, especially with popular songs both Chinese and Western played at record and cassette stalls. It is also brightly lit. Until 1970 lamps for each stall were prepared daily in the forecourt of the temple, but since that time electric light has been usual, taken by cable from the fixed property.

The organization of the Temple Street evening fair is obscure. Responsible officers in government service say that the fair takes place virtually without administration. Local people say that the market is administered in practice nevertheless—sites allotted, disputes resolved, thieving prevented—by private societies who levy protection money and provide protection. Business meetings of stall-holders also take place.

There are no official records for the fair. People say that twenty-five or more years ago, after the Pacific war, hawkers' stalls were set up in the evenings in both Temple Street and Shanghai Street, but in those days the market was much smaller. A comparison of lists in the directories for 1951 and 1940 shows that restaurants proliferated in and around Temple Street after the war. Before the cooked-food stalls were removed from the Public Square, the night fair in Temple Street was more closely related to them. The whole complex of hawkers, cooked-food stalls, restaurants and entertainments which occupies street space and property around the Public Square and the temple has origins which go back certainly to 1946. No clear evidence has been found for its extent before the war, but some people say that the fair is forty or fifty years old.

Temple Street is a kind of shadow to Nathan Road and the other regular business streets of the locality, such as Reclamation Street with its day-time hawker market for vegetables and other kinds of food. Nathan Road is the smart shoppers' street, with plate-glass windows and fancy prices. Shanghai Street and Reclamation Street are respectable family shopping streets. Compared with either, Temple Street is as much an economical and profitable form of amusement as a commercial enterprise. The Temple Street fair has its own shadow in its turn, in its own buildings and in neighbouring streets like Woosung Street, in the form of businesses offering illegal gambling, blue films and cheap prostitution.

THE RATIONALE OF BUSINESS CLUSTERING IN YAUMATI

It is clear that clustering of businesses engaged in the same or related trades is an important feature of the Yaumati streets. A number of clusters have grown up during the past forty years. Others have decayed, but can be deduced from the directory for 1927. At that time, there were clusters of various degrees of intensity of wine merchants in Temple Street and Reclamation Street, salt dealers and coal merchants at the northern end of Canton Road, old clothing dealers in Shanghai Street, metal workshops and dealers in charcoal and firewood in Reclamation Street, and pig dealers in Portland Street, among others. Some of the diversity and character of these old streets, block by block, derives from inherited fragments of these former clusters. Shanghai Street has not only its clusters of Chinese jewellers, but also a loose group of hardware merchants at the Jordan Road end, where there have been hardware shops for fifty years.

There are obvious fundamental parallels between the business clusters of Yaumati and those which have been studied in Sheung Wan. Shopkeepers in Yaumati who gave their opinions were more explicit than those in Sheung Wan, rather than less, on the total dependence of individual businessmen on personal contact in business, and on the interdependence of the businesses in a cluster. In spite of this, clusters in Yaumati appear to be more diffuse than in Sheung Wan, both in terms of the spread of linked trades which belong to a cluster, and in terms of the spread of a cluster through the streets. Interspersed among the businesses representing the local specialism there are many others which belong to the locality in a much more general sense. In Yaumati, there is a kind of matrix of common day-to-day business within which the specialist cells settle and colonize, or wither and decay.

In this respect, Yaumati does differ considerably from the specialist business area of Sheung Wan, where there is nothing which could be called a 'matrix'. The difference is a fundamental one, as further consideration will show. It is of value here to look back to the realities of growth and change in the area during the past thirty years.

The property uses of 1941 were not very different from those of the present—locality specialisms (not all the same then as now), standard convenience shopping and marketing, workshop manufacturing and service trades, and upstairs the cubicles. During the generation since 1945, there has been change in personal and individual situations, change within kinds of business and the introduction of new kinds of business, building and rebuilding, increased density of residential and business use of the area, and change in the whole status of Yaumati. During this intensely active and varied phase and up to the present, each locality, each street and each property block has both contributed to change and experienced pressure from other localities; specialisms whether local or city-wide in significance have grown up and have colonized territories whether symbiotically with others, in competition or in indifference.

What has continued throughout all this change has been residence on the upper floors, and to a great extent the cubicle system. The contribution of the cubicles to the structure of the locality has been to ensure the nourishment of universal high densities of business use of the street property (and the street) through universal high densities of custom for all kinds of convenience business. This is in addition to important parts of Yaumati which are occupied as specialist cells of day-to-day vegetable and other marketing business. Custom from the cubicles is continuous, and still growing in density as rebuilding continues to lead to gradual increases in residential population densities.[14] Hence when specialist clusters form they compete for ground-floor and street space with miscellaneous convenience demand in businesses such as laundries, grocery stores, cafes and restaurants of all kinds, barbers and small workshops—a kind of generalized small business assemblage without beginning or end. They also compete in the same way with hawking whose resistance to the government's policy of hawker bazaars is a resistance to a clustering principle in the name of the generalized small business assemblage. All these kinds of ground floor use symbiose visibly with the cubicles on the upper floors, through dependence on the high densities of convenience custom which the cubicles create, and through access to labour supplied by people who live close by. Residence is the essential component of the matrix of miscellaneous uses which fills the streets and in which the speciality areas arise.

High densities and the extreme versatility of any locality, even of quite small size, are the central conditions of symbiosis of the kind which underlies Yaumati business distributions; and high densities in business and residence respectively also operate in a symbiotic relationship. In this respect as in others, the upper floor uses in the tenement districts function in relation to but differently from those at street level. In all this, Yaumati differs from the *nam-pak-hong* streets in Sheung Wan, where cubicles are uncommon and residence on upper floors is not the rule. Decay of the residential function of Sheung Wan after 1941 did lead to decay in residence-related street and property uses in that area, and is one main reason for the generally depressed state of Queen's Road in Sheung Wan.

THE REBUILDING PROCESS

Rebuilding is one of the characteristic features of business experience in Yaumati and Mongkok, and of course in many other parts of the city. Typically, rebuilding affects business tenants first by depriving them of their business premises for the period of building work; and second by putting up properties which are usually much more expensive to rent than those which were pulled down. In the case of ground floor shop premises in this kind of area, rents in the rebuilt property may easily be five times those charged at the same addresses before the property was rebuilt. For both of these reasons, tenants do not usually return to the same addresses after rebuilding; instead, they usually adopt one of several courses of action. They may take their compensation money[15] and go out of business, especially if the proprietor is elderly. They may seek fresh cheap accommodation locally, or even two or three miles away, and hope to carry on their business as before—of course, cheap accommodation in these conditions is not easy to find. If they can afford it, and are satisfied with the original locality, they may move immediately to freshly completed new property in the vicinity. Rebuilding is after all done on the assumption that somebody can afford the new high rents; new property does not remain unlet. Or they may seize the opportunity—if the business is prosperous and the proprietor is energetic and successful—to move into potentially much more profitable premises in Mongkok or Nathan Road. Removals of this kind have been in turn one of the springs of the phenomenal business growth in these two places. Meanwhile, the new property in Shanghai Street or Reclamation Street is taken partly by local businessmen performing short moves when their own properties are in turn pulled down; partly by successful people moving to the area from shabbier districts, or people starting new businesses; partly by banks, which have taken up a good deal of new property; and in some areas partly by expanding specialisms, especially engineering.

Family business continuity is not strong in Shanghai Street, in spite of the slow relative decline. Discussing this point, local shopkeepers point to the disruptive effects of rebuilding, but they also point out that in contemporary conditions there is no special likelihood that a man's sons will succeed him in business. This is partly because sons now do not feel much filial obligation, partly because shopkeepers' sons are very likely to be educated men living abroad or working for the government. And in this walk of life, it may be the security which is represented by a man's educated sons which enables him to go out of business.

It may well be asked, how does the business cluster survive the rebuilding process, with the need for removal and the steep rise in rents? Physically, survival in a certain locality appears to owe much to the fact that rebuilding is always done piecemeal, a few properties at a time, according to ownership and the age of the lease. Alternative premises are always available close by, at a price. Economically, rebuilding appears to be simply another of the hazards which afflict the individual business; for the cluster as a whole, and the network of contacts which it represents, prosperous conditions at the time of rebuilding (as for engineering) enable sound businesses to take good new property; whilst poor conditions (as for old-fashioned trades) result in rapid loss of businesses at the time of rebuilding, so that the cluster falls further into decay, and perhaps disappears altogether.

YAUMATI, NATHAN ROAD, TSIMSHATSUI AND MONGKOK

Yaumati is an old town, as many examples have shown. It is now surrounded on three sides by newer, more fashionable, more specialized and more profitable districts which represent the fundamentals of the transformation of Kowloon in the post-war expansions. These areas are Tsimshatsui and Mongkok, with Nathan Road joining them.

Nathan Road occupies a special place in this discussion. It was laid out between 1904 and 1907 with a spaciousness which took the growth of two generations to give it justification. Until after the Pacific war, Nathan Road was very mixed, part suburban, part commercial, with vacant sites even in prominent locations, and a tendency to attract the new space-consuming businesses like motor-cars and the cinema. Nathan Road was ready at that time to form the centre of a new Kowloon town which could break away from the small scale and restricted layout of old Yaumati. In the expansion after 1947, this is what happened. The older Yaumati was by-passed physically and in development by a newly dominant Nathan Road.

At the same time, partly in response to this growth of Nathan Road, Tsimshatsui experienced a radical reshaping of its seafaring heritage. In the decade from about 1955 to about 1966 the formerly quiet streets of Tsimshatsui—mainly residential to the east of Nathan Road, mainly commercial to the west—were rebuilt and adapted to the new bar and shopping trades oriented towards Western customers, both civilian tourists and servicemen. The first round of new building, to the east of Nathan Road, took the form of conventional tenement blocks and hotels of moderate size. But from about 1960, much bigger buildings based on the 1956 Buildings Ordinance were being erected, especially in Nathan Road. These two kinds of building form the bulk of the property stock of contemporary Tsimshatsui. Both are occupied typically by smart tourist shops and restaurants on the ground floors, with complexes of workshops and factories (particularly in the tailoring trades, based on tourist custom on the ground floors), brothels, offices, boarding houses and cubicles on the upper floors. To these have been added, during the past ten years, much better planned and better managed big buildings, mainly in shop, office and hotel uses, of which the Ocean Terminal of 1966 is one of the prototypes. New hotels, with elegant shopping arcades, cafés and restaurants on the ground and first floors, belong to the same phase. In these buildings, and some very similar new office buildings in Mongkok, the separation of uses is experiencing its first trials in metropolitan Kowloon.

Tourism and spending by the garrison and visiting naval personnel occupied a special place in the balance of payments in the industrial expansion of the 1950s. In 1954 tourism was bringing in an invisible income of the order of 21 per cent of the value of all domestic manufactures.[16] The equivalent figure for 1973 was about 13 per cent, but even this figure 'compensated for Hong Kong's entire balance of trade deficit in visible imports and exports'.[17]

The influx of spending by the troops and the tourists in the ten years after 1945 was the critical external factor in the growth of the new Tsimshatsui. Chinese people who know the trade say that there is certainly business and personal continuity from the bars and restaurants catering for Western tastes in Tsimshatsui in 1946 and 1947 to their successors of the present, and are able to give examples, though direct continuation is exceptional. Today, provision for the tourists includes Western-style hotels and bars, restaurants of many different kinds, and the businesses which cater for the main form of entertainment for the tourists—shopping.

In the late 1960s, spending by American soldiers on leave from Vietnam brought a period of exceptional prosperity in the tourist industry, but since that time there has been extensive contraction, partly because of the collapse of this business, partly because of the new factor of keen competition from Causeway Bay, especially since the cross-harbour tunnel was opened in 1972, giving direct access to the island from the airport. Recession has brought to light some fundamental weaknesses of Tsimshatsui—particularly the backwardness of most of the area in property terms. Tsimshatsui has too many low-built tenements without lifts, too many big buildings of the 1956–66 phase with showy ground-floor shops and cubicled slums above, and too many mixed side-streets and alleys where Chinese domestic life is fused with small businesses selling magazines, paintings and sandals to tourists. Tsimshatsui today in part continues its old business with Western tourists, whether in old property or new; in part it has turned over to night-clubs and shops oriented towards Japanese tourists; and in part it has converted its Western restaurant and bar inheritance to Chinese restaurants and night-clubs catering for rich local people. In some spots there has been expansion of an indigenous 'village' inheritance akin to the service streets in prosperous parts of Western cities a century ago.

The experience of Mongkok in growth since the Pacific war has been even more remarkable. Mongkok in 1945 was a depressed semi-commercial periphery, gloomy and impoverished. By 1960 it has already attracted more adventurous investment than Yaumati, especially the big new bank premises, departmental stores, and big restaurants, whilst Shanghai Street still stood for the older kinds of business.[18] During the decade and more which have followed, Mongkok has increasingly strengthened its hold on the entertainment business of Kowloon, and the department store and restaurant businesses. The fundamental tone of Mongkok remains working-class; the best shopping business in Kowloon continues to be done in Tsimshatsui. But semi-luxury and luxury business among the masses has now grown sufficiently in Mongkok to be the foundation of the biggest and most dynamic of all the new districts of the city, and one where average standards of luxury and elegance rise visibly year by year, *pari-passu* with those of the mass of the people.

It is not altogether clear why all this has taken place in Mongkok, and there is no received opinion on the point. It is sometimes said that growth in Mongkok is more apparent than real, especially by comparison with Tsimshatsui: thus rentals remain 10 or 20 per cent lower for comparable properties, and hotel charges are much lower. This view has substance, but most of it is subsumed by the recognition that in terms of shopping and entertainment Mongkok is still basically a working-class area. Really, this view explains why the biggest money cannot yet be made in Mongkok, rather than that the growth of Mongkok is not really substantial. In part this view also depends on a comparison with Tsimshatsui which is quite unrealistic; in no Chinese district can money be expected to flow as freely as in the tourist area. To some extent the view of Mongkok as relatively undynamic rests on unfamiliarity with the extent, quality and diversity of recent growth.

Realistically, two important circumstances appear to have been influential in Mongkok during the 1950s, when the die of contemporary conditions was cast. One was the fact that the localities where the most important squatter settlements grew up during the refugee phase from 1947 onwards were mostly more or less tributary to Mongkok as their shopping and service centre. Shek Kip Mei lay about a mile to the north, on the Taipo Road which continues Nathan Road, and Argyle Street gave main access to the new communities of north-east Kowloon. From this standpoint, Mongkok lay at the north-eastern fringes of Yaumati, in a situation where most of the big new communities lay to the north and east of Yaumati. Moreover, Nathan Road and its northern and eastern tributaries provided both access and—so to speak—the opportunity to intercept business. Mongkok, unlike Yaumati, is unthinkable without Nathan Road. The change in scale in Kowloon and the swing to the north and east changed the fundamental balance of Kowloon; the centre of gravity shifted decisively from Shanghai Street in Yaumati to Nathan Road in Mongkok.

Mongkok itself appears to have made some contribution to this growth, and this is the second of the two circumstances. Before 1941, Nathan Road and the linking main roads like Argyle Street were already laid out and developed, but loosely. The grid of streets mainly to the east of Nathan Road which now accommodates hinterland Mongkok—streets like Sai Yeung Choi Street—were also laid out before the Pacific war, and likewise were only loosely developed, to some extent with factories. Both the main thoroughfares and the side-streets were by any standards ripe for redevelopment in 1950. The streets were wide and relatively uncluttered, and the property low-built and cheap to clear in terms of both purchase and compensation. All this must have provided ideal conditions for redevelopment, given the demand for expansion.

Looked at in these terms, Mongkok in the ill-documented and hectic 1950s seems to have been a kind of Mahagonny, a place to make quick profits by discreditable means. This image is seductive, and it relates to an image for the city as a whole. Mongkok is still noisy, brash, and mercilessly commercial. Many people would say the same of the whole city. Yet like most other parts of the city, Mongkok is primarily a community of ordinary people working and spending month by month. It is powerful and stable, with visibly rising standards among the mass of the people. A Mahagonny can perhaps still be found there, but it takes its place alongside other specialisms within the fabric of the area.

1 G.B. Endacott, *A History of Hong Kong* (1958), p. 111.

2 Osbert Chadwick, *Report on the sanitary condition of Hong Kong* (London, Colonial Office, Eastern No. 38, 1882), Paras. 290 and 300.

3 Office of the Commissioner for Rating and Valuation, *Valuation list for Kowloon*, 1880.

4 In Seoul in Korea, there is a very similar engineering complex, at least double the size of that in Kowloon, with sub-specialisms more closely grouped than in Kowloon, and with less relation to motor-cars and ships, and more to watches, jewellery and electrical goods. This complex in Seoul extends for about a mile through the city very close to the centre. Seoul is 1,300 miles from Hong Kong; the resemblance between these clusters in the two cities, particularly in an untraditional field like engineering, is a noteworthy tribute to the persistence of Chinese concepts and institutions.

5 These views come in detail from one manager, but they represent the general trend of the opinion which has been heard in the area.

6 T.G. McGee, *Hawkers in Hong Kong* (Hong Kong, 1973), p. 4ff.

7 C. Geertz, *Peddlers and princes. Social change and economic modernisation in two Indonesian towns* (Chicago, 1963), Chapter 3, esp. p. 29.

8 John L. Espy in 'Some notes on business and industry in Hong Kong', *Chung Chi Journal* 11, 1 (1972), (Special issue on Hong Kong), pp. 172–81, discusses the relations between the small scale and labour-intensive practices of the typical Hong Kong factory and its capacity to work effectively for export markets. He calls these relationships 'the bridge between How Ming Street and Main Street'.

9 The Urban Council, *Hawkers, a report with policy recommendations,* December 1957, p. 11. Pages 10–14 of this report contain a very interesting account of these stalls as they were in 1957.

10 Information on points of this kind, even of a kind which might be called raw material, is of course often hard to obtain, though some stalls will give figures freely. Figures have been suggested with range from $1 per table per day to $10 for corruption money paid to the police, without taking account of protection money which local black societies may demand. A big pavement restaurant of the kind described here must be saving at least $20,000 per year in rent. $20,000 per year is about $55 per day. This kind of figure must put some sort of limit to what can be paid out of the advantage of paying no rent. As a result of the institution of the Independent Commission against Corruption, police demands are reported to have diminished, but many stalls—perhaps most—still pay allowances to the local police even without being asked for money.

11 Cooked-food-stalls, with equipment not readily portable, and with or without seating arrangements, have been a regular feature of Chinese cities and towns, certainly during the nineteenth and twentieth centuries. The system is thought to have existed in something like its present form throughout the history of Hong Kong, though in earlier generations usually with more portable equipment. It must have owed something to the consistently high ratios of immigrants and of men in the community. In the scale and sophistication of the individual enterprise, and in the number and density of the enterprises, however, contemporary Hong Kong is certainly exceptional, and perhaps unique. In contemporary Canton, similar stalls can be found, though without the free-standing street structure; but their scale is quite small, their menus strictly limited, and their numbers few. In Singapore, a few celebrated streets, Albert Street especially, have establishments which in scale and grouping resemble those of Hong Kong. Taipei also has a famous nucleus of fixed stalls.

12 T.G. McGee in *Hawkers in Hong Kong* (op. cit.) draws on an extended survey of hawker markets in the island city (not Kowloon), made in 1969, and produces a large quantity of fresh material. There is also extensive material in F.Y. Tse, *A preliminary report on the size, daily turnover, and gross profit variables of street traders in Hong Kong* (Hong Kong, 1971).

13 *Hong Kong 1974, Report for the year 1973,* pp. 84–5.

14 In Yaumati south of Waterloo Road, the average occupancy rate in pre-war property is 39 sq. ft. per person, against 92 sq. ft. per person in post-war property. Average plot

ratios are however 3.6 floors in pre-war property and 10.7 in post-war, giving an average increase in residential density of 27 per cent on rebuilding. (Figures from sample data kindly made available by the Colony Outline Planning Officer.)

15 A landlord who wishes to rebuild may evict his tenants, but he must pay compensation on a scale which in the last resort may be settled in court.

16 *Annual Report*, 1954, pp. 15, 51.

17 *Hong Kong 1974, Report for the year 1973,* pp. 121, 220–2.

18 The point is made explicit by the anonymous author of *Hong Kong Today* (1960), p. 45 (Chinese text).

5 Causeway Bay

TOPOGRAPHY AND GROWTH

A number of the localities discussed in this book have been dominated since the Pacific war by their experience of increasing densities of investment and use, which have led or are leading to the growth of communities which in the Hong Kong sense are now mature—high-built, varied and diverse in use, and congested. Mongkok is one such locality. Causeway Bay is another; although smaller, it has increased densities and intensified uses as completely and successfully as Mongkok. The surviving nondescript inheritance from its industrial and warehousing past, distinguished only by its association with the 'princely hong', Jardine Matheson's,[1] the Yee Wo Hong of Yee Wo Street, is now fast disappearing. Causeway Bay, whose significance in the entertainment field in 1945 was practically limited to the Lee Theatre (a smart air-conditioned cinema at that time, and still in business) has become the principal focus of entertainments and restaurants in the island city. In so doing, it has drawn away some trade from Central District and from the old, congested streets of Sheung Wan as those increasingly approximate to business streets in Western cities and residence diminishes; and more important, it has dominated the vast total increase of business in entertainments and restaurants which has been created by the new growth and new prosperity. There are now nine cinemas in Causeway Bay, most of them new and very smart, against about ten in Mongkok. Causeway Bay has also achieved distinction in two other fields at least: in retail shopping, based on four big and several smaller departmental stores, specialist shops in fields like fashion and teenage boutiques, Western supermarkets, abundant smaller shops and extensive specialist hawking; and in high-class residence, especially in the big blocks between Great George Street and the sea. Causeway Bay is also now a major focus for hotels, originally catering mainly for good-class non-Western customers such as Japanese businessmen, but now increasingly competing successfully with Tsimshatsui for the main tourist traffic. The exit of the new cross-harbour tunnel is at the north-west extremity of Causeway Bay; where formerly for tourists to use a hotel on the island side involved a ferry journey, now taxis and hotel minibuses can make the journey direct.

The British War-Office map of 1930 (Figure 14) is the most revealing introduction which can be made to the layout of Causeway Bay. It

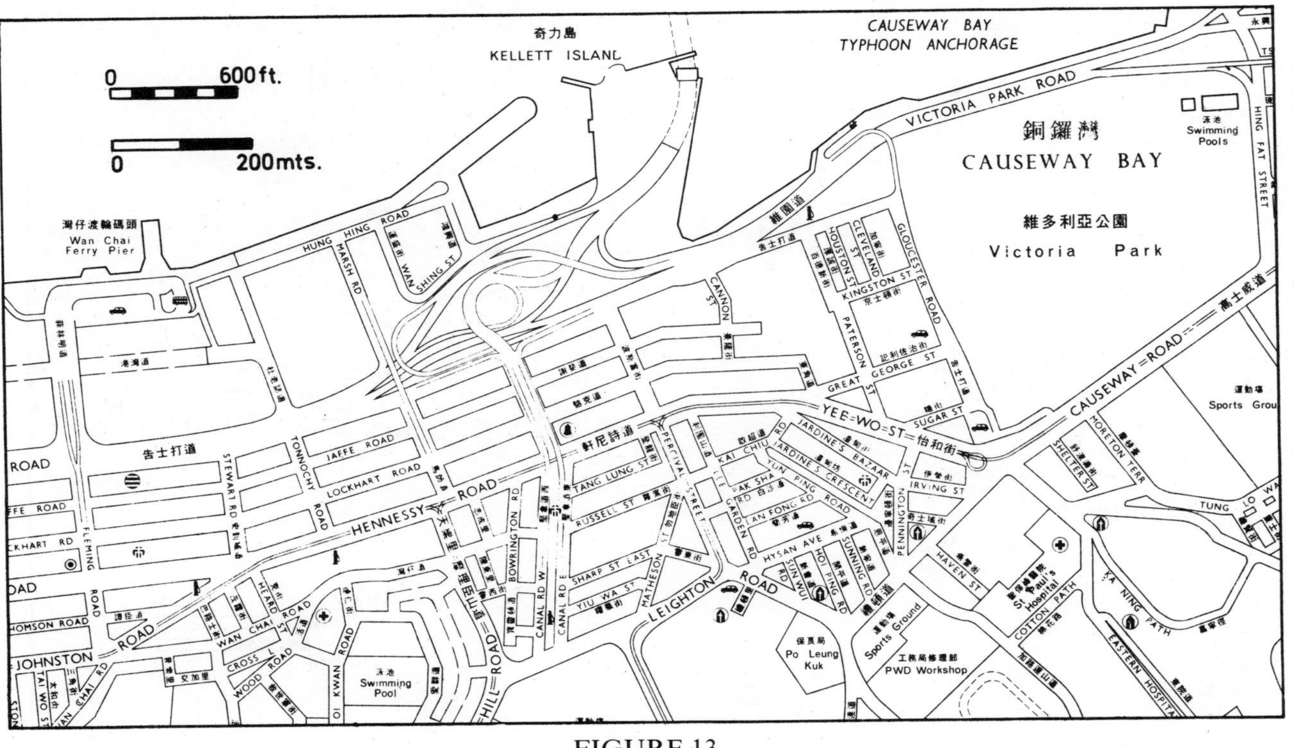

FIGURE 13

STREET PLAN FOR CAUSEWAY BAY AND PART OF WANCHAI (1974)

Scale: 8 inches to 1 mile.

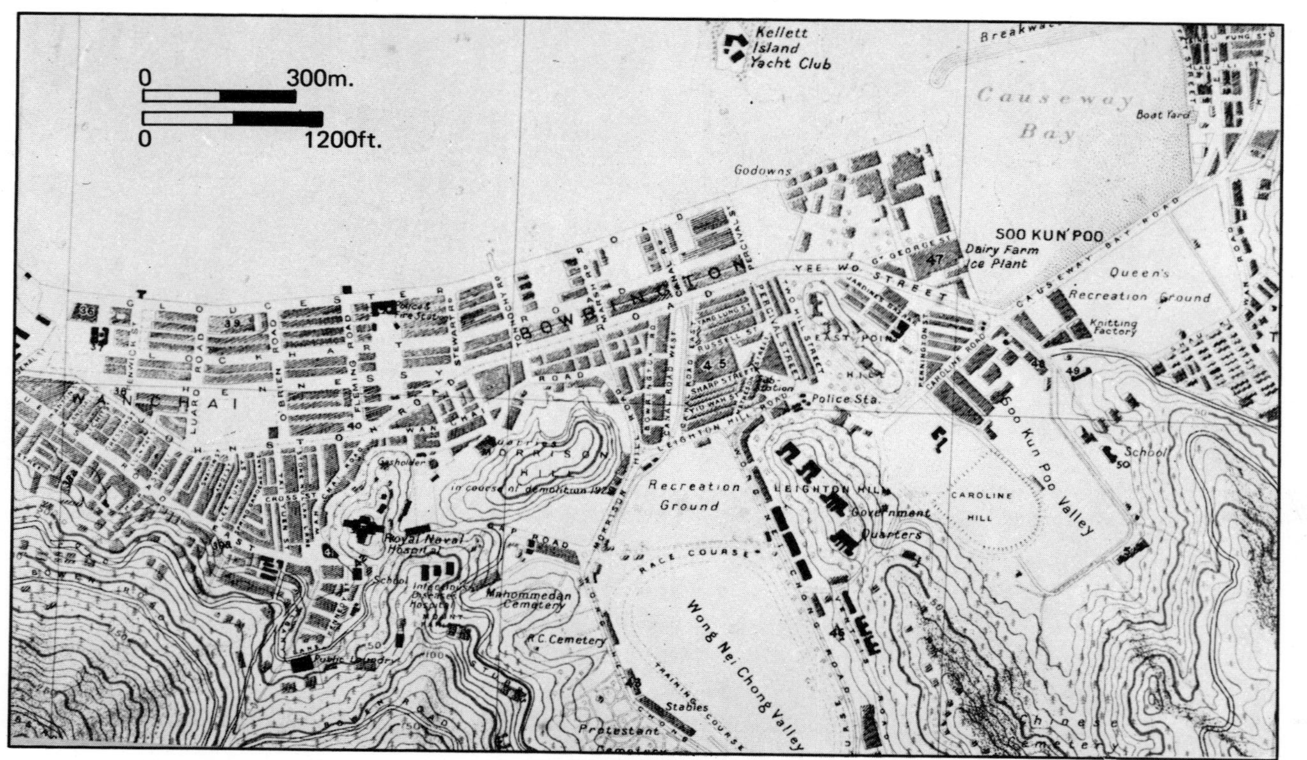

FIGURE 14
CAUSEWAY BAY AND WANCHAI, 1930
(REVISED 1931, 4TH EDN 1949). W.O.

supplies the clues to three things which are, of course, related: the earlier state of the terrain in the area, the earlier phases of land use, which matured gradually during the century before 1941, and the relations of the relatively small Causeway Bay area itself to the neighbouring areas.

The essence of the whole site in 1930 was the abrupt hill masses which punctuated the low-lying level ground. East Point Hill and Morrison Hill have since been removed. The main thoroughfare was already what it is today—Hennessy Road and Yee Wo Street, carrying the tram route. This road was originally built under Sir John Bowring in the 1850s as Praya East. It then represented both reclamation of a slice of the shore, and road access along the sea's edge to East Point, as the Jardine's land opposite Kellett Island was called.

Between Morrison Hill and the precipitous slope above the south-eastern corner of Victoria Park lies the world of Causeway Bay and the areas directly tributary to it. Yee Wo Street, now the heart of the whole area, was in 1930 little more than the tram-route running through a quiet district of godowns, tips and yards, suburban housing, small bazaar and tenement developments, and vacant sites. Most of Yee Wo Street itself, as this map shows, had no permanent buildings.

The whole area between Morrison Hill and the Bay had no single centre in 1930, or even in 1950. The most developed district then was that which is still in most dense working-class use: the Bowrington area, centred on Canal Road East; but this area was then and still is today an eastward extension of Wanchai, rather than a part of Causeway Bay.

To the south lie the two important spurs which separate the three north-facing valleys which are now all, in their various ways, tributary to Causeway Bay—Leighton Hill and the Tai Hang Road Hill, separating out Happy Valley (the most important of the three, with the racecourse and middle-class residence), Sokonpo Valley, and Tai Hang Valley. None of these valleys has experienced much fundamental change since 1930, though there has been building in all. Eastward of Yee Wo Street then lay the old reclamation called Queen's Recreation Ground, and the bay itself, then used as a typhoon shelter and anchorage, and reclaimed as a public park during the 1950s.

The area between Yee Wo Street and the sea, land created by reclamation subsequent to Bowring's Praya East scheme, which in 1950 was still occupied by Jardine Matheson's godowns, has been transformed. Daimaru, the big Japanese departmental store, took up its site in Great George Street in 1960. Mainly since that time, incessant building has brought up the level of investment in this area, taking density and quality of the property together, to one of the highest in the city. The transformation of this area from Victorian warehouse to contemporary hotel, shopping and residential complex was being brought finally to completion in 1974, with two elegant and spacious new hotels in use, together with some related mixed shopping, office and residential developments.

Already during the 1960s, Yee Wo Street was transformed into a principal shopping and entertainment street, lined mainly with high property.

The old domestic shopping streets of the area, especially Jardine's Bazaar, have retained much of the old style, but virtually none of the pre-war property remains, and there has been a vast influx of people and prosperity. The experience of Percival Street has been less drastic than that of Yee Wo Street, but it too has been fundamentally transformed—from a quiet, rather suburban street with the dignity of a tram-line but the indignity of the tram-sheds and hawkers at Russell Street, into a bustling and prosperous mixed shopping and restaurant thoroughfare in main-road style.

One other hill appears on the map of 1930—East Point Hill, also former Jardine's territory. This hill has been removed since the Pacific war, and most of its site has since been built over. The building of this new ground is typical of the experience of Causeway Bay during the past twenty years. The first building was in the middle, with good but very ordinary tenements in six floors. The southern end was built later by Lee Hysan Estates and finished in 1967; it comprises offices, distinguished and expensive shops and very good residential apartments. The northern and best end of the site, fronting on Yee Wo Street, remains unbuilt.

Contemporary Causeway Bay is in short a quite distinctive area of limited size (Plate 17). Something more specific remains to be said on each of these points. To take its size first: Causeway Bay is based on its main street, Yee Wo Street continuing Hennessy Road, in length from Percival Street to Leighton Road only about 1,600 feet. It is bounded quite sharply to the east by Victoria Park and the playing fields, and to the south by the more extensive land uses of the three tributary valleys, and it merges rather abruptly on the west side into Wanchai. It is the smallest of the major areas of the city.

The distinction of Causeway Bay is harder to define than its extent. Yet it is not hard to recognize. Its essence is that to which attention was drawn at the outset: the creation through ceaseless investment, and concomitant inexorable increases in densities everywhere except in the very best residential areas, of a new prestigious metropolitan complex of restaurants, entertainments, shops, hotels and apartments based on Yee Wo Street.

The investment process in Causeway Bay is linked to rapidly rising standards of amenity and modernity—and Westernization. Westernization in this sense means a complex of things whose origins and implications are of more than one kind. Some of these things, such as cleanliness, appear now more than formerly to be no more than the suppression of bad features from the older Hong Kong. Some of them, such as elegance, luxuriousness, diversity, prettiness in decoration, and even the use of written English in advertising and the shops, are as much Japanese as Western. Some of them, such as the acceptance of the physical separation of property uses and the building of big and comfortable flats for the occupation of prosperous single families, are among the central features of the contemporary absorption of well-off Western attitudes in the upper strata of the Hong Kong community. They can also find parallels in

Japan. They represent, it may reasonably be thought, much less a slavish imitation of alien cultural habits, than one phase in the adaptation of Cantonese cultural style to the bourgeois part of modern urban living.

Attitudes and standards in these respects have evolved rapidly during the 1960s throughout the community, and they did so with special force in some suburban districts which were then becoming richer and more varied, especially Causeway Bay. In the competition for prestige through visible smartness and elegance, the newest buildings have obvious advantages; but in Causeway Bay standards can be and are maintained in buildings no longer new, as in the West and in Tokyo, by redecorating, rearrangement and refitting; new signs and new pots of flowers. But meanwhile, to a considerably greater extent than in London or Tokyo, cleanliness, order and elegance in the front hall tend to have an accompanying descant of dirt, chaos and convenience somewhere close at hand—but less so, as always, in the newest buildings.

It follows from what has been said, that Causeway Bay as a locality must be thought of as comprising a series of related but distinct units, with related but dissimilar origins and histories, which during the expansion and intensification of use of the post-war generation have converged to create an unmistakable locality, with a range of characteristic functions. From a wasteland of suburban terraces, empty sites, old tenements, godowns, hill masses either removed or developed, the tram-route, the reclamations, and a new centrality depending on the growth of North Point beyond it to the east—a new contemporary Causeway Bay has assembled itself, through incessant investment and constant increase in densities of use, which is strong in entertainments, departmental stores, restaurants, and a wide range of middle-class housing, but weak in manufacturing and offices, with no government housing, relatively limited working-class residence, and relatively scanty use of street space for business. This new Causeway Bay is now the main centre for entertainments and restaurants in the island city, a major shopping centre, a large and growing centre for tourists, and one of the main middle-class residential areas.

THE BUSINESS HEART

The heart of Causeway Bay is the Hennessy Road–Yee Wo Street thoroughfare and business complex. One foundation of the present prosperity and style of this complex is the departmental stores. Daimaru, the big Japanese store in Great George Street, just off the main thoroughfare, is the most important both in contemporary shopping terms—and,fifteen years ago, as a catalyst for other development. The others are branches of the Wing On, Pearl City and Chancellor departmental stores, and a big China products business, which sells mainland China goods of all kinds, and acts, as do all these stores, as a centre for mainland China consciousness and mainland propaganda. A second foundation of the business style of the area is the cinemas. There are six cinemas in, or very close to, Yee

Wo Street, all usually showing English-language films. The functioning of the area as a business centre is strengthened by a number of bank offices. A big English-language and Western-style supermarket occupies a site just off Yee Wo Street. There are a number of good hotels, and many specialist smaller shops, especially in fields like fashion and tailoring, electrical machinery and photography. The area has night-clubs and various kinds of houses of entertainment. The Ruby Restaurant in Great George Street opposite Daimaru is one of the biggest in the city, and there are many other restaurants of various kinds, including many which use English. Bars are relatively scarce but becoming commoner, and there are a number of Japanese night-clubs. What all this adds up to is a consumers' spending centre which can appeal to most middle-class groups in the resident city population, including Europeans and Japanese. At a window-shopping level, Causeway Bay competes increasingly effectively with Tsimshatsui and Central District.

Most of the property in Yee Wo Street has been rebuilt since 1965, though some remains to be redeveloped. Upper floor commercial uses in the centre are usually in either entertainment or professional kinds of business; the extent of these uses varies a good deal from building to building, and is generally less in workshop trades, and less in total amount, than might be expected. Much more than half of the upper floor accommodation in Yee Wo Street is in simple residence, without cubicles. Generally speaking, commercial uses are confined to the lowest two or three floors only, and comprise photographers, doctors, teachers of various arts, offices, health clubs, dance halls, billiard rooms and brothels. Most ground floor restaurants occupy upper floor accommodation as well. In Hong Kong Mansion, built in 1967, the most central building in the whole complex, the Ruby Restaurant occupies the first and second floors and also part of the third as stores and offices. This building is typical of many in the area. It is clean and contains no factories at all. By the time the fourth and fifth floors (there are 23 floors in all) are reached, flats in business uses have shrunk to a quarter or less of the total. About one-quarter or one-third of the residential flats are partitioned internally to the extent that the main room has no direct window light; but this does not necessarily indicate commercial use of the residential space.

Something more remains to be said, in the context of the business heart of Causeway Bay, about Daimaru, the Japanese departmental store. Daimaru came to Hong Kong in 1960. It is a big shop—probably the biggest single shop in Hong Kong—and its layout and style, at least on the all-important ground floor, are both inviting and undemanding. The shop is not particularly cheap, but it has no exclusive tone at all, and its merchandise, which is by no means all Japanese in origin, is varied and up to date.

The site of Daimaru was formerly part of Jardine's godowns. It lies just off Yee Wo Street, and the site was cheap, no doubt partly for this reason. By 1960 Causeway Bay had big blocks of four-floor and six-floor tenements with varied commercial uses, and some of the new high buildings as well. It was already a centre for cinemas and night-clubs, and was a centre for investment of capital from overseas Chinese communities.[2] Development at that time was strongest towards the eastern end of Yee Wo Street. Daimaru created a new focus, and brought a new scale and fresh impetus to this expansion. The opening of the store had some of the quality of a self-fulfilling prophesy. But Causeway Bay (below Happy Valley, and with North Point filling up) was a convincing enough prospect for further growth in 1960; the decision of the Daimaru managers to come here was a perceptive as well as a prophetic one.

The setting-up of Daimaru was one major step in the creation of Causeway Bay as it now is. It is possible to point to another special feature of the area which in its time may well have had a comparable catalytic function. This is the very long range of four-floor tenements, built in 1953, which lies on the north side of Hennessy Road between Percival Street and East Point Road (Plate 15). In spite of the advanced age of this property, the ground floor shops are still extremely busy. When these tenements were built, on land which was previously used for storage, a timber yard and sawmill and a skating rink, they must have contributed richly to the growth of Causeway Bay in city terms; they probably doubled the number of well-situated shops in the area. Yee Wo Street at that time had no good property; Causeway Bay itself was little removed from the conditions of a company village with a bazaar.

Ground floor property use in this big group of forty tenements is now very mixed, but concentrates mainly in the clothing-shoes-household goods group. Upper floor uses differ markedly from those in the newer high property in Yee Wo Street, except that here too there are very few factories. The great bulk of the property is occupied by cubicles, in some places very crowded. The social level, commercial as well as residential, is lower than in Yee Wo Street, no doubt because this is old property without lifts. One typical address has a ballroom, a dentist, a Chinese doctor, a photographer, a store, and residential flats with cubicles. Others have tailors, a ping-pong parlour, a teacher of Chinese boxing, more dancing and photography, and brothels. These tenements are a very good example of properties almost the whole of whose value lies in the localities which they occupy. Physically they are due for redevelopment, though because of the shape of the sites this will present difficulties.

BEYOND THE BUSINESS HEART

Most Causeway Bay property is occupied at street level by business uses of one kind or another, and because the total area is small, most though not all of the ground floor business areas are appendages of some kind to the Yee Wo Street complex.

DENSE USES

To the south-west, Percival Street and Lee Gardens Road and their connecting streets like Foo Ming Street are solid business streets very like Yee Wo Street, but operating at a somewhat lower economic level, with fewer prestige businesses (departmental stores, hotels and fashion shops) and more convenience shopping (food shops), more service businesses (radio, tailoring) and more business use of street space (key-cutting, fruit hawking). Business use other than lodgings is common in the tall buildings in this area below about the fourth floor; and there are fewer doctors and more Chinese gymnasts, more tailors and more places where business and residence are visibly combined, than in Yee Wo Street. Pak Sha Road and Russell Street represent in their separate ways further steps along the same social and economic continuum. Russell Street is in part a tenement street with standard convenience shops, and in part a hawker-market, extending from the official market at the Canal Road crossing, now rehoused beneath the new flyover. It is famous for its assemblage of cooked-food-stall restaurants. Between Russell Street and Hennessy Road lies Tanglung Street, a Hogarthian little street of about 50 addresses, with ground floor premises occupied by small shops and tenement engineering, joinery and printing works; cubicles and whorehouses upstairs; and its own cooked-food-stall restaurants—a quintessential tenement street which belongs in spirit to the older Wanchai. Many eating places in this area work through the night and virtually until dawn, with night-time customers coming from the tram-sheds, newspaper offices and late-night entertainments.

Pak Sha Road is a service street of a different kind, occupied mainly in tailoring, but also with other trades such as air-conditioner and refrigerator repairs. It subserves a situation which exists in Western cities (as in Soho in London) but usually in less developed form: the sumptuary demands of well-off customers create a need for manufacturing and manufacturing-service work which it is convenient to meet in premises not far from the fashionable shop-fronts (and high rents) which draw the demand. Pak Sha Road specializes in this function.

Close-knit business clusters are rare in Causeway Bay. The keynote of most localities seen at street level is diversity, and where neighbouring businesses or streets do have complementary functions, suggesting symbiosis, the functions are not narrow agglomerations of groups of related commodity or activity specialisms, as is the case in most of the clustering situations which have been reported from Sheung Wan and Yaumati, but mixed groupings of activities which typically all relate to an economic stereotype. A number of complexes whose rationales are of this kind have been discussed.

Why is this so? The obvious reason appears to be the right one: that in Causeway Bay, where growth has been rapid and change fundamental, and the essence of this growth and change has been the adapting of Western ideas of consumption and leisure to the instincts and tastes of a Chinese community, a more or less Western system of catering for the relationships between specialism and diversity (or, to put it in another way, between finite location and potentially infinite demand) has evolved. Economic relationships, rather than individual agglomerations, are the key to business distributions in Causeway Bay. Seen in this economic light, the business complexes of this area, even if less conscious and less organized, are not less functionally adapted than those of Sheung Wan itself; but to a Western observer they appear less individual, and they are certainly less conspicuous. Nor is there any reason to think of them as arising out of any network of business relationships.

Jardine's Bazaar, appropriately named, is the old market street of Causeway Bay. It is now a daily marketing street of very good class and evident prosperity. About half of the ground-floor businesses sell food of some kind. At night, here and sometimes in neighbouring streets, hawkers sell clothing. Use of street space for business is relatively common, especially around the market, where there are also a few cooked-food-stall restaurants. Yards and alleys in this area are very densely used: the yards of the buildings are roofed in plastic to accommodate cooking and mahjong; the alleys, also sometimes partly roofed, have carpentry, soft drinks cafés, scullery work, marketing of fowls, and in some places huts where people live.

SPACIOUS USES

In Causeway Bay, all the property may be classified within one of two easily-recognizable categories, which might be called respectively 'congested' and 'spacious'. The streets and buildings which have so far been discussed fall, of course, into the former category; they have important central functions, they are densely occupied in both residential and business terms, and they generate encroachment on public or private circulation space wherever that is possible. Most of the smaller, more old-fashioned, and less metropolitan property in Causeway Bay, in Pennington Street and Sugar Street for example, also falls into this category. These properties belong to the standard Hong Kong system, operating at various social and economic levels. The 'spacious' group, on the other hand, are exceptional. They are properties where residential occupation is not dense per unit of floor space (though it may still be quite dense per unit of the site), where street encroachment and staircase encumbrance are both low by Hong Kong standards, where space is used relatively extravagantly in the shops and other ground floor businesses—these being in many cases showrooms in Western style—and where on the whole there is effective separation of property uses. Naturally, the 'spacious' sections stand out as oases of space and calm. Several distinct areas are of this kind. One is the big group of blocks of apartments, built on former warehouse and factory land which was originally reclaimed about 1884, lying between Daimaru and the sea. These blocks have only limited ground floor commercial use—food marketing, restaurants, tailors and hairdressers—most of which are obviously very prosperous. Another is the big Lee Hysan Estates group of showroom, office and hotel properties on the north side of Hysan Avenue, occupying the southern end of the site of the former East Point Hill. The third occupies much of Leighton Road and also, extending southwards, Wongnaichung Road and the northern end of Tunglowan Road. A fourth is emerging in the most recent years—new buildings in or very close to the business heart in which social and prestige pressures exert economic force sufficient to separate uses convincingly, to keep places clean, and to preserve low densities. The most important developments of the past few years have all been of this kind, for instance the Pearl City and Excelsior developments.

There are two different kinds of underlying social dynamic involved here. One, particularly in the areas to the south where continuity through time is visible on the ground, is clearly the 1960s' and 1970s' reinterpretation of the tradition of extensive suburban land use which has always existed in Causeway Bay. In and around Leighton Road, a variety of relatively extensive land uses—institutions, mostly with gardens, apartments, and even a few villas—survive from various phases of the past. New buildings carry on this essentially suburban, residential tradition. The new extensive *commercial* uses in this area—motor-car, furniture, carpet, decorators', fashion and office equipment showrooms, represent a fresh development of the suburban heritage of the past and a fresh extension of money-making. The same is true in Happy Valley, where similar business uses arise out of similar conditions of relatively loose land use and relatively concentrated middle-class demand.

The other kind of dynamic underlying the spacious land and property uses is new, urban and 'foreign'; it relates afresh to Western standards of cleanliness, privacy and calm where these are used for making money; its prototypes are the bank buildings in Central District. Properties where this type of situation arises are those in the business heart, or on the old godown land where redevelopment did not take place until the influence of Western standards was already being felt in these respects.

The distribution of the motor car business throws some additional light on this distinction between two kinds of area. The motor business is essentially suburban: it is the oldest and most space-consuming of the businesses which typically arise in middle-class residential areas, and the one which introduces both the flashiest showrooms, and the least inconspicuous workshops. Causeway Bay, together with Happy Valley and Wanchai, has been the main locale of the motor-car business in the island city since the 1930s.[3] Two-thirds of the motor-car sales firms in the island city named in the Yellow Pages for recent years have been located in one or other of these three eastern districts, and especially Causeway Bay; and most of the rest were in North Point still further to the east. All this is what may be expected of a business tied on the one hand to middle-class consumption and the luxury end of the business spectrum, and on the other to a need for space. There are few motor salerooms, or none, in the newer and more densely used of the 'spacious' areas to the seaward side of Yee Wo Street.

Car repairing, as might be expected, follows a different but related rationale. By far the biggest contribution in this industry is made by the north-eastern third of Wanchai, on the reclaimed land where access is good. In this workshop and cubicle area, motor vehicle repairing is one of the staple trades. A good deal of vehicle repairing also takes place in basements and side streets in Happy Valley.

THE WANCHAI FRINGE

On the north-western fringe of Causeway Bay, in the little Cannon Street complex which includes the eastern end of Lockhart Road, Causeway Bay uses have in the past few years advanced steadily against older uses more akin to those of Wanchai. In this part of Lockhart Road (Plate 16), the property is mainly tenements built soon after the war, and the older uses included restaurants, a Shanghai bath-house, some workshops, and convenience shops. Most of these can still be found, though the bath-house has moved and a sauna has been opened; but in addition to the old uses a fresh crop has grown up in recent years, including Japanese-style night-clubs and American-style steak houses. These certainly represent the authentic direction of fresh growth.

Closer to the sea, in Cannon Street itself, and like Lockhart Road adjacent to the new prestigious Excelsior development, uses are still rather equivocal. Uses in one building, which dates from the early 1960s, will illustrate this point. The building is arranged on a corridor principle; the bulk of the residential flats are subdivided into small rooms, and many into cubicles; there are a few brothels on the lower floors, and a garment factory on the first floor which employs about fifty women. The assemblage of ground-floor uses reveals marked diversity of both function and class; it includes motor repairs, a waste paper business, a ballroom, an engineering works, small shops selling groceries and Western pharmaceuticals, a fashion boutique and a coffee-shop. This building is extremely well situated in a general way, being only about 250 yards from Yee Wo Street. It stands in a cul-de-sac, which encourages vehicle repairing and other workshop trades. There is some business use of street space, and of course no attempt to create a 'spacious' atmosphere; nor is the place particularly clean. Money which in Paterson Street nearby is made by charging customers high prices for privacy, space and quietness, is made in Cannon Street by high densities and multiple use, and keeping overheads down, as it is in the city as a whole. What this case shows with particular clarity is that the extent to which closely adjacent localities may have divergent schemes of subsistence, and the extent to which uses which might be thought incompatible in Western conditions may in fact share properties. This tolerance is clearly one means by which change takes place in locality style and the general character of the local business assemblage; and there is every reason to think that what emerges from adaptations of this kind is usually a fresh and individual locality business grouping.

RETROSPECT

It has been shown that close, narrowly-defined and technically homogeneous cells of business activity are not common in Causeway Bay, as they are in other parts of Chinese Victoria to the west. In Causeway Bay their place in the streets is taken by technically heterogeneous but economically related groups of businesses. Shanghai grocery businesses (to take one example) are quite common, but there is no cluster of them; they occupy locations in assemblages of businesses which occupy similar premises and have equivalent economic needs and qualities, such as good-class tailors, banks, electrical appliance dealers, and fashion businesses. Shanghai restaurants and Chinese bookshops fit readily into the same kind of assemblage. This observation on the small scale may be adapted on the large to interpret the functional layout of the whole area. An area like Hysan Avenue has showrooms, offices, hotels, medium-to-good and often specialized restaurants; an area like Cannon Street has density-based and entertainment-based businesses; the area of middle-class apartments between Daimaru and the sea has middle-class service trades like tailors, hairdressers, good grocers and butchers, and a range of restaurants. Yee Wo Street, the 'business heart', has no specialist business clusters, but instead an assemblage of uses—shops, restaurants, entertainments, residence—which is technically quite wide for so small an area, but also quite narrowly defined in terms of function and to some extent class. Here, apparently, the operation of a Western kind of business rationale—based on a kind of customer rather than on a kind of tradesman—has led to the establishment of a Western kind of urban landscape, at least in terms of business groupings. At the same time, study of the situations in detail, including change over time, shows that marked changes in class basis of the Causeway Bay business assemblages have taken place in the past generation, and that in some places such changes are still going on. Phenomena of the kinds identified here for Causeway Bay can also be found in other parts of the city where similar forces are at work—particularly in Mongkok.

1 Jardine's has not been quite the area's only early claim to distinction. In 1878 John Jack's rum distillery at Caroline Hill was producing 14,520 proof gallons per quarter. (*Hong Kong Government Gazette*, 16 February 1878, p. 55).

2 *Hong Kong Today* (Hong Kong, 1960), p. 10 (Chinese text).

3 *Business directory of Hong Kong, Canton and Macao* (Hong Kong, 1939). Seventeen out of the nineteen businesses named as selling cars on the island side in this directory were located in one or other of these three districts. It was not quite so in the 1920s. In 1927, according to the Chinese Chamber of Commerce's *Business guide and directory* for that year, twelve of the thirty-two equivalent businesses were at the time located in Central District, eleven in Wanchai and four in Causeway Bay. No doubt this change was the outcome of increasing pressure on space in both buildings and streets.

1. Wellington Street, Central District, about 1870. The original tenement landscape.

2. Sheung Wan. The nam-pak-hong landscape. Part of Bonham Strand West, showing rebuilt tenements and a new office block, (1971).

3. Sheung Wan. Part of the salt fish cluster in des Voeux Road, (1971).

4. Sheung Wan. Jervois Street, showing part of the property which houses the textile cluster, and also the scale on which rebuilding has taken place in parts of Sheung Wan, (1974).

5. Sheung Wan—the Taipingshan town. Hollywood Road, part of the Urban Renewal District. Some demolitions for the pilot scheme have already taken place on the left, and the space has been partly occupied by stalls. A new building can also be seen on the left, (1974).

6. Sheung Wan—the Taipingshan town. The Circular Pathway, now demolished, (1970).

7. Sheung Wan—the Taipingshan town. Mixed hawker market, shops and teahouses with tenements, at the foot of Possession Street. Part of the Pilot Scheme for urban renewal, (1970).

8. Yaumati and Mongkok looking north along the line of Nathan Road, 1968. Yaumati lies to the left, with Mongkok beyond, and in the left background, Taikoktsui. Left foreground is part of the former Whitfield Barracks, now Kowloon Park.

9. Yaumati. Shanghai Street, showing property between Pak Hoi Street and Saigon Street—high buildings of about 1964, and two old tenements, (1974).

10. Mongkok. An industrial street off Canton Road, at the edge of the engineering cluster. Dense use and congestion, (1971).

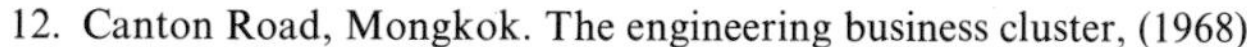

11. Yaumati. Temple Street at dusk; setting up the evening fair, (1974).

12. Canton Road, Mongkok. The engineering business cluster, (1968).

13. Yaumati. Cooked-food-stall restaurants in a group with (right) a big fixed fruit stall, (1970).

14. Yaumati. Daily marketing stalls and shops in Reclamation Street, (1974).

15. Causeway Bay: Hennessy Road (north side) looking towards Yee Wo Street. Tenements built in 1953; newer high property beyond, (1974).

16. Causeway Bay. Lockhart Road looking east towards Daimaru and the Excelsior development, (1974).

17. Causeway Bay from Tai Hang Road, looking north-west across the stadium towards the harbour and the Kowloon peninsula, (1974).

18. Taikoktsui: looking towards Beech Street. Licensed and squatter industry; beyond, big mixed buildings of the 1955–1966 phase, (1970).

19. Taikoktsui. Tung Chau Street. Industrial property in tenement form, 1950s, (1970).

20. Taikoktsui. Fuk Sing Factory Building seen from a remnant hill site with licensed industry and some new building, (1970).

21. Taikoktsui. A small cafe occupying hall, staircase and pavement space, (1970).

22. Taikoktsui: Man On Street, a tenement industrial street of 1958, (1970).

23. Behind Man On Street, Taikoktsui. The back of the range of buildings shown in Plate 22, (1970).

24. Kwuntong, 1961. Early days. Kwuntong Road crosses the picture from left foreground to right middleground. The factories occupy sites on the reclaimed land. Hillside site formation is taking place in the foreground. The site of Yue Man Square is right, middleground. Extreme right foreground, the edge of the resettlement estate.

25. Kwuntong from the air, 1967. Kwuntong Road runs through the middle of the picture, from left foreground to right background. The industrial zone lies to the left; the commercial centre and Yuet Hwa Street in the middle, flanked by the resettlement estate. Early stages in the building of Ham Tin (left foreground) and Sau Mau Ping (right, foreground to middleground) can be recognized. Reclamation in Kowloon Bay, background, with cottage and squatter settlement, and a boat village, cleared in 1970. (Hunting Surveys Ltd. *HSL HK* 67, 7, Run 4 5573.)

26. Kwuntong—Hung To Road. Factory landscape; restaurant on the left.

27. Kwuntong: Sau Mau Ping. New-style resettlement block in 16 floors on the left. On the right, hawker stalls forming a business lane alongside the block, (1971).

28. Kwuntong: the housing zone. Resettlement property (group B) on the left; former housing authority property (group A) on the right. Between, the roofs of stalls in the hawker market.

29. Kowloon City and the villages, looking west. The former walled city lies on the right-hand side of the picture, marked by the high buildings. The low village property lies to the left, with Lung Chun Tou between, (1970).

30. Kowloon City. View in the former walled city, 1970.

31. Kowloon City. Lung Chun Tou, close to the site of the former main gate of the walled city. Dentist and restaurant, (1970).

32. Kowloon City area. The road to addiction. One route to a place where drugs are sold. Hoklo Tsuen, (1970).

33. Kowloon City area. 'Tung Tau Tsuen Main Street', as the sign proclaims, (1970).

34. Clearwater Bay Road Village, looking towards Kowloon, 1970, showing the dye-works which dominated the village, the quarry above, and the relation of the village to the rest of north-eastern Kowloon (in the background beyond the spur).

35. In Clearwater Bay Road Village, 1970. Access by a rough but practicable road. Dyeworks with yarn drying on poles.

36. Clearwater Bay Road villages area, 1974, after clearance and site formation. Clearwater Bay Road Village (plates 34, 35) lay in the right middleground.

6 Taikoktsui

INTRODUCTION

TAKEN as a whole, Taikoktsui is the creature of its location. It lies just within the northern edge of Old Kowloon, where the frontier of 1860 to 1898, now represented by Boundary Street, cuts the western coast of the peninsula. For half a century and more, Taikoktsui had a sort of fringe status in Kowloon, and much of it was rather isolated. In 1972, the Mongkok ferry to Hong Kong island was removed to new reclaimed land at the tip of the promontory, and a bus station has been built alongside; but apart from Cherry Street, Taikoktsui is still to some degree cut off from the main traffic streams, which pass through Nathan Road and Shanghai Street some blocks to the east. The street pattern which Taikoktsui has inherited from a chequered past is laid out on four differently-oriented grid systems (Figure 15), which also tends to isolate the area by creating traffic difficulties. The area is quite small; Taikoktsui Road is only about half a mile in total length. For all these reasons, and also by reason of special features of its economic history, Taikoktsui is an area of quite marked individuality. It is an industrial area, and its history has been that of successive phases of growth of factory industry. Taken street by street, Taikoktsui is the creature of the history of its industrial sites. The various kinds of landscape and locality which are the present result of its industrial history form the central topic of this chapter.

Taikoktsui was originally a high, sharp promontory, partly separated from the mainland by a south-facing sea-bay occupying the space to the north of Cherry Street. Early Taikoktsui was essentially an industrial and seafaring periphery. It now has more than double its original area, due to successive phases of reclamation; and the original coast of the promontory, like that of all urban Hong Kong, now lies wholly inland. Sites have also been formed by the removal of most of the hills. Even less than most parts of the city, Taikoktsui has few sites which are quite natural.

TAIKOKTSUI, CONTEMPORARY STREET LAYOUT

Figure 2 shows that the first major phase of marine reclamation took place before 1887, and the second, together with the formation of the Cosmopolitan Dock, between 1887 and 1904. Two more big blocks of land were reclaimed before the Pacific war. By the late 1920s, when most

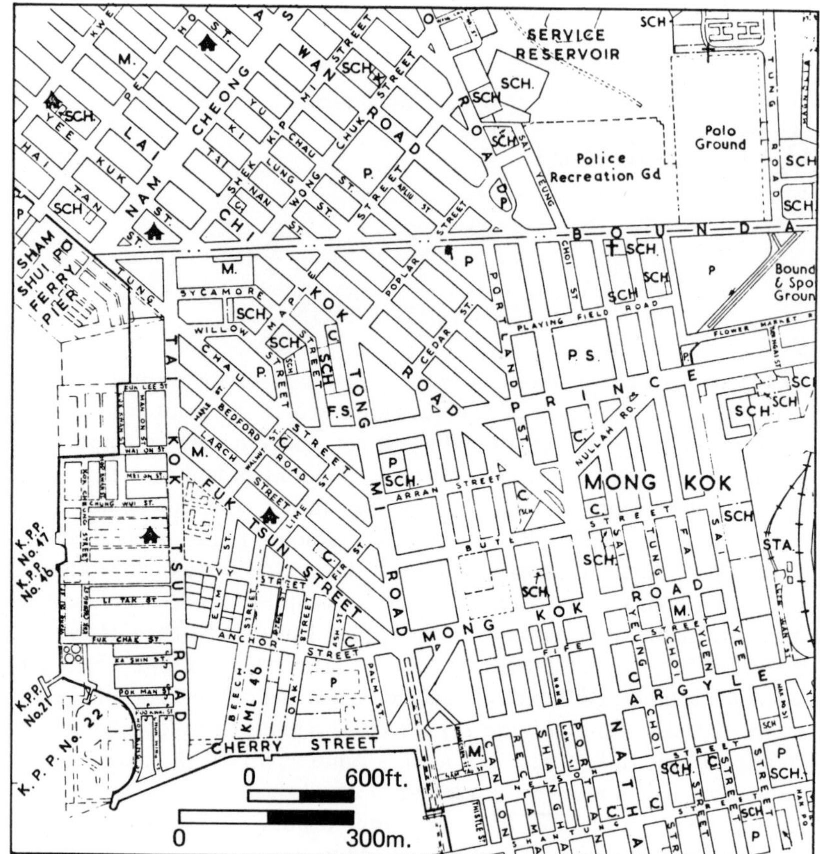

FIGURE 15

STREET PLAN FOR TAIKOKTSUI (1974)

Note: The new ferry and bus station reclamation has been added to this map. Some other developments which have not yet taken place have been anticipated by the cartographer, especially the fresh reclamation at 'Sham Shui Po Ferry Pier'. The dock area is not yet built upon, and squatter or permit areas at Cherry Street and the northern end of Fuk Tsun Street are treated as cleared and marked as a park.

of the work was finished, there was a good deal of unoccupied land in Taikoktsui.

In other respects apart from the reclamations, the early form of Taikoktsui was different from that of the present. The central ridge of hills which formed the spine of the promontory ran roughly north-south, slightly to the east of the modern Taikoktsui Road; it separated the dockyard area from the two or three streets of what must have been a sailors' and dockers' village, which lay between the old sea's edge and the eastern foot of the ridge. Nothing at all remains of this village, except a few yards of the street-lines of Beech Street and Elm Street. In the 1920s a fresh start was made with the main grid of streets like Fuk Tsun Street. Building on the new lines in Taikoktsui began in the 1920s, mainly with tenements, and increased in scale in the following decade.

The development of Taikoktsui since 1945 has continued to be based on this fresh start. The substance of this development has been the building up of empty or nearly empty sites, the removal of the hills and the village, the building of new streets, and the intensification of use on all kinds of sites, all in the context of the tremendous expansion of Kowloon during the past twenty years. During these years, Taikoktsui has changed through investment in buildings and machinery from a scattered and neglected periphery of Yaumati into a solid industrial area in its own right, providing about 40,000 manufacturing jobs in all. In due course it has gone on to begin the development of entertainment and shopping facilities. In terms of land use and property use, the first of these groups of processes has reached a degree of maturity; but the second has still a long way to go, even by the standards of consumption which obtain at present.

AREAS WITHOUT PERMANENT BUILDINGS

At the turn of the century, Taikoktsui formed part of the northern fringe of Kowloon town, and it had an early dock. Consequently, the area has a relatively long history as a place for dumps and depots, the storage of oil (before 1896 and on a small scale up to the present), storage of coal and wood, sheds and workshops, and various kinds of offensive land use. In the early 1920s, there were already some tenement blocks in Taikoktsui, no doubt partly in industrial use, and industry also occupied workshops and sheds. Some individual small workshops of this phase still exist, and there are a number of groups of workshops with shacks, yards, stores and dumps, some old and some new, but all representing the heritage of Taikoktsui as a kind of industrial frontier.

The biggest area of this kind lies between Anchor Street and the south-facing sea-front at Cherry Street (Plate 18). This area occupies land which was reclaimed in the phase 1924–45, and which has never been properly built up. The property comprises partly old workshops, partly unpaved yards with sheds, partly dumps and huts. There is an old-established small steel-rolling mill in Cherry Street. Land is used for storage by a coal-yard, a big saw-mill, and a business dealing in metal drums. The workshops are occupied by a variety of engineering and metal-work businesses, and by factories making baskets, food products, umbrellas, rubber, plastic and glass products.[1] There are also some businesses which reclaim refuse, including bottles, a number of cafés and working men's restaurants, and of course some residence in the factories and workshops, and in adjacent shacks. Most of the factories have 'permit' status, that is tenure liable to termination without compensation at three months' notice; but some are thought to be illegal 'untolerated' squatters.

Many of the firms started business only in the middle 1950s, when the last of the land was taken up. The vast majority of the buildings have only one floor, and many small buildings are made of timber. Indeed, there is not a solid building in the area, though there are several big ones. The area is rat-infested and very squalid in appearance; access is poor and space scarce, and there is serious danger of fire. Some premises have uneven workshop floors of bare earth. Capitalization throughout the factories is minimal; machinery is simple in the extreme. Single-floor land use is extravagant by Hong Kong standards, but in spite of the high values of the sites in areas like these, there is no particular tendency for land use to become more dense within an individual site in terms of either capitalization or use of space. Saw-mills retain their sites for storing timber, glass-furnaces remain elemental. Each business simply goes on conducting its affairs along simple lines, drawing what advantage it can from its location, until the sites are cleared by the government. Industry such as garment manufacture needs better shelter, better light, more security of both tenure and property, and perhaps a better address; but even more to the point, industry here is both older and simpler than the contemporary phase of industry in the city.

The clearing of unsightly, extravagant and insanitary remnant areas like these for building, for playgrounds or for planting as much-needed small public gardens, cannot be long delayed, whatever they have contributed in economy and enterprise in the past. Most of the people who hold permits will be sorry to have to go. Local industrialists, both people occupying shack property such as this and people occupying regular factory buildings, agree in regarding the 'backyard' status and quality of Taikoktsui as the central feature of its economic history. The rolling-mill in Cherry Street has been located here for thirty years; it has grown up with the district, depends on local custom and local labour, and is reluctant to leave. But it occupies what in modern conditions is a very choice site. Its old-fashioned and untidy premises are an anachronism, but a productive and (for the firm) an economical one. They form part of a spectrum of anachronism which runs from junk-yards and coal-dumps, through cooked-food-stall restaurants and pavement industry, to the big bamboo and timber yards on the northern fringes of Taikoktsui and the older factory buildings themselves. The central experience of Taikoktsui is now, and has been for forty years, a revolving process of investment in buildings and machinery by which in each succeeding phase parts of the old structure have been brought up to date. The spectrum of anachronism is also a spiral of renewal.

THE FACTORY STREETS—TENEMENTS AND OTHER SIMILAR BUILDINGS

By 1947, there were clearly two distinct phases of industrial property in Taikoktsui, apart from the tenements; there were the one- or two-storey workshop and storage buildings, some of them no more than sheds, which have been discussed; and there were also some solid Western-style factories which are still in use, most or all of them individual factories built for individual firms.

After the Pacific war, the typical industrial property built in Taikoktsui was one which fused elements of both the tenement tradition and the Western-style factory. The new buildings were intended for industrial use throughout, but were built with several floors and let unit by unit to individual industrial tenants. Several different kinds of buildings represent phases of this fusion. The earliest phase is represented by properties of essentially tenement form, built on tenement-like sites, with four floors all intended for factory use, and without lifts. These were built until about 1956. The most recent phase of the same fusion is represented by high buildings, typically of 10 to 15 floors, built on square or nearly square sites, usually with bigger units of space, and arranged on a hallway plan with access from lifts or stairs in the middle of the block, but still let unit by unit. These buildings were introduced in the middle 1960s. Between these two phases in time came the vast corridor buildings built under the 1955 Buildings Ordinance, typically in mixed use. Multi-storey factory buildings, of which all three types are representatives, are part of the community's characteristic response to two of its characteristic features —the multiplicity of small industrial firms, and the nexus of physical crowding conjoined with resistance to isolation.

The blocks of tenanted factories are the most important single feature of the Taikoktsui scene. They represent a group of concentrated industrial landscapes.

Figure 16 represents the assemblage of uses for all floors in part of the south side of Tung Chau Street in 1974, in property which inherits the tenement tradition in a number of respects—size of building lots (typically 15 feet by 60 feet, though there are variations), and access by a staircase at each address or each pair of addresses. The property (Plate 19) was built in or around 1956, on land which up to that time was unbuilt, or virtually so. Above ground level, the property in this block—in this and other respects it is typical of its kind—is heavily committed to the garments industry, textiles (mainly knitting) and plastics. At present, the typical factory occupies a double flat—two addresses on one floor; but in 1970 some occupied five or six units of space. Employment, investment and output per unit of property vary from trade to trade. Some units are used only as stores. The warehouse at the end of the block occupies not

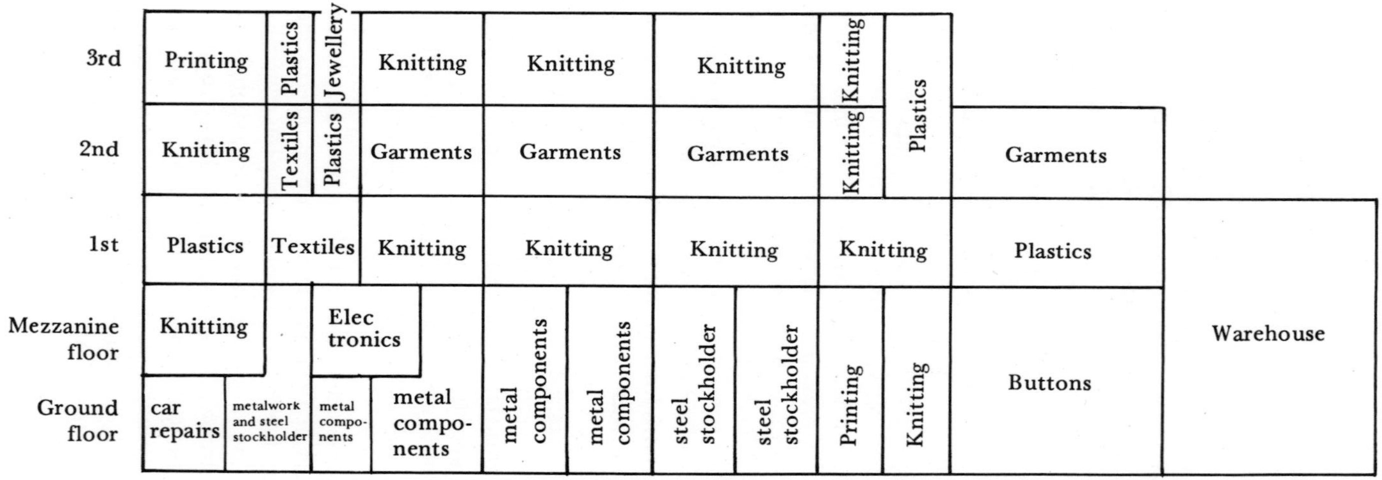

Floor	Uses (left to right)										
3rd	Printing	Plastics	Jewellery	Knitting	Knitting	Knitting	Knitting	Plastics			
2nd	Knitting	Textiles	Plastics	Garments	Garments	Garments	Knitting		Garments		
1st	Plastics	Textiles		Knitting	Knitting	Knitting	Knitting		Plastics	Warehouse	
Mezzanine floor	Knitting		Elec tronics								
Ground floor	car repairs	metalwork and steel stockholder	metal compo- nents	metal compo- nents	metal components	metal components	steel stockholder	steel stockholder	Printing	Knitting	Buttons

FIGURE 16

TAIKOKTSUI—PART OF TUNG CHAU STREET. ASSEMBLAGE OF PROPERTY USES, AUGUST 1974

Note: Considerable alteration in the physical arrangement of the space inside the buildings takes place from time to time—e.g., part of the property now occupied by 'Electronics'.was united with the floor above in 1970, and then formed part of a garments factory.

tenement-style property but individual premises on three floors, built in 1956 as the factory of a thread business.[2] The next building is one floor lower than the rest of the range. Each of these occupies two addresses, and hence each has a more or less square site, being in that respect prototypical of the later factory buildings. In the mixed-tenancy buildings there are no lifts. These buildings, and others like them, house many 'stair shop' businesses in odd corners on the ground floor, usually at the foot of each flight of stairs. These perform canteen functions, the kitchen lining the stairs (Plate 21), or furnish small-scale services like electrical and plumbing repairs. The pavements outside these blocks are more or less fully occupied by a combination of industrial work and canteen services. Ground floor tenancies are more varied, and have a stronger retailing and service side, than those on the upper floors.

This block in Tung Chau Street is one of those for which Dwyer and Lai recorded parallel assemblages in 1962.[3] There is also a record of the property use of this block in 1967, floor by floor, in the office of the Colony Outline Planning Division.[4] Property use in this block was also surveyed in 1970. Comparison of the detail of the four assemblages reveals a feature already familiar from other phases of economic life in the city: the type of use of the properties as a whole has remained stable, but individual properties have changed use, and presumably tenancy, with surprising speed. The overwhelming majority of businesses were in 1962, 1967 and 1970, as they are now, firms engaged in the garments, textiles, or plastics industries, with metal trades on the ground floor. But about half of the individual factories changed use between 1962 and 1967, about half also changed use between 1967 and 1970, and about half also between 1970 and 1974.

What may be called by analogy with wholesale business clusters in Sheung Wan the network system appears to operate also in the world of manufacturing industry in Taikoktsui. Continuity of management in a general sense and of business relationships as a whole appear to be what furnish continuity of the industrial grouping, whilst individual firms display only limited stability at a given address because of both removals by the successful and failures by the unsuccessful. It is remarkable that what may be called the network system can work effectively in localities which are no more than twenty years old.

The Tung Chau Street block is typical of many. The character of several sectors of Taikoktsui has been fixed for the present, and the foreseeable future, by the style of this kind of factory property built around 1955.

Man On Street, which lies to the west of Taikoktsui Road and very close to the sea, represents the continuing use of ground floor workshops in simple tenement property to create an industrial street (Figure 17, Plate 22) and may serve as an example of the common phenomenon of the tenement industrial street.

Man On Street was built in 1958. It comprises tenement buildings with ground and mezzanine floors in industrial occupation, and with the ground floor premises open to the street. With a few exceptions, the upper

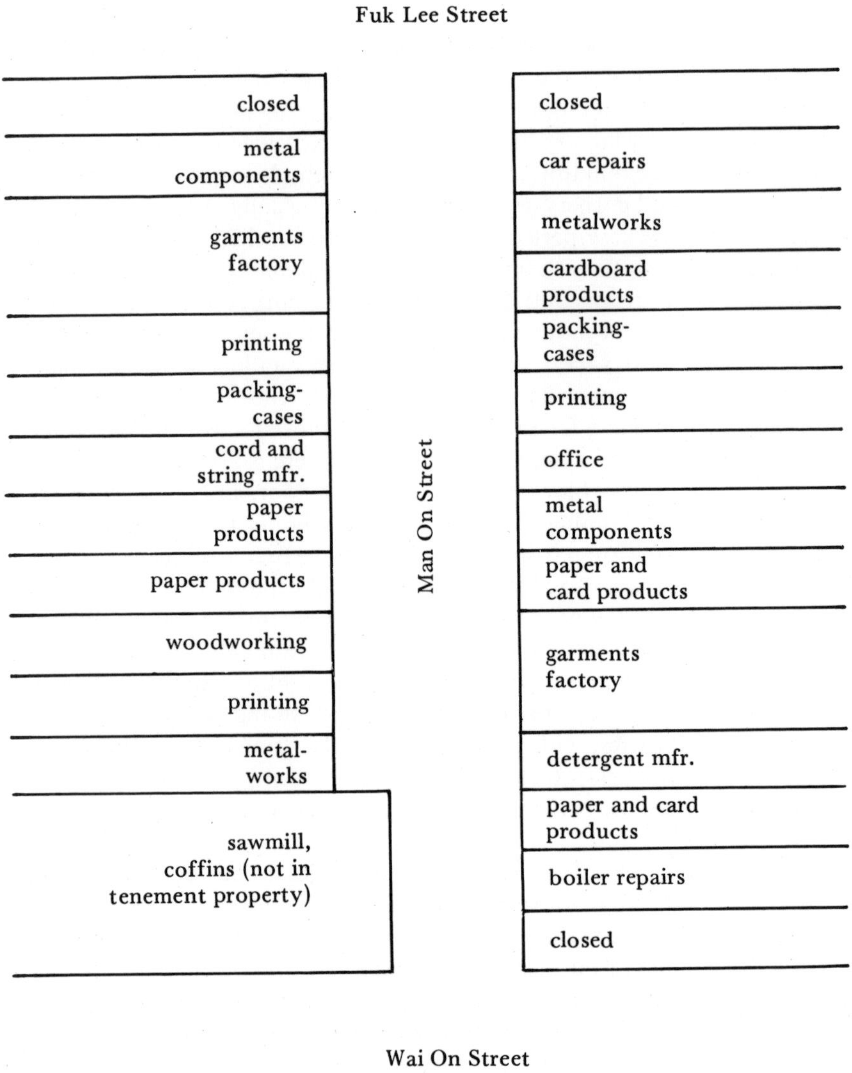

Fuk Lee Street

West side	Man On Street	East side
closed		closed
metal components		car repairs
garments factory		metalworks
		cardboard products
printing		packing-cases
packing-cases		printing
cord and string mfr.		office
paper products		metal components
paper products		paper and card products
woodworking		garments factory
printing		
metal-works		detergent mfr.
sawmill, coffins (not in tenement property)		paper and card products
		boiler repairs
		closed

Wai On Street

FIGURE 17

MAN ON STREET, TAIKOKTSUI, ASSEMBLAGE OF GROUND-FLOOR PROPERTY USES, AUGUST 1974 floors are used for residence only. The front street itself is partly occupied by motor-car repairing. Woodworking, printing and packing businesses also use pavement and road space. On the factory premises in the evenings, workers watch television, play mah-jong or continue working, and some sleep there. Business activities here are very mixed, as the plan shows, but there is a long-standing degree of specialization in the paper, cardboard and printing businesses, for instance the manufacture of advertising and packing materials. The bigger businesses employ 15 to 20 men, except the two garment factories which each employ up to 40 women. Turnover of businesses has been extremely rapid here as in Tung Chau Street. About one-third of the properties changed use between August 1968 and November 1969.[5]

For Man On Street, an attempt was made in 1970 to find out the reasons for this rapid rate of turnover by asking the firms then there why their predecessors left the property. The information obtained was not complete, but its direction is clear. A few businesses failed, but the majority did well, expanded, and moved to bigger premises, generally in new factory buildings. At that time small industry was very prosperous. In 1974 Man On Street was visibly less prosperous, and local businessmen were short of orders, and said so. Movement in this phase was much less; between 1970 and 1974 only one-third of the properties changed use, and in three cases the change was the closure of the premises. Rapid movement appears clearly to arise out of prosperity.

New tenements, no less than old, create their characteristic human landscapes; although this locality is only 15 years old, the back streets at Man On Street are crowded with the activity and objects which are typical of their kind throughout tenement Hong Kong (Plate 23). Baskets, empty or full of rubbish, potted plants, boxes wrapped in plastic sheeting, crates of bottles, earthenware jars, piles of planks and trestles, polythene baths hanging up, refuse underfoot, people doing scullery work such as cleaning chickens and washing crockery, boys doing factory work, other boys having a bath, chickens pecking about, barbers working, cooked-food stalls and their kitchens, piles of metal, paper and cloth waste from the factories, derelict kitchen equipment, washing hanging up to dry on poles, corrugated iron sheeting, piles of old newspapers, water dripping from air-conditioners and pipes overhead, beds and chairs. Man On Street, back no less than front, represents the habitual terminus of life in the tenement streets: a state of acute and profoundly human congestion.

BIG MIXED BUILDINGS (1955–1966 PHASE)

The increases in density of building permitted under the Buildings Ordinance of 1955 led to the construction of a number of very big tenement buildings, arranged on corridors and with mixed uses. The interior landscape of these big mixed buildings, quite hidden from the streets, is a special and characteristic, extremely crowded slum landscape.

Hoi Hing Mansion in Li Tak Street is typical. This very big building has 9 floors including the ground floor, with 44 flats on each upper floor. There are no lifts. Its total site area is about 20,000 sq.ft. It was built about 1964, in the phase when these big mixed buildings, their height limited to the 9 floors which was the highest limit permitted for a building without lifts, reached their maximum development. They represented at that time the main achievement of the movement of developers, working within the framework of the 1955 Ordinance, in moving away from the tenement concept of a multiplicity of staircases to a new ill-named 'mansion' idea of a complex of corridors.

The occupance of Hoi Hing is very mixed. The ground floor is predominantly in industrial use. About half is occupied by various metal trades, the rest by a mixed group including plastics and paper. There is a mezzanine floor, but this is normally used as part of the ground floor premises.

Above this, the first and second floors have many factories, occupied by such trades as machine-knitting, clothing manufacture and the manufacture of metal components. From the third floor upwards factories become relatively scarce, no doubt partly because there are no lifts. There are only a handful of factories on the top four floors of this building, but in neighbouring buildings of similar design and age which have lifts, there are factories throughout.

Residential occupance is also quite mixed. Many flats are fully fitted with cubicles; many have various compromise arrangements. Some 'domestic' flats have manufacturing machinery installed, such as knitting machines; some 'factory' flats have cubicles which are used for residence. Oddities in buildings of this kind take such forms as offices, kindergartens and baby-minding businesses, occasional amateurish soft-drinks cafés, and in some places kitchen businesses furnishing cooked meals which are distributed on a contract basis to groups of workers in the factories. Some 2,500 to 4,500 people must live in Hoi Hing, and about 400–500 must work here in factories. The interior of Hoi Hing illustrates with particular force the achievements of the Clean Hong Kong campaign. In 1971 the seven staircases and long corridors were not only dark but very dirty indeed, in many places encumbered by refuse, and fouled by dogs and cats. At that time it was hard to resist drawing parallels with alleys such as those behind Man On Street, or those in squatter villages. In 1974 these passages were adequately clean, and unencumbered except in some particularly squalid spots; and the air was proportionately fresher. Surprisingly perhaps, some of the best achievements of the campaign have been made in the dirtiest places. Taikoktsui as a whole is visibly cleaner than formerly.

In buildings of this kind, a proportion of the factory workers live in neighbouring flats. Because of the system of rented cubicles and bedspaces, it is relatively easy for people to move to an address very close to their work if they are housed within the private sector, and many people do so. But there is no reason to think that in the big buildings, new or old and of whatever style or class, there is any special tendency for community or association to arise from the fact that various people and organizations are sharing a roof, beyond the practical needs of the day.

The new legal framework of 1970 for the joint management of the common areas of multi-storey buildings arises from this situation. It is interesting that in some buildings, the process of management itself is tending to create a community of interest among at least some owners who occupy their properties themselves.

RECENT FACTORY BUILDINGS

The elephantine mixed buildings like Hoi Hing represented, in building terms, the last phase of the old Hong Kong. Under the pressures of the new Buildings Ordinance of 1966, increasingly sharp administrative control, and rising standards of expectation among businessmen and people, a new kind of factory building, flatted and intensively used but without provision for residential use, began to appear. Many streets are now dominated by these new-style factory buildings.

Fuk Sing Factory Building in Fuk Tsun Street may be taken as typical, although some lack the complicating feature of small properties with street access on the ground floor (Plate 20, Figure 18). Here as elsewhere, the ground floor properties appear to belong to a street-level community of uses, whose content—engineering works, packing, services such as plumbing and catering, and some other trades which usually come in small units, such as plastics—is in general terms rather uniform for the district. This street-level community of uses usually bears rather little resemblance to the upper-floor uses, which generally include bigger units, much more dependence on all the textile trades, and much more process manufacturing of standard objects. In so far as the upper-floor businesses depend on the street-level assemblage for services, increase of density above, due to higher building or other causes, contributes directly to increased congestion in the streets. At the same time, industries which typically occupy street-level property (such as motor firms and the developing machinery-building industry) are tending to proliferate and to occupy bigger premises than formerly. There is no lack of competition for space in the street property or in the street itself.

Compared with the tenement-based factory buildings of the 1950s, Fuk Sing and its fellows are in every respect bigger in scale—higher, with much bigger units, and wider and deeper; the building itself occupies the width of two of the old building blocks, and so faces two streets, not one as the older buildings did, and is roughly square in plan. Fuk Sing Building is also provided with lorry access off the street in a basement, and with a number of big lifts for goods. The assemblage of trades in this building is however only slightly more varied than those typically found in the older buildings. Separation of uses is more complete than in the older buildings, though uses other than manufacturing are not common in the latter either.

There is not very much difference between Fuk Sing and later flatted factory buildings. The newest factory buildings are generally the biggest in both height and area, and their units of tenancy are generally proportionately bigger as well. Newer generally also means cleaner and tidier, upper floors

knitwear garments	hairdressers' accessories	3
printing leather plastics	garments garments metalwork	6
garments		1
garments		1
garments printing	knitwear knitwear	4
paper bags knitwear		2
knitwear metalwork	printing printing printing	5
garments garments garments	knitwear	4
garments garments	printing	3
knitwear optical products	embroidery embroidery embroidery	5
plastics plastics plastics	printing printing printing	6
wigs knitwear knitwear	printing printing	5
watch bracelets		1
mixed, as shown		16

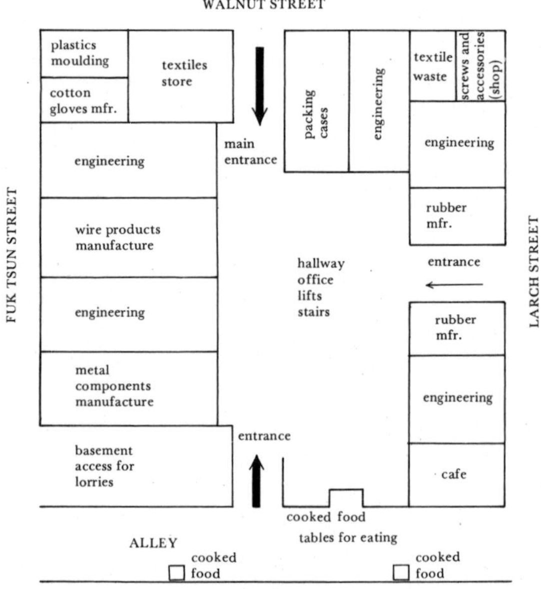

FIGURE 18

TAIKOKTSUI: FUK SING FACTORY BUILDING.
PROPERTY USES, GROUND FLOOR AND UPPER FLOORS, JULY 1970

but there is as yet no way of knowing whether this will endure as the buildings age, or whether it is no more than an attribute of newness itself. On the showing of Hoi Hing, there is room for optimism.

Fuk Sing Building directly faces a very squalid rocky hill site occupied by permit or squatter industry (gloves, garments, soy sauce) with a shrine and some residence. In this area, the oldest type of Taikoktsui landscape is giving way rapidly and directly to the newest. It is revealing to recognize how much change there has been, in less than twenty years, in the kind of new building which occupies such sites in Taikoktsui. The Sycamore Street development at the northern end of Taikoktsui was built on a new site by the Hong Kong Economic Housing Society in 1954 as low-cost suburban housing for middle-class workers. These quiet blocks of flats without shops or workshops, with schools, a church, a playground and two small shrines form an enclave in which is fossilized the earlier Taikoktsui whose northern end, at least, could then invite quiet housing development.

HAWKING AND THE SERVICES TRADES

Hawkers seek out potential customers, and once established, they attract them. The main hawker assemblage in Taikoktsui is a complex one centred on part of Larch Street. It is about ten years old. Its customers are partly the workers from the factories and partly the people who live nearby. Part of it, especially the restaurants and some of the stalls in Larch Street, is fixed; part of it, especially the cooked sea-food stalls in Bedford Road, is reassembled every evening on street space which by day is occupied mainly by parked vehicles.

The day-time hawker assemblage comprises in all about 200 separate businesses, and it has two main features. The first of these is the textile and garment trades. The second, involving less stalls but probably more business, is the group of cooked-food-stall restaurants. There are thirteen of these in the assemblage, in groups of three or four, with seats for 500 or 600 people in all. At lunch-time, most of the seats are occupied by relays of customers for upwards of an hour. Business in the evening is slower, but occupies several hours.

Apart from textiles, clothing and meals, many other things are also sold in this market—shoes, flowers, vegetables, fruit, and small eatables hot and cold for immediate consumption. Evening customers in the restaurants are mostly men, no doubt many of them tenants of bed-spaces in the locality, who may well take all their meals in restaurants or at stalls. During the lunch-break, the customers at the cooked-food and other stalls are working-class people both men and women. At the textile and clothing stalls, most of the customers are women and girls, especially at lunch-time when they come from the factories. Evening business is not very brisk. At the mid-day break, when the whole area is at its busiest, there are up to a thousand people there at any one time. This hawker assemblage is still growing quite rapidly. Hawkers in a street are usually thought to be good for trade in neighbouring shops in spite of the congestion which they create and in spite of the tendency of big fixed stalls like those in Larch Street to form virtually a second frontage to each block, hiding the shops.

On the seaward side of Taikoktsui Road, in more recent property, a different kind of service assemblage is in the course of development, based on very high density residential and mixed use, with ground floor shops and hawking concentrating on vegetables. In Chung Wui Street and its neighbours, a shopping and service landscape has already made its appearance which is close to the Hong Kong average, but which is a new one in most of Taikoktsui. Most of Chung Wui Street was built in 1966.

In terms of kinds of business, the shops are of good tenement type, serving the day-to-day needs of the local people in food, drink and hardware; and the vegetable hawking at the corner supplements what they sell, as is usual throughout tenement streets. The shops are big, well-stocked and busy—better than average. Shops in Chung Wui Street, and the hawkers still more, occupy sites which follow standard Hong Kong principles: they line the routes which are most used by pedestrians. In places which are not through ways for pedestrians, like the side-streets, about half of the ground floor property is used for factories, generally very like those in Man On Street, which lies only a block to the north. These are now creating afresh the characteristic forms of the tenement workshop street.

The big and prosperous convenience shops which typically occupy the street property in Chung Wui Street are a kind of use very unlike the engineering works which occupy the street property in Hoi Hing Mansion, yet bearing in mind that the buildings in Chung Wui Street are higher (16 floors) and have lifts, the differences in upper floor style and use are not marked. Here too the flats are arranged in long corridors, and there are many factories. Some residential flats have cubicles, some not. A few factories also have cubicled living-space, but most do not. The formidable degree of activity in these high blocks must be the context of the new servicing assemblages at ground floor level. So must the increasing consumer demand of the past decade. Chung Wui Street must be one of the last developments in which permission was given for high corridor blocks.

During the 1970s, the old Cosmopolitan Dock has been filled in, and the site is now occupied by the most recent big private housing venture in Taikoktsui, Tai Tung Sun Tsuen, a development which in layout and physical style rises considerably above most of the other property in the area, and whose ground-floor properties are likely, when completed and occupied, to add considerably to the diversity of shopping and restaurant facilities in Taikoktsui.

One other means by which services and shopping facilities have been expanding in Taikoktsui demands comment. This is the reconstruction of some of the old streets, and investment in shops and cinemas. Anchor Street, one of the oldest streets in the area, has a new cinema, whose site was formerly occupied by an important metal and engineering works. The sites of the adjacent new shops were occupied, fifteen years ago, by old factories and a timber yard. Until 1971, this new assemblage faced an area of temporary factory buildings and dumps, now cleared.

Service business is likely to expand further in Taikoktsui, both in consequence of growing local demand, and as a result of the transformation of part of the area from a backwater in terms of public transport into a transport focus of some importance. What can be expected to expand most of all is the restaurant business, which is the heart of the service and entertainment industries throughout the city, and which until 1971 was notably backward in Taikoktsui.[6] There are already signs that this expansion of the restaurant business has begun.

THE PROGRAMME OF GROWTH AND CHANGE

Forty years ago, land in Taikoktsui was only very loosely occupied. Much of it was used for dumps and stores. Local businessmen nowadays agree in the belief that the real origin of industry in Taikoktsui (apart from the dock and the ship-yard) was cheap land of poor physical quality and isolated location, as in the conditions of 1930 it must have been. On this 'bad land', untidy or noisy trades, those producing fumes or those needing plentiful space for open-air storage, could all be carried on cheaply and without interference. Shacks could be used as factories at minimal cost. These advantages were regarded as continuing, by the standards of other areas which generated business, such as Yaumati, until twenty years ago. In some ways, such as public and official tolerance of noise and dirt, and tolerance of industrial activity and storage on the pavements, they do so even up to the present, although tolerance of these things is high in some other parts of the city as well, especially areas with similar histories such as Togwawan. Moreover, 'bad land' advantages continue to be represented by the intensification of use of the surviving dump and shed areas which took place in the 1950s. But these areas of the style of forty years ago are by any standards obsolete, and will not survive much longer.

During the past twenty years, in the context of the galvanic economic expansion of Kowloon since 1949, Taikoktsui has ceased to be a periphery. Most of the land has been taken up for long-term building. Land use and property use have been greatly intensified, and the area has become filled up, or nearly so, as it certainly was not in 1930 or 1950. There are, it is true, a number of ways in which Taikoktsui is not yet completely occupied, even by buildings—the remnant 'bad land' areas, the residual site-formation areas where hills are now being removed, the under-utilized sites of older properties, perhaps even of the older specialized factory blocks—all these represent space which can be put to fresh use. But local businessmen agree in regarding Taikoktsui as having become more or less saturated by industry, in present conditions, by about 1966. Since that time, new or incoming firms have not found it easy to gain a foothold.

In these conditions, one question which naturally arises is that of the removal of established factories to Tsuen Wan or other peripheral areas. It is not a question which arouses much enthusiasm. Of course, those who have businesses here now are those who have not been keen to leave. One usual view of Tsuen Wan is that it is preferable in property and technical terms to Taikoktsui, but much inferior in terms of access to labour and customers; this applies particularly to firms which belong to local specialist clusters of businesses, like the metal trades. Businessmen who produce mainly for export, and those whose factories are big enough to find it difficult to fit into the factory premises available in Taikoktsui, think better of Tsuen Wan. Of these three considerations, the third is perhaps the most pressing, though adjacent premises can generally be found. None of the three carries imperative weight.

It is clear from what has been said that fresh demand for space in Taikoktsui is now as likely to come from the tertiary sector as from the secondary. The tertiary sector is in no sense complete. Taikoktsui is not well supplied with shops, restaurants or entertainments. Only street trading approaches the norm. Even in day-to-day terms, a good deal of purchasing power must go out of the area. There has been significant vitality and growth in this respect in the past ten years in the hawker bazaar, in streets like Chung Wui Street, and in the new cinemas and groups of shops and (most recently) big new restaurants. This vitality represents one phase of the continued raising of the level of economic and social life in Taikoktsui from the 'backyard' levels of the 1920s towards those of metropolitan Kowloon, especially in terms of diversification. What is surprising is that there has not been still more growth of this kind. Whether in the future the government offers new leases mainly for industry or for mixed development, there is surely much more growth of this kind to come.

During the past twenty years, Kowloon has grown from a moderate-sized provincial industrial town into a great metropolitan city. In Tsimshatsui and Mongkok, great new business centres have been created since 1945 from relatively humble beginnings, by a characteristic programme of expansion of business, congestion, rising land and property values, investment in high buildings, further expansion, further increase in land values, further congestion, and more investment. Taikoktsui was not favourably placed, by either location or prior industrial structure, to attract central business functions. The programme of expansion took a parallel but different form, through expansion and investment in industry. Hence Taikoktsui remains an industrial area, though no longer a backward one; and her tertiary functions remain both local in orientation, and inadequate in extent. In diversity and social provision, there is still lost ground from before 1945 to make up.

In these respects, and in respect of increasingly high densities of activity on each plot of land, the programme of growth and change in Taikoktsui is still widening as the years go by. Each block of land and property in the area occupies its own position in relation to this varied and still developing programme. Some sites have changed during the past thirty years only in degree of density of activity. Some, which fifteen years ago were in the forefront of change, are becoming obsolete. Some older properties have already been replaced, at densities at least three times what they were, and up to ten times or more. All this is the essence of the physical fabric and economic functioning of Taikoktsui in the present generation.

1 It is of interest that ten out of the sixteen glassworks named for the whole colony in 1955–6 were in Taikoktsui, all apparently on squatter or permit sites *(Hong Kong industrial and commercial views, 1955/56)* (*Hsiang-kang kung-shang-yeh pao-dao*, in Chinese), published by the Wah Kiu Industrial and Commercial Press). Comparison of this list with the telephone directory for 1971 shows that some of the works named in the *Views* are still occupying the same sites, that some are defunct, and that all the rest have moved to sites in the New Territories—presumably still seeking low-priced locations and relative freedom from planning restrictions. The valuable detailed paper by Barbara E. Ward, 'A small factory in Hong Kong. Some aspects of its internal organisation', in W.E. Willmott (ed.), *Economic organisation in Chinese society* (Stanford, 1972), relates to a glass factory.

2 In 1947 this business already occupied about 10,000 sq.ft. on two floors at an address in Shumshuipo. The firm—typical of many—was started in 1933 by a Cantonese (born in 1887) who gained his knowledge of the industry in America. (Wang Chu-Jung, *Hsiang-kang kung-chang tiao-ch'a* (*Survey of Hong Kong factories*), (Hong Kong, 1947), section *tzu-tsao-lei* (textiles), p. 51.) This business moved in 1972 to bigger and less congested premises in Tsuen Wan.

3 D.J. Dwyer and C.Y. Lai, *The small industrial unit in Hong Kong. Patterns and policies*, (Hull, 1967), p. 41. There is an interesting account of small-scale industry in Taikoktsui in pp. 39–46 of this book, relating mainly to conditions in 1960–5. The substance of this account appears also in D.J. Dwyer (ed.), *Asian urbanisation, a Hong Kong casebook* (Hong Kong, 1971), pp. 124–8.

4 Hong Kong Government, Colony Outline Planning Division. *Existing land-use plans*. The author thanks the Colony Outline Planning Officer for allowing him access to this material.

5 Data for 1968 from MS. records of the Colony Outline Planning Division, *Existing land-use plans*.

6 Since 1971, the government has allowed a group of cooked-food-stall restaurants to occupy a vacant plot in Taikoktsui Road. No doubt this development is strictly temporary, but it is welcome to the people.

7 Kwuntong

INTRODUCTION

In most people's opinion, Kwuntong represents a radical new departure in Hong Kong public life. Certainly it is one of the most remarkable cases of urban development within a narrow space of time, and guided by a comprehensive plan, to be found anywhere in the world. Yet at the same time much that has happened at Kwuntong goes only a little way beyond kinds of developments which have been commonplace in the city for fifteen years, and some for more than a century. On the one hand, Kwuntong is a distinguished successful essay in the building and peopling of a great industrial town on an empty site, within the space of half a generation. On the other, the creation of land by reclamation follows many precedents on both sides of the harbour, and the big-scale building of public housing and other features of the planned town have been typical of Kowloon during the 1950s. Kwuntong is remarkable in Hong Kong terms mainly for the adoption and implementation of a *comprehensive* plan, with public housing built *pari passu* with the building of factories. The decision to build a Kwuntong town was taken in 1954, at a time when both public housing on a big scale as a permanent part of social policy, and and manufacturing industry as the solid foundation of the whole Hong Kong community's future livelihood were both new ideas arising from novel situations, and when neither was yet standard orthodoxy.[1]

The plan for Kwuntong was based on a zoning concept. As the map (Figure 19) shows, there are industrial, housing and commercial zones, though of these broad categories the second and third by no means represent uniform types of land use. Also shown on the map is the realistic limit of the commercial centre as it could be recognized on the ground in 1970–4. It has encroached on the housing zones to west and north. In this chapter, it is intended to document the various kinds of landscape which can be recognized in Kwuntong, and to isolate characteristic features of the forms which are developing. Clearly the zoning of the areas as planned comes into conflict to some degree with the habits of the people. It is not the purpose of this account to try to castigate the planners with the wisdom of hindsight. But it is intended to investigate the influence of the plan in this kind of situation, and at the same time to investigate the pressures put upon the planned town by the people.

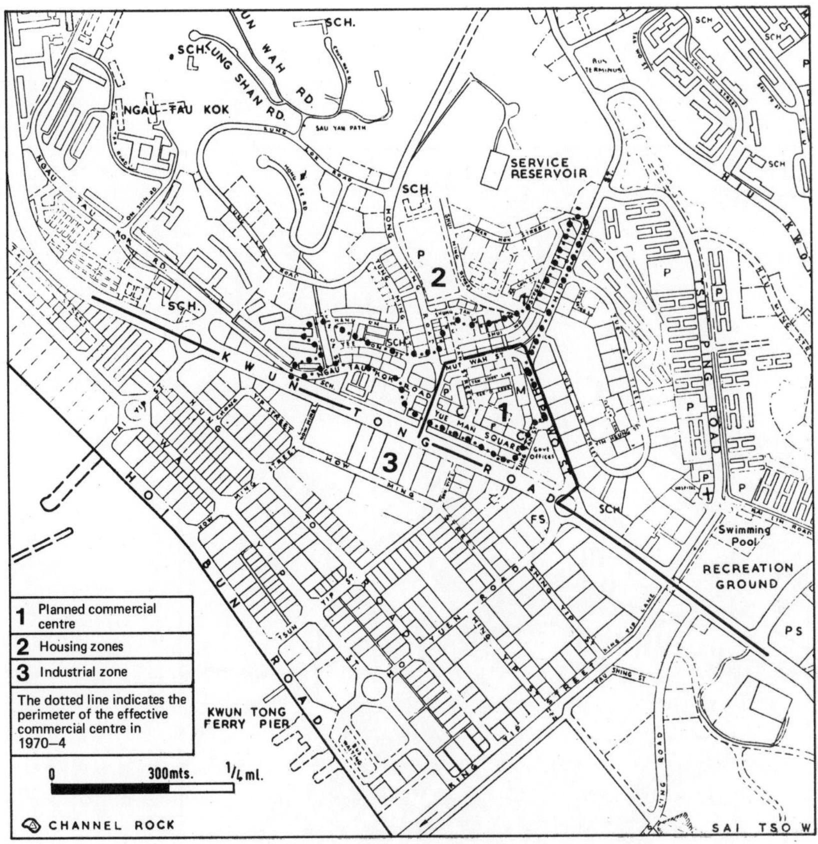

FIGURE 19

KWUNTONG: CONTEMPORARY STREET LAYOUT, THE PLANNED LAND USE ZONES AND THE EFFECTIVE COMMERCIAL CENTRE (1974)

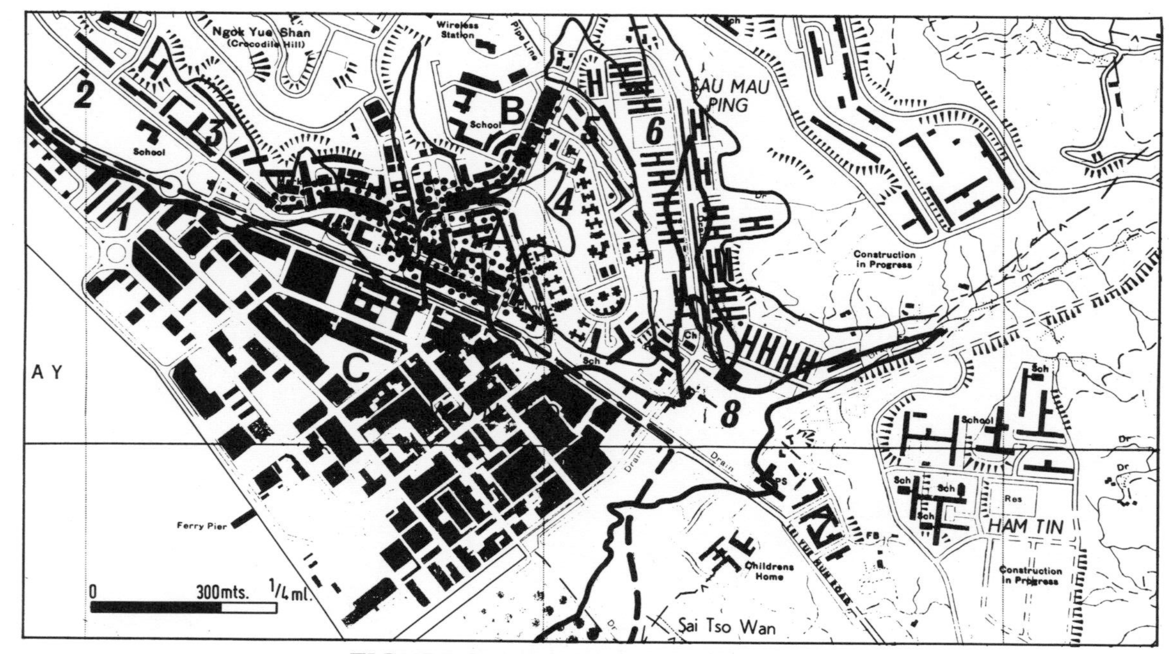

FIGURE 20 THE LAYOUT OF KWUNTONG

The continuous black lines indicate the former sea level and the former 100-ft contour line. These are taken from the 'Paras Ram' map, 1902 (London, Public Record Office, MPH), 149 (C)

Key to symbols: A Commercial centre B Housing zones C Industrial zones—separated by heavy broken lines

1 resettlement factory blocks
2 site of the former Ngautaukok village
3 the Housing Society's Garden Estate
4 the private housing zone
5 the Wo Lok (group A) public housing estate
6 the resettlement (group B) public housing estate
7 the former low-cost housing estate (group A public housing)
8 area zoned for community uses (swimming pool, etc.)

Sau Mau Ping and Lam Tin (here called by its earlier name Ham Tin) are shown in the eastern half of the map.

THE PHYSICAL GROWTH OF KWUNTONG

The chronology and rationale of the growth of Kwuntong have been recorded up to 1963, when most of the reclamation work was already finished, by Lai and Dwyer.[2] In their article they point out that the comprehensive plan at Kwuntong arose partly out of the government's unsatisfactory experience at Tsuen Wan, an earlier, more distant and less planned industrial satellite on the coast to the north-west of Kowloon, where up to the present the burden of squatter settlements of all kinds remains a heavy one. They show that the site of Kwuntong, since 1933 a refuse dump and in part since 1947 a Shell oil depot, involved both marine reclamation and the removal of hill masses. Figure 20 shows the original physical features of the area which was to become Kwuntong, and the relation of these to the layout of the town. Work began on reclamation in 1954 and was finished in Kwuntong itself in 1965; levelling and terracing of hill sites began about the same time and was finished in 1971 or 1972. At first, industrialists were slow to take up land and build, partly because of the deep piling needed, partly because of poor public transport and road access and poor supplies of water, electricity and telephone services. These inadequacies were mostly rectified by 1959.[3] From that time, factories proliferated, and zoning became realistically operative. The figures given by Lai and Dwyer for acreages of reclaimed land and numbers of factories and factory workers are reproduced here by permission, with continuations beyond 1963 and population and planned population figures added from other sources (Table III). Plate 24 shows the situation in 1961.

By 1963, the physical reclamations at Kwuntong were approaching completion, though a further reclamation of most of the rest of Kowloon Bay to the north-west was then under consideration.[4] The factories were coming in at the rate of about forty a year. The resettlement estate was finished, and so was the smaller first phase of the Housing Society's Garden Estate. The Housing Authority's Wo Lok estate was begun but not completed. In January 1963, about one-third of the planned industrial zone between Kwuntong Road and the sea was occupied by buildings. Flatted factory buildings were beginning to make their appearance. The resettlement flatted factories came later. Private building apart from factories was still quite limited in extent. The main middle-class suburban housing complex at Yuet Hwa Street was barely started, and only two or three of the big buildings of the intended commercial centre were finished. More big buildings were finished in the housing zone to the north-west, based on Ngautaukok Road. The early completion here of what are essentially mixed buildings, with ground-floor shops, must be the origin of the present marked north-western extension of the commercial centre. But the photograph of 1967 (Plate 25) shows Kwuntong complete in all essentials as it is today.

By 1963 or 1964 however, before Kwuntong was finished, and in terms of development other than public and aided housing almost as soon as it was begun, radical changes were being introduced. These were above all

TABLE III

GROWTH IN KWUNTONG, 1954–1973

Year	*Total Acreage of Reclaimed Land*	*Number of Factories*	*Number of Workers in Factories*	*Population*	*Planned Population*
1954	5.5				
1955	14.5				
1956	52.5				120,000[1]
1957	66.6	1	80		
1958	89.1	10	3,014		'nearly
1959	112.3	22	7,372		250,000'[2]
1960	133.0	90	13,877		
1961	180.0	134	18,589		
1962	230.0	146	19,758		
1963	250.0	170	22,000	110,000[3]	
1964	250.0	197	25,336		
1965	261.0	343[5]	30,500	160,000[4]	
1966	Kwuntong	468	49,378		
1967	reclamation	503	48,445		
1968	completed 1965	642	63,000		
1969	Reclamation				
1970	continues	1,098[6]	84,970[6]		
1971	elsewhere in Kowloon Bay	1,362[6]	89,498[6]		
1973	618 acres[7]		95,000[7]	530,000[7]	

1 Kwuntong District Kaifong Welfare Association Ltd., *Kwuntong Today* (1969) English text, p. 6.
2 *Annual Report*, 1959, p. 63. "Estimated".
3 *Annual Report*, 1963, p. 255.
4 *Annual Report*, 1965, p. 174.
5 *Annual Report*, 1965, p. 45. Page 174 in the same volume gives a figure of 226.
6 Figures issued by the Labour Department (April-June quarter). The Labour Department's corresponding figures for 1968 were 687 and 64,224.
7 *Hong Kong 1974, Report for the year 1973*, pp. 92–3.

the resettlement estates at Sau Mau Ping and Lam Tin, on high sites inland from Kwuntong, the one to the north-east, the other to the south-east. Even at their first planning, each of these projects was intended to house about 50,000 people, roughly the same number as were then living in the Kwuntong resettlement estate itself. In 1973, the authorized population of the Sau Mau Ping estate was 116,000 people, and that of Lam Tin 68,000.[5]

Sau Mau Ping and Lam Tin are not the only contributors to the growth of the hinterland of Kwuntong. In all, government housing projects on the east side of Kowloon Bay, counting only those to the south of Ping Shek, and not including Kwuntong itself, have a total population of about 400,000 people; Kwuntong itself contributes about 80,000 in government or Housing Society housing, and about 150,000 in private accommodation.[6] All these people live in an area which is in some sense tributary to Kwuntong. In the resettlement estates like Lam Tin whose communications with Kowloon are necessarily through Kwuntong, most people visit Kowloon only exceptionally, at holiday times and for special reasons.

All this means that Kwuntong has become or is becoming the main business and social centre for a population of half a million or more. There are frequent buses to various parts of Kowloon, and since 1970 bus fares throughout urban Kowloon (including Kwuntong and its elder sister Tsuen Wan) have been charged at a flat rate (now 30¢), which of course favours the more distant areas such as Kwuntong; still, the journey by bus may well take an hour. The journey by public light bus takes about half an hour, and costs 80¢ or $1. There is an adequate ferry service to North Point on Hong Kong island and a limited service to Central District. Nevertheless, Kwuntong necessarily remains by Hong Kong standards somewhat isolated. Pressure on the commercial centre of what was designed as essentially an industrial town, consequent upon these great numbers of people and their visibly growing prosperity, has led already to some inadequacy and some unplanned development in Kwuntong, and can hardly fail to lead to more. In these respects, Hong Kong has already far outgrown the Kwuntong which was planned in the decade from 1954, and which has taken shape on the ground up to the present. Growth on the east side of Kowloon Bay has not yet ceased. Expansion of public housing is still taking place in the Clearwater Bay Road area and at the southern end of the peninsula. Exploitation of new industrial land still has far to go on the reclaimed northern half of Kowloon Bay opposite the Kai Tak runway, and at Junk Bay to the east where since 1960 the government has been systematically relocating the ship-breaking and steel-rolling industries. These expansions must create increased demand for central services of all kinds in Kwuntong, even though the government is now tending (rightly but too slowly and still with too little sense of creating town centres, rather than estate centres) to provide more sites for restaurants, shops and entertainments in the big new estates themselves.

ZONE, LANDSCAPE AND ACTIVITY: THE COMMERCIAL CENTRE

As the map (Figure 19) shows, the Kwuntong commercial centre as planned was a compact central area whose boundaries, all dividing streets down their length, can never have been quite realistic. The map also shows the commercial centre as it has emerged in real terms up to 1974.[7] Various differences can be seen. The light-bus park on the Kwuntong Road fringe, and the government offices in the south-east corner, qualify only very marginally if at all. At the same time, circulation pushes the commercial centre northwards of the market, so that it occupies most of the west side of Hip Wo Street, and also westwards along the old main road, Ngautaukok Road, so that it takes in part of the hawker bazaar area. A number of anomalies of different kinds arise. One factor which has weakened the zoning concept in practice here is the adaptability of private 'housing' property to commercial and industrial use. In practice, zoning in Kwuntong has operated with real effectiveness only in keeping non-industrial development out of the industrial zones; and that, as will be shown, is not an unmixed blessing. A market and a hawker bazaar were planned for the housing zones on the inland side of the planned commercial centre, in addition to the town centre's own market. These can be expected to generate activity at a commercial centre level, though up to the present they have done so to only a limited extent. Both lie at the fringes of the extended commercial centre which can be recognized in real terms, and neither has much function beyond the daytime supply of vegetables. So far, where the commercial centre of Kwuntong has extended beyond the area intended by the planners, the degree of specialization and central-shopping character is not high, except in the oldest area in Ngautaukok Road. The truth of the situation is not only that the planned commercial centre is small and too compact in shape, but also that Kwuntong as a whole is still rather sparsely furnished with businesses of all kinds, apart from factories. It is remarkable that the commercial centre identified 'in real terms' grew in extent very little indeed, if at all, between 1970 and 1974.

One reason for the failure of the more-than-local central business functions of Kwuntong to grow very much has been the failure of business to bring in investment. Central Kwuntong had in 1970 the two cinemas provided for in the original plan, but no dance-hall; only half-a-dozen big restaurants, no night-clubs, and few big shops. The situation was the same in 1974. The two departmental stores which exist (one is very small) are both mainland China products businesses—it is remarkable that only the mainland products businesses open departmental stores in the industrial suburbs. It may be that they do so for political reasons. Certainly businessmen in Mongkok are reluctant to do so for business reasons.[8] This reluctance appears to be based partly on ignorance of Kwuntong, partly on a view that the positive side of the agglomeration of businesses demands a negative component: that because Mongkok is the focus of entertainment and shopping for Kowloon, Kwuntong is not. The limitations of the planned commercial centre of Kwuntong and the prejudices of the business community—and perhaps of the community of potential customers as well—tend each to fortify the other, and growth remains limited. Yet it must be remembered that the centre of Kwuntong is little more than ten years old; even in Hong Kong, the growth of variety and maturity in new streets can be expected to take time.

By the standards of old Kowloon, the commercial centre of Kwuntong is distinguished in detail by some lack of diversity and by relatively low densities of property use, both business and residential. Crowded apartment blocks with very mixed functions are less common than in Kowloon, but those which do exist contribute much to what metropolitan character the area has.

In Ngautaukok Road, one such building, built about 1963, has eight floors above ground level, and occupies twelve addresses. There are no lifts. Access is by open corridors along the back face of the building. Ten of the sixty flats on the five upper floors are in non-residential use, as factories (knitting, plastics) or stores. About one-third of the flats on the lower floors are in business use, as offices, hairdressers, a tailor, a fortune-teller, and so forth, or as factories. Several flats are totally occupied by bed-spaces—in one case the dormitory of a factory, in others the commerical renting of bed-spaces in three-tier bunks. This property represents perhaps the maximum level of congestion which exists in contemporary Kwuntong.

Here as elsewhere, ground-floor occupance has little in common with that of the upper floors, apart from the extension of peripheral town-centre businesses like hairdressers to the first and second floors. Ground-floor occupance of this building is partly in town-centre businesses, including four premises selling furniture imported from mainland China, and partly day-to-day businesses like a kindergarten and a grocery store. In terms of Yaumati, this part of Ngautaukok Road has the same kind of status as Shanghai Street. It compares surprisingly closely with other big buildings in the commercial centre, though newer buildings are usually much cleaner and rather less mixed, especially those with good-class residential flats.

The official market building in Kwuntong, which lies at the eastern edge of the commercial centre, is quite small and in no way distinguished. It had the customary appendages of a group of cooked-food-stall restaurants, also rather small, and a planned hawker market selling vegetables, pets and clothing. An attempt has been made by the planners to create a pedestrian precinct on the inner, busy side of the market area, centred on Yan Oi Court and the little public garden off the north side of Yue Man Square. This initiative has been welcomed by the people. Yan Oi Court has come gradually to be almost wholly lined with restaurants, which use much of the space in the court to deploy tables. In the evening, a large area of adjoining pavement space becomes the site for an evening fair—but not the garden, where hawkers are not allowed, and where people play chess, talk or sleep. Property belonging to the hawkers is left about to encumber the pavements, and domestic washing is sometimes dried on railings. It is hard to say whether this kind of use of traffic-free space ought to be condemned as dirty and offensive clutter, or welcomed as the wholesome result of the use of the city as a place for human beings to live. The limited field evidence is that the government has in recent years moved to some degree from the former standpoint towards the latter.

ZONE, LANDSCAPE AND ACTIVITY: THE HOUSING ZONES

It has been shown that given the normal conditions in Hong Kong, there was a certain ambiguity lodged within the concepts of commercial centre and housing zone. Upper floors in a commercial centre are expected to be more or less in residential use, and ground floors in a housing zone may be expected (depending mainly on social class) to be in commercial or even light industrial use. In practice, and from the point of view of both the urban landscapes and the economic structure of the localities, the housing zones in Kwuntong fall into groups which are differentiated in two kinds of way: according to whether they are government-financed or government-sponsored on the one hand, or private on the other; and according to whether the ground floors are in commercial use or not. This unorthodox but realistic division distinguishes four kinds of development.

One of these has already been discussed, namely private housing with commercial development on the ground floor, which is typical of the commercial centre.

A second type is that represented by the Yuet Hwa Street development. This is an area of about 160 acres, occupying a high spur which in human amenity terms is the best group of sites in Kwuntong, and which is frankly the middle-class residential area. It has a central open space laid out as a public park. Building takes the form of residential blocks which are usually in thirteen floors. Some professional services are offered in some blocks, but there are no shops at all. There is no fixed-pitch hawking and little hawking of any kind. All buildings and forecourts are clean and tidy. Inside these flats, main sitting-rooms may be cut off from the windows, but if so then usually by glass panelling only. There are no cubicles of any kind.

Since all the various kinds of public housing in the city are represented in Kwuntong, it will be useful at this point to discuss each type.[9] One feature which they all have in common is that the managers and staff on the estates are all Chinese. These public estates are now regarded as falling into two classes—Group A, comprising the former low-cost and Housing Authority estates, and Group B, comprising the former Resettlement estates.

In the Group A estates, where for historical and practical reasons conditions are generally better than in Group B, most domestic flats are self-contained with private balcony, kitchen, and toilet with shower. Provision of shops, markets, schools, clinics and other amenities varies considerably from estate to estate, but there is always some provision. In these estates, the principle of the separation of uses is operative to the extent that convenience shopping in the estates is limited in scale, style and distribution, and that whilst some blocks do accommodate parts of the estate's shopping centre on their ground floors, most do not. There is in principle no hawking and no manufacturing. To qualify for a tenancy in a Group A estate, a family must comprise at least four people and have an income within or somewhat above the ordinary working-class range; there is an upper limit which depends on the size of the family. The rent for a 6-person flat is $51 per month in 1974, and the space allowance is 35 sq. ft. per adult.

There are two Group A estates in Kwuntong. One is small and unremarkable. The other, Wo Lok, lies in a situation which obviously owes something to opportunism, if not cynicism, about social class; it occupies the very steep south-east-facing slope which separates the smart Yuet Hwa Street development on the spur from the resettlement estate which occupies the valley beyond. Hence it serves as a screen. Wo Lok has shops and some social amenities including two kindergartens. There are no hawkers. About half of the flats have extensive interior subdivision.

Something may be added here about Ping Shek, which lies to the north-west of Kwuntong itself. Ping Shek is also a Group A estate, but is new and very smart, and may indicate the direction in which official housing provision is likely to develop as time goes on. Ping Shek was opened in 1971. There are two housing blocks of 8 floors and five of 28; car-parks, a pedestrian shopping-centre, a market, schools, and a big restaurant of the kind most patronized by the people in the city itself. There is no manufacturing, the shops do not encroach on the pavements, and there are no hawkers. In the residential property on the upper floors, some rooms are cubicled, including some on the old-style tenement plan. Population capacity at Ping Shek is 29,208 people.

Ping Shek is quite strictly controlled. Hawkers are turned out, if necessary by the police. Meetings are held at which groups of new tenants are introduced to the rules of the estate, which include, for instance, the prohibition of mah-jong (which as played in Hong Kong is a very noisy game) after 11 p.m. Quarrelsome tenants are reasoned with: as an ultimate sanction, a persistent trouble-maker can be evicted. Bad shopkeepers are not evicted, but they do not get their tenancies renewed. The range of shopping provision is decided by the estate manager and his staff, and the shop tenants are selected by them. A magisterial, benign, broad-minded and sympathetic, but in the end powerful and ruthless, public authority guides, protects and instructs good people whose best interests lie in cooperation with the authority and with one another. Harmony and cooperation are the ideals of the system; corruptibility is its characteristic weakness. All this seems to take us surprisingly close to the ideals and weaknesses of the bureaucratic system of imperial China. It is sometimes argued that in a Chinese community a Confucian authority must perform the work of creating positive respect for other people and for the community which in a Western community is performed by the force of public opinion.[10]

In some physical respects, calm and quiet within the Ping Shek precinct are paid for in disorder outside it. Immediately outside the precinct, jammed into the narrow space of the verges, hawkers congregate, selling food, clothing and toys. Immediately across Clearwater Bay Road, and serving the adjoining Choi Hung Housing Authority estate as well as Ping Shek, is a moderate-sized hawker market of some dozens of stalls, occupying the south-eastern end of the squatter estate. According to stall-holders, this market took its rise at the time that the Choi Hung estate was opened in 1963. Prices in the hawker market do not appear to be lower than in the small official market inside Ping Shek, but choice, as one customer pointed out, is much better.

It is typical of Hong Kong that Ping Shek was barely finished, and the symbiosis with the hawker market established, when the government began to build the Choi Hung interchange, a series of flyovers designed to ease traffic flow, on the edge of the estate, and in part on sites occupied by the hawker market, which has been proportionately reduced.

Also belonging to this broad group are the estates of the Hong Kong Housing Society. The Society builds in order to let to families with incomes around or rather above the working-class average. The Society's estates are generally distinguishable from government housing by reason of various superior features—better finish, rather more space and trees, and so forth. The Society's estates are those which most resemble the low-cost housing estates of Singapore, though the resemblance is not very far-reaching, particularly in allowance of space per person, which is much greater in Singapore, as are rentals.[11] Rentals in Housing Society property generally fall within the spectrum $10–$20 per person per month, according to levels of amenity, and the allowance of space is 35 sq. ft. per person—the same as in the other 'better' types of public housing.

The Housing Society's property in Kwuntong is the Garden Estate, at the north-western and oldest end of the town, on Ngautaukok Road. It has its own shops and restaurants, but there are no hawkers.[12]

It is the Hong Kong government's 'resettlement' programme, rather than other aspects of its vast public housing programme, which has attracted most attention, especially abroad. Resettlement estates are now known as Group B estates. They accommodate about two-thirds of the people in government housing in the urban area, 1,001,000 people in all in 1973.[13] Resettlement has attracted attention partly for this reason; partly by reason of the characteristic appearance of the older blocks, partly by reason of its being tied in principle and practice to the squatters. Resettlement was introduced, in general terms, to house former squatters, and this remains the central function of Group B estates.

Much discussion of housing in Hong Kong over the years has revolved around the existence of the squatters. In the simplest terms, squatting is the illegal use of land, usually unoccupied public land, to build a house and set up a home. It has been a continuing problem since the early days. After 1947 it grew rapidly to crisis proportions. In 1954 there were thought to be 260,000 squatters in Hong Kong.[14]

Resettlement in its modern and characteristic form—multi-storey blocks of government housing—began in 1954 as a result of the great squatter fire at Shek Kip Mei during Christmas 1953. This and other fires

> . . . had two important results. First, they transformed the squatter problem from a stubborn and apparently endemic evil into an emergency of the first order; and second, the fires freed for proper development substantial areas of valuable land which the presence of squatters had rendered unusable and whose removal had defied all ingenuity.[15]

Colonel Clague's sub-committee recommended multi-storey resettlement, to be financed and undertaken directly by the government. This decision has turned out to be one of the most momentous ever taken in Hong Kong.

In fact 'resettlement' was not a wholly new idea in 1954. The first 'resettlement areas' of 1948 were areas of land set aside for homeless people to build huts, the government providing services. These have their present equivalent in the licensed and resite areas. A later phase of 'cottage' resettlement enterprise began in 1952, when some thousands of cottages were built under various charitable schemes.[16] The fires of 1953 and 1954 led away from piecemeal and amateurish approaches of this kind.

The first harsh, ugly six-floor 'Mark I' resettlement blocks made their appearance at Shek Kip Mei in 1954, less than a year after the fire. In the years which followed, the resettlement estates came to be one of the characteristic features of the whole city. By 1961, 115 of the original Mark I, H-shaped blocks, each with 64 rooms on each floor, with communal lavatory and washing facilities and communal water-taps, and with access to each room by open corridors around the blocks on each floor, had been built. Allowance of space in these blocks was and is basically 24 sq.ft. per person. Between 1961 and 1964, 94 Mark II blocks were built, with the arms of the 'H' connected, and the open courts closed.

In 1964, Mark III blocks were introduced, with access to the rooms by a central corridor, giving private balconies, and also with refuse chutes and semi-private lavatories; 142 Mark III blocks were built in 1964 and 1965 when the new high Mark IV blocks appeared. These have sixteen floors, and access is by lift and central corridors; the blocks are also much bigger. Each room now had a private water tap and private lavatory on the balcony. The Mark IV blocks brought the standard of resettlement accommodation close to that in the government's low-cost housing, and represented a vital change in approach. Some Mark IV blocks have breath-taking views from the upper floors. Mark V blocks, which are not radically different, followed after 1967. In all, 95 Mark IV and Mark V blocks were built between 1965 and 1970. In 1970, the first Mark VI block was opened. Mark VI offers at last the same space provision, 35 sq.ft. per adult, as low-cost and most other public housing.[17] At the same time, the government has embarked on an ambitious programme of modernization of some of the earlier blocks.

Rents in Group B estates are low—for a standard room of 120 sq.ft. in a Mark I or Mark II block, only $18 per month; for a room of 140 sq. ft. in a Mark VI block, $38 per month. Social provision on the estates varies very much, but all have schools and clinics, and all have shops and workshops. Generally speaking, the ground-floor premises of Group B estates are occupied by either shops or workshops, and generally speaking hawkers are allowed to encumber at least part of the precinct. Even so, separation of uses is generally enforced to the extent that commercial and industrial activities are not allowed on the upper floors. Many of the squatter factories which would potentially have been occupants of resettlement estate ground floor workshops were siphoned off into resettlement factory blocks.

Resettlement tenants, by and large, are former squatters; hence the study of the resettlement estates is the terminus to the study of the squatters. It is generally agreed that the squatters form a part of the whole urban system in Hong Kong; they are not a group in any sense which overrides their status as squatters. In the same way, what resettlement tenants have in common is, by and large, the experience of life in a squatter community. Moreover, cleared squatters have a right by law to accommodation within the resettlement system.

From this point of view of the resettlement administration, this is important because it means that they are in no position to pick and choose their tenants. Moreover, because hawkers form an important part of most squatter communities, they are common in the resettlement estates, and include people such as 'hawker barbers', who ply their trade from room to room. In the earlier 'marks' of resettlement buildings, physical standards were low, due to economy or over-economy in their construction; provision for disposal of refuse in these buildings was and still is poor. As a result of the union of these with other parallel factors, resettlement communities practise dirty habits.

Resettlement emerged, not primarily as a means of housing the part of the community which was too poor to pay commercial rents, or of improving housing standards, but as a means of tackling the central problem created by squatter communities everywhere: the physical occupation of exactly that unoccupied land close to the city which is next in line for urban development. Resettlement up to the present is still by intention an exercise in the orderly and humane removal of illicit settlers from land which is needed for permanent uses, although it has certainly served ends which belong to social policy, especially in furnishing adequate dwellings at low rents with security for very many poor families. Once inside the resettlement system, few people leave it.

The part of the government's housing programme whose direct purpose is one of social policy is represented by low-cost housing. Present trends are that the low-cost housing programme is being progressively strengthened, for reasons essentially of social policy, and that standards in resettlement (hitherto low both for the sake of keeping the rents low, and because it was felt that social policy demanded that former squatters should not get particularly favourable treatment) are rising towards those in other kinds of government housing—in the first place in management and in such features as lighting in public areas.

The resettlement system provides to a degree for business, as well as for homes. Each squatter area, as it is cleared, yields its crop of shops and factories. During 1972–3, 58½ acres of squatter land were cleared, and 39,000 people resettled in consequence. These clearances yielded 273 factories and workshops, 281 shops and 101 piggeries. Eligible shopkeepers and pigbreeders were paid *ex-gratia* cash allowances in compensation by the government, and 145 factories were allocated a total of 304 units of accommodation in resettlement flatted factory buildings.[18]

There are two such flatted factory blocks in Kwuntong, very well located at the north-west end of the factory zone. Each has seven floors, connected by incline and stairs, but no lifts. In 1969 they housed 164 factories employing 610 workers. Tenancies include a wide and representative range of Hong Kong light industries—wood-carving, rattan manufacture, metalwork, plastics, printing, engineering, weaving, knitting, rubber and furniture. Some of the factories are big and professional in style; some littered with piles of materials and waste; some, especially the smallest, have a domestic air, with only two or three men working, some domestic washing drying outside, and perhaps a shrine. But in these blocks separation of uses is complete, or nearly so. Tenants do not sleep or cook on the premises, and the stairs and the rest of the circulation space are perfectly free of storage or litter. Rents in these factories are low—often only about one-half of normal commercial rents. Physical restrictions are sharp, but tenancies are usually considered quite advantageous. It would be hard to overstate the differences in physical conditions between these premises, and the average squatter factory.

The resettlement housing blocks at Kwuntong were begun in 1958. They belong, consequently, to the original Mark I type (Plate 28). They have few visible peculiarities. A few rooms are used for frankly commercial purposes such as as offices, though people also live in them. A few double flats are cubicled right through on the old corridor principle used in the tenements; one at least is filled with bunk beds like a bed-space business. Most tenants have television. Densities here are in principle based on the standard of 24 sq.ft. for each adult, and overcrowding may be permitted down to 16 sq.ft. It is not surprising that in these conditions (where a standard room of 120 sq.ft. serves for all purposes for a father and mother, a grandfather, and four children under ten) a room is intolerably crowded —or, more broadly, that the community's tolerance of noise, litter, nuisance and proximity generally is extraordinarily high. The tradition of explicit tolerance of other people's nuisance, and the limited intake of alcohol, are two of the factors which make for acceptance of crowding without acute tension. But acute crowding at home is thought to be one reason for the rising rates of crime, especially among the young.

The ground floor premises in these blocks are in a mixture of industrial, commercial and residential uses. Figure 21 shows the assemblage of these uses for one court, chosen at random, for 1974. Surveys were also made of the assemblages of uses in the same court in 1970 and 1971. Among the 35 business tenancies in 1970–1, there were 5 changes of kind of business during 20 months, representing a rate of change per annum of

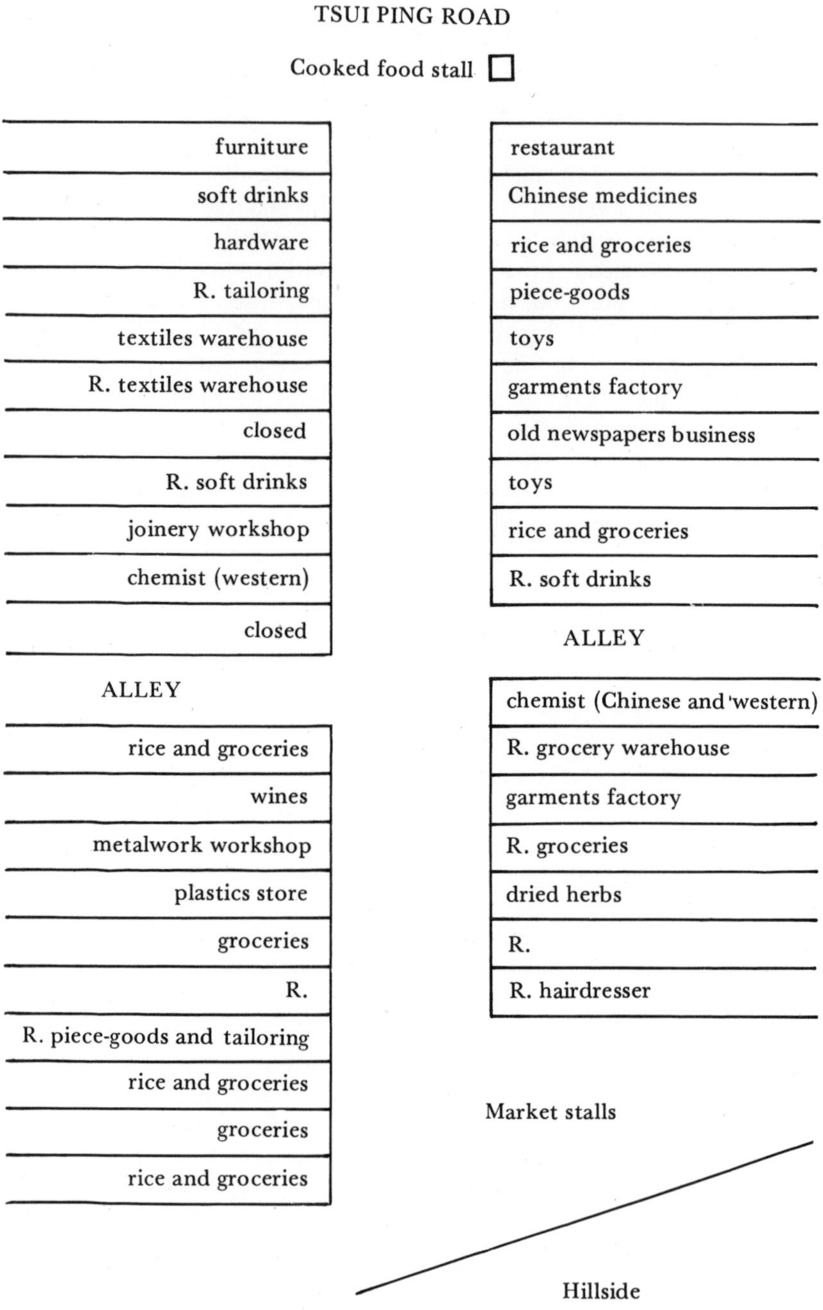

R=Residence
Commodity only (e.g. 'piece-goods') indicates a shop

FIGURE 21

KWUNTONG: THE RESETTLEMENT ESTATE. ASSEMBLAGE OF GROUND-FLOOR PROPERTY USES IN A TYPICAL COURT, AUGUST 1974

8 per cent. Among the same 35 tenancies, there were 24 changes in 1971–4, including both new businesses and closures. This represents a rate of change of 23 per cent per annum—though probably not all changes in kind of business were changes in tenancy. Lowered prosperity in this case seems to have speeded firms out of business. There are now fewer factories than formerly, especially in the metal trades. In this court their place has been taken mainly by residence, sometimes with a very small shop element. In some other courts in the same part of the estate there has been a marked growth of the restaurant function in these years; one court now has about one-quarter of its total area roofed to provide eating space. Naturally, in these cases there has been a corresponding tendency for scullery work to occupy space in the back court.

ZONE, LANDSCAPE AND ACTIVITY: THE INDUSTRIAL ZONE

Kwuntong is an industrial town in planned origin and present reality. The flat, reclaimed land on the south side of Kwuntong Road is almost wholly in industrial use, and comprises a vast industrial estate whose visible peculiarities arise quite simply from the wishes and needs of the developers on the one hand, and the stipulations of the Crown Lands office on the other. The landscape of the industrial zone in Kwuntong is the most recent addition to the extended family of Hong Kong street landscapes (Plate 26). The streets are wide and laid out on a regular grid plan. Building heights however are far from uniform, because the present standards of height—twelve storeys is usual—did not operate in the early days; at that time four floors was considered normal, and six floors high.

In some places, building is still going on, creating piles of debris. Street litter is plentiful. Chinese signs are strangely absent from the buildings, and in this and other respects the street landscape is somewhat drab. Hawking comes and goes according to the times of day when there are workers in the streets; midday is busiest. Alleys are less regular in form than might be expected, often rich in industrial refuse, and often partly occupied by cooked-food stalls. The Kwuntong industrial zone is the place where the new policy of the separation of uses has so far been pushed furthest in a large area. The policy has given the city a new industrial zone with industrial conditions generally much above average, but also with a range of characteristic problems, of which the most important is the lack of places to eat. This is of course *par excellence* the landscape of the export manufacturers. The newest member of the extended family brings a great deal of money into it.

The assets of the area as a new industrial zone are both clear and solid. They include level sites, modern factory buildings, access to supplies of labour, good street access, and a long stretch of waterfront with cargo handling facilities. Supplies of water and electricity are now satisfactory. Congestion is not in general a problem.

The first reclamation at Kwuntong was that occupied by the Shell oil depot to the south-east of the nullah, which still forms the south-eastern periphery of the town. The next section was that between the now culverted stream and Tsun Yip Street, and building of factories began first in the north-eastern half of this section. This part of the industrial zone still has a more established look and more hawkers than the rest. By 1967 almost the whole of the industrial zone of the new town was laid out, and in the larger half, where development was almost non-existent in 1963, about half of the sites were either built or building. At that time, in 1967, there were 503 factories in Kwuntong, employing 48,445 people; the industrial zone was not full, but it was within sight of being so. By 1971, with 956 factories employing 85,695 workers in the industrial zone alone, and nearly all sites in the industrial zone built (at densities which have continued to rise) and in production, the Kwuntong industrial zone was considered filled up.

In bringing this study of the industrial zone of Kwuntong down to the human scale, it is intended to illustrate conditions in the older area from Tsun Yip Street at its north-western edge, and in the newer areas from the south-western side of Hung To Road, which may be thought transitional, and the north-western end of Wai Yip Street in the newest part of the zone. The main points of discussion are the use of the factory premises, and the question of activities other than manufacturing.

Tsun Yip Street is lined with factories on its south-eastern side, all built before 1963 and varying in height from two floors to six. These buildings are of the Western factory type. Each address is a separate building, occupying a government 'lot' of 10,000 sq.ft. of land—a size which was standard in the early days, but was later given up as being too large for convenience. Each building accommodates one firm only. Some of these buildings have lifts, but by no means all.

Land on the north-west side of Tsun Yip Street is partly occupied by factory buildings, some big, some much smaller, built mostly about 1964. Until 1971, it was also occupied in part by a big group of cooked-food-stall restaurants, which grew up between 1963 and 1967, but this land has now become a recreation ground.[19]

This restaurant assemblage represented one phase where the separation of uses has given less than total satisfaction in industrial Kwuntong. Tsun Yip Street also offers evidence of another problem created by the separation of uses. Tsun Yip Street ends to the north-east in a broad alley called Tsun Yip Lane, which gives access to Kwuntong Road and, the traffic overcome, Yue Man Square and the Kwuntong town centre, and the residential zones beyond. The obverse of the coin of the separation of uses must be the movement of people. Distances are not great in Kwuntong, and most people perform short journeys on foot. When people leave work, large numbers walk through Tsun Yip Lane either to go home or (at midday) to pass an hour outside the environment of the factory and the factory streets. Kwuntong Road is an important traffic road. Those who cross on foot cannot well be less than 10,000 in number in each direction per day. In most parts of this most human of cities, wheeled traffic is still not dominant. But in some places, of which the Kwuntong Road crossing is one, motor traffic and pedestrian come into a conflict which appears far from resolution. In this case, the planned separation of uses on a big scale by an arterial road is directly responsible.

Tsun Yip Lane itself has responded to this situation in a way typical of Hong Kong. At busy times twenty or thirty hawkers line the route taken by the work-people, and others line Tsun Yip Street itself, though much less densely. Tools, clothing, toys, fruit, and sweet and meat titbits of various kinds, are all sold, and sometimes a gambling school is set up. All this has the same tone as of the evening fairs, no doubt for good marketing reasons.

Some fresh points, and some related ones, arise in a group of factories which has been studied on the south-west side of Hung To Road. These are flatted factory buildings in mixed occupation, on sites of 12,000 sq.ft. or thereabouts, built between 1966 and 1969. It is clear that the introduction of flatted factory buildings in the 1960s brought a welcome versatility into industrial building custom. In one building, two weaving firms occupy four floors with a total of about 140 automatic looms, and the roof is used for the preparation of yarn. In the next, a factory building with 8 floors above the ground/mezzanine premises, there are four factory units on each upper floor, and a total of about twenty businesses, very mixed in type and in density of use. Some of the units appear to be wholly or mainly in storage use; a garment factory, on the other hand, has about sixty sewing-machines. This building has two multi-purpose lifts. On the ground floor, there are two industrial servicing businesses, one with engineering supplies, the other repairing machinery. Part of Hung To Road is shown in Plate 26.

In streets which are even newer than most of Hung To Road, such as the northern end of Wai Yip Street, built mainly since 1967, the overall proportion of the property which comprises flatted factory buildings is higher. In the newest streets, these are generally smaller in site area, and much more consistently built up to a height of ten or twelve floors, than in the older streets. Building on the remaining sites, at densities which rose steadily during the period, rather than either rebuilding or the raising of rents, was the characteristic form taken by the property side of continuing industrial expansion in Kwuntong during the phase 1960–9. By 1969 and 1970, rents throughout the city, including Kwuntong, were rising steeply, and Kwuntong was nearly physically full. It is interesting to observe that in these respects Kwuntong has been moving consistently towards the Hong Kong norm of high densities and small units. Both in total numbers employed, and in density of industrial workers per unit area, Kwuntong has continued to register growth, to an extent considerably greater than was originally expected.

Hung To Road, like other industrial streets in Kwuntong, is a cheerless spot, apart from the sunshine. It is concrete-grey in colour, and dusty, and the factories make it noisy. In terms of scale and consistency of use alone it is impressive. Even the *praya*, though impressive in scale, lacks the variety and complexity which arise everywhere in the old Hong Kong. If trees were planted on the *praya* they would bring a welcome touch of diversity. It is sad that variety and complexity seem to exist in industrial Kwuntong only in the form of litter. The separation of uses operates quite strictly in the factory buildings; apart from caretakers and watchmen there is little or no residence. What diversity of property use exists in the industrial zone is almost confined to eating places, and a high proportion of these are essentially temporary.

Eating facilities represent a weakness which is real and large-scale, and perhaps even critical, in the separation of uses principle which lies at the heart of the zoning of Kwuntong, and affects above all the industrial zone. It has been demonstrated that the commercial zone is rich in residential uses; that is not surprising. It has been demonstrated too that the housing zones generally do not lack commercial uses, though the extent of these varies with the kind of housing and its location. It has been shown in the study of Taikoktsui, moreover, that an older and less specialized but not wholly dissimilar industrial area has tended to diversify during the past decade, with the restaurants and hawkers as the spearhead of an invasion by new tertiary trades, responding to custom arising from factory workers as well as residents. In recent years, Taikoktsui has tended to generate building for residence as well. Taikoktsui of course is not zoned; control of property use is enforced only through conditions of lease imposed when sites come up for lease or re-lease. Industrial Kwuntong, shackled by the zoning concept, can show nothing to compare with the varied developments in Taikoktsui. In terms of diversity, by comparison with other parts of Kwuntong or with industrial areas elsewhere, the Kwuntong industrial zone was and remains uniquely narrow. Both the design of the buildings and the conditions of lease of the sites seem likely to ensure that little or no growth of a more varied kind can take place in the future. This is really a new kind of situation in the city, and in some respects it is surely a bad one.

There are two big restaurants in the industrial zone, both at intersections with Hung To Road. There are also a few smaller restaurants, and some shops which sell cakes, sandwiches and other kinds of eatables, in the fixed property. A number of semi-permanent stalls also sell light refreshments, especially of a Western kind such as sandwiches. At the western end of Hoi Yuen Road lies one big group of cooked-food-stall restaurants; that in Tsun Yip Street was cleared in 1971. At the seaward end of Lai Yip Street, backing on to a dirty stretch of new reclaimed land where lighterage, car repairs and refuse sorting are going on, is a small group of kitchens which provide contract meals for the factories, the meals going out by bicycle and the water supply coming in by means of a tank on wheels. At various spots throughout the industrial zone, makeshift restaurants occupy alleys, parts of building sites, and other kinds of adventitious space, often forming clusters. One cluster close to Tsun Yip Street has four assorted businesses, with a few others in alleys nearby. The four open kitchens serve in all sixty or seventy tables—that is, about

300 people at a sitting, about the size of one biggish restaurant floor. At lunch-time they are always crowded.

Physical conditions in these places are not good. There is a family resemblance between alleys here, and their prototypes in Taikoktsui and Yaumati. An alley in industrial Kwuntong is wide—perhaps 30 feet wide—and can take both parked and moving vehicles. But there is still a deep mulch of litter, albeit usually industrial and not domestic in origin, and water still drips from overhead. Bits of industrial detritus stand derelict among parked motor-cycles, and the air, hot with the discharge from ducts and fans, is thick with noise from machinery. Whether emotionally or rationally, it is hard to know whether the state of the less formal streets of Kwuntong is a victory or a defeat for natural man against official management. But what it is surely a defeat for, sadly, is sound conditions of the social environment by either Chinese standards (too cheerless and too restricted) or Western (too inconvenient and too dirty).

In industrial Kwuntong, the community and the government have between them created an economic organism of great effectiveness, but one whose efficient functioning makes it more difficult for the people to live like human beings. At one level, this is a problem of some industrial streets in a new town in Hong Kong. At another, it is an aspect of the immense tension set up within the fabric of the civilization of ordinary Chinese people when it begins to carry the weight of Western technology, organization, demand for change, and social experience. At a level somewhere between these, what has been described is a deep-rooted problem of the management of community life throughout the city, involving characteristic weaknesses of both the community and the government. The community insists on pressing diversity to the point of chaos, grumbling but indifferent towards the resultant problems of dirt, noise, congestion and corruption. The government plans for the separation of uses as a remedy for dirt and congestion, but fails to insist on an adequate provision of elements in the town layout to provide for diversity, such as trees, places to sit, places to buy and sell, and above all, places to eat. The result, in the Kwuntong industrial zone, is an environment with a depressing tendency to display the faults of both schemes and the virtues of neither. Things are better in the commercial and housing zones, but still far from ideal. It is perverse to seek to press the logic of the separation of uses to the point of separation of human beings from factory workers.

1 The public evidence is that the new town concept for Kwuntong existed in 1954, but was not necessarily paramount. The *Annual Report* for 1954 indicates (pp. 8–9) that Kwuntong was to be a factory area probably served by commuters, but in the Town Planning section (pp. 135–6) it is stated that Tsuen Wan and Kwuntong 'will amount to new towns'.

2 D.C.Y. Lai and D.J. Dwyer, 'Kwuntong, Hong Kong. A Study of Industrial Planning', *Town Planning Review* (35), 1964–5, pp. 299–310.

3 Ibid., pp. 304–5. The present view of the Crown Lands officials is that important lessons have been learned from the experience of Kwuntong in all these respects. It is intended

that the new development at Sha Tin, across the watershed to the north of Kowloon, the first big urban development away from the harbour, shall not experience problems of these kinds.

4 *Annual Report,* 1963, pp. 254, 255.

5 Commissioner for Resettlement, *Annual Departmental Report,* 1972–73, Appendix 3, p. 28.

6 *Kwuntong Today* (op. cit.), Chinese text, p. 75.

7 The identification of the commercial centre 'in real terms' was made through study on the ground of the kind and degree of commercial activity, mainly on ground floors and in the streets, which it was thought proper to recognize as 'central' in the context of Kwuntong. The following considerations were borne particularly in mind: bright lights in the evenings, variety in goods sold in the shops (e.g. whether both Chinese and Western goods were sold), numbers of assistants in the shops, degrees of specialization and the extent to which shops were of a specialist kind (e.g. selling sewing machines or furniture), and physical continuity with the rest of the centre. The evening 'bright lights' area is that in which shops remain open after about eight o'clock, and where streets attract pedestrians in the evening.

8 One important businessman gave his reasons for reluctance to open a departmental store in Kwuntong as the thin spread of population and the convenient communications to Kowloon. The interpretation which is expressed here takes a number of opinions into account.

9 Public housing in Hong Kong is a relatively well-documented topic. The government publishes *Annual Reports* of the Commissioner for Resettlement, of the Housing Authority (dealing with Group A housing), and of the Housing Board, an advisory body concerned with all aspects of housing policy. The Housing Society also publishes annual reports. Most books on contemporary Hong Kong contain discussions of housing and housing policy, often with special emphasis on the squatters. E.g. Keith Hopkins, 'Public and private housing in Hong Kong', in D.J. Dwyer, *The city as a centre of change in Asia* (Hong Kong, 1972), and the same author's paper 'Housing the poor', in Keith Hopkins (ed.), *Hong Kong, the industrial colony* (Hong Kong, 1971); L.F. Goodstadt, 'Urban housing in Hong Kong, 1945–63', in I.C. Jarvie and J. Agassi (eds.), *Hong Kong, a society in transition* (London, 1969), D.W. Drakakis-Smith, *Housing provision in metropolitan Hong Kong* (Hong Kong, 1973). The factual account of function and status of the various public and semi-public housing bodies given in this account is based on notes in Chapter VIII (pp. 99–100) in *Hong Kong 1974,* and in *Housing Board Reports.*

10 Outside a public housing block in north-east Kowloon, a man empties out a big wooden box infested with scores of cockroaches on the pavement, without making any attempt to kill or catch any of the creatures, which run in all directions, some into drains, some into the building. No neighbour or passer-by complains or remonstrates. Local people say that to do so would be thought very odd.

11 This topic has been explored by Y.M. Yeung and D.W. Drakakis-Smith, 'Comparative perspectives on public housing in Singapore and Hong Kong', *Asian Survey,* xiv, 8 (1974), pp. 763–75.

12 It is revealing that at Kwuntong the Society found it advisable to allow the tenant of a restaurant to enclose part of the precinct as an extension of his eating space, in order to deny the same favoured spot to hawkers. *The Hong Kong Housing Society, 1969* (Annual Report), p. 9.

13 Commissioner for Resettlement, *Annual Departmental Report*, 1972–73, Appendix 3, p. 28. The total figure for people living in Group B accommodation, including 'cottage areas' and the rural New Territories, is 1,234,000 people, that is almost 30 per cent of the whole population of Hong Kong. The total figure for all persons housed in public or public-aided housing for 1972 was 1,667,000, or 41 per cent. (*Housing Board Report,* 1972, Appendix iv, p. 18.)

14 *Annual Report*, 1954, p. 3.

15 *Annual Report,* 1954, pp. 132–3.

16 Commissioner for Resettlement, *Annual Departmental Report,* 1968–69, paras. 101–2, pp. 36–7.

17 Because of the central corridor plan of these blocks, the ground floor commercial uses also have central corridors, forming a complex of rear access facilities and storage space. These dark and ill-kept alleys, littered with bits of property and puddles of water, are a kind of counterpart to alleys in squatter villages, or behind tenement streets in Yaumati or Taikoktsui. Improvement is now being attempted.

18 Commissioner for Resettlement, op. cit., paras. 28–31, pp. 7–8.

Big factories (over 5,000 sq. ft.) and factories which because of noise, dirt and fire hazard are unsuitable for accommodation in flatted factory blocks, are expected to find their own fresh accommodation, which may be in a licensed area. Shops and small workshops may be accommodated in the ground floor premises of residential blocks. The older resettlement estates still have a problem of workshop industries in upper floor domestic rooms. The estates were originally conceived as residential alone. Ground floors in commercial use, and the resettlement factories, were both responses to real needs which were recognized during the first years, from 1954–7, of multi-storey resettlement. The growth of a commercial and industrial side to squatter life was not immediately recognized by the authorities outside the resettlement administration. Squatter factories are reckoned a standard feature of life in Hong Kong and a standard problem. But that they exist at all is a remarkable testimony to the vitality and competence of the Chinese squatter community.

19 The sports ground is welcome, not least because before it was opened young men had nowhere to kick a ball about at lunchtime except the traffic island. It is regrettable that the price of this improvement has had to be paid in loss of places to eat.

8 Kowloon City

PAST AND PRESENT

THE expression 'Kowloon City'[1] has several meanings. Properly speaking, it is the name of the small former walled city close to Kowloon Bay, whose status was the subject of special mention in the Kowloon Extension Agreement of 1898. In common local use, the expression 'Kowloon City' means the former walled city plus an area occupied by old villages, and this twofold area is that which is described and discussed here. The villages form a very conspicuous feature of the landscape, because most of the property there is low-built and very shabby, and appears particularly so since much of the area lies up to 10 feet below the general local street levels. Partly because the villages are so conspicuous and so shabby, most Hong Kong people are unaware of the distinction between Kowloon City itself (which as will be shown is generally high-built) and the villages, and it is common, even in the press, to find the villages confused with the former walled city.

The fundamental condition of life in Kowloon City itself is that the area was at first excluded from the cession of the Leased Territories to the United Kingdom in 1898, but in 1899 included within the cession unilaterally by Order-in-Council in London, invoking a defense stipulation in the original agreement.[2] It is for this reason that the administrative status of Kowloon City is, or appears to be, anomalous.

The government makes no attempt to 'administer' Kowloon City in any normal sense. Moreover, although the legal status of the villages area is in no way different from that of the rest of New Kowloon, physical proximity to the walled city has had the effect of extending some of the city's immunities into the villages, which are also considered politically sensitive.

At the same time, administrative neglect in long-term matters is tempered throughout by some sensible administrative action in short-term. The Urban Services Department makes itself responsible for sanitation, such as it is, even in the former walled city, and the public water-supply is available through standpipes in the villages area. There are public wells and some public taps in the walled city area, and people also carry in water from outside. There is also a limited amount of police activity.[3]

The reason for the original exclusion of the walled city from the Kowloon Extension Agreement must have been its status as an administrative centre, however insignificant. The city walls were built in 1847[4], according to the inscription formerly at the main gate—presumably as a precautionary measure after the cession of Hong Kong island. At the time of the lease of the New Territories to Britain, Kowloon City may have had about 500 inhabitants.[5] The villages must have had some thousands, with an economy based partly on marketing but also on gambling and other kinds of illicit entertainment catering for Hong Kong people, though in decline after the cession of the New Territories.[6]

At that time the walled city was a terminus in the area, not a centre. Routeways passed either immediately below the walls on the south side or between the walled city and the head of the bay. On the other hand, the main village, which lined the route from the south-east corner of the walls to the pier, a third of a mile continuously built up, was obviously a place of some importance. It was called Tung Tau Tsuen.

Fresh growth began in the area in the 1920s. The northern part of the bay—roughly northwards of the old pierhead—was reclaimed before 1924. The old coast route became a main road, called Saigon Road. By 1927, as the directory for that year indicates by its lists of businesses for the area (partly shops, partly factories), the western end of this new land was already occupied, presumably by standard 3-floor Kowloon tenements like those which in the succeeding decade filled up some of the space to the west, between Kowloon City and Prince Edward Road. The commercial airport was opened on the eastern end of the reclaimed land in 1936. During the Japanese occupation, Saigon Road and the other early blocks of tenements lying close to the airport were pulled down, together with part of the eastern end of the old villages, in the course of building extensions to the airport. At this time 'Saigon Road' was removed to the present line of Choi Hung Road. The later blocks of tenements in the area, those further to the west centred on Nga Chin Wai Road, still remain.

In 1941, partly in the tenements and partly in the old village property, there was already an industrial periphery, however haphazard, dirty and marginal. The directory for 1940 names some 20 cotton-weaving businesses in one part or another of the complex. It is remarkable that a survey of 1947 names just over 100.[7] The area was also considered a centre of soy sauce factories; 16 are mentioned in the 1940 directory.

The experience of the walled city in the same phase was very different. Inside the walled city, the government in 1933 embarked on a slow-moving policy of resumption and clearance. By 1940 this was said to have resulted in demolition of every building inside the walls, except the *yamen*, free school and one dwelling.[8] People can be found who lived in the walled city throughout the Japanese occupation. They recall that at that time some plots of land inside the walls were planted with vegetables; elsewhere grass grew man-high. After 1945, north-east Kowloon acquired the heavy population of squatters which has been one of the dominants of development in the whole area ever since,[9] and Kowloon City shared this experience—indeed was probably one of its determinants. Sites could be and were acquired in Kowloon City by squatting on them during and probably before the war, as well as for some time after it.

Squatters settled in large numbers in north-eastern Kowloon for reasons which are not really documented but which may be readily conjectured—relatively plentiful space, the attraction of Kowloon City itself and the many old villages surrounding Kowloon Bay northwards from Ma Tau Kok, and weak government control of development partly because unlike most of north-west Kowloon (not including Shek Kip Mei), which in 1941 already had the essentials of a planned street layout, north-east Kowloon was still something of a hinterland in terms of urban development potential.

The remaining pre-war tenement blocks to the south of the walled city formed the local western limit of squatter settlement. The walled city area itself, freed from its massive walls and now much less peripheral to the new expanding settlements, was violently stimulated into growth. At the end of the war, industry in the walled city was quite limited, though there were already some weaving, rattan and metalwork businesses. Industry expanded from 1948 or 1949 onwards, and again, more rapidly, in the 1960s. The same happened in the adjacent villages. Land formerly used for farming was built up, and manufacturing expanded. The population of the walled city and adjacent villages must have increased in this phase by at least ten times, from a few thousands to perhaps 30,000 or more. It may now be about 20,000. As a result of the general expansion of north-eastern Kowloon, Kowloon City, far from being peripheral, is now located close to the geographical centre of Kowloon.

Although all the inhabitants of the area are usually thought of as squatters, much of the land in the villages is held on regular tenure from the government, and some properties pay rates. In the villages, high building is not permitted, and is not often attempted.[10] In recent years, in addition to occasional nibbling at the fringes of the area in the course of road works, the government has started to reserve sites in the villages which have been cleared, for instance by fire, no doubt with the intention of making a start on the clearance of the whole area.

Inside the limits of the former walled city, rebuilding takes place without Hong Kong government approval, and most of it without adequate provision of light and ventilation. Nearly all the property in the walled city has been built or rebuilt since 1945, much of it in buildings with six, eight or even ten floors, lining lanes which range between three feet and ten feet in width. This high building, taken in conjunction with streets which are very narrow indeed, makes most of the area dark at ground level, even on a bright day. Some streets, especially behind the northern frontage, run virtually through the basements of tall buildings, lined by open drains. High building began about 1962, mainly at the eastern end of the walled city; it is now proceeding, generally to rather greater heights, in the less accessible western part.[11]

Some of this rebuilding has been done by people who live there and own property, but some represents investment by absentee landlords. Landholding in the walled city is said by local people to be based on customary recognition of squatters' rights among neighbours; these rights

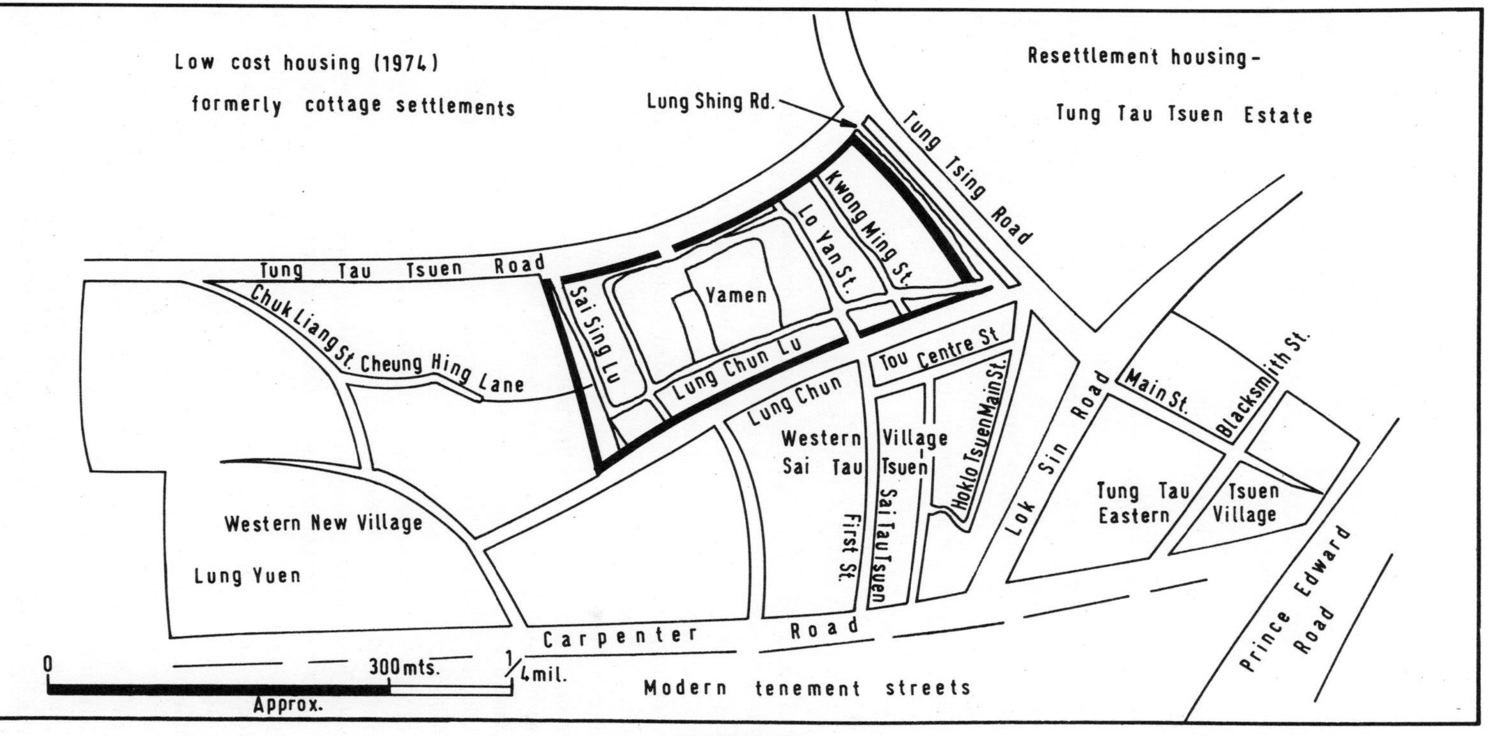

FIGURE 22

KOWLOON CITY AND THE ASSOCIATED VILLAGES—SKETCH PLAN

The heavy block line shows the former walls, with breaks to indicate the gates.

Tung Tau Tsuen formerly extended much further to the east. Many streets and alleys in both areas are not shown. The sketch is diagrammatic and not exactly to scale. Scale about 400 feet to 1 inch.

can be 'sold' or rented like squatters' rights elsewhere, but unlike those elsewhere they are not registered or recognized by the government—nor, during the foreseeable future, will they lead to resettlement tenancies.

The population of the whole area is generally believed to be of the order of 20,000. This has been the figure most commonly adopted in guesses by local people for a number of years, and some 'unofficial' official guesses have been the same. Since most people agree that the population of the villages area and the walled city are roughly comparable, this figure also has the support of the Census figure of 1971, which was 10,004 for the walled city.[12]

Since the area of the walled city is about one-quarter of the total, density of population must be about three times as great in the city as in the villages. This is made possible by the high buildings; and density of population may be increasing quite rapidly in the city, as more high buildings go up. In any recent year, there have been four or five such buildings in the course of construction. Comparable population densities exist in the villages only where there are densely-packed lodging-houses.

THE LAYOUT OF THE CITY AND VILLAGES

Apart from drains, nothing now marks the line of the city walls on the ground to east, south and west, but it is well known to many local people, including those responsible for the new high buildings. Only on the northern side, where the line of the outside of the wall forms the building line on the south side of Tung Tau Tsuen Road, is the walled city area fringed by an open street; but on all sides the edge of the walled city is recognizable from a distance by the line of high buildings (Plate 29). On all four sides, the thickness of the walls, typically about 15 feet, is now occupied by buildings. The city faces roughly but not exactly to the south, and it lies in what must be a geomantically favourable position, on the south side of a hill facing the sea. In form it is a rough oblong, longer in the east-west dimension (Figure 22).

The central position in the plan of the walled city is occupied by a group of traditional-style buildings grouped round a court and surrounded by a high wall. These buildings originally housed the *yamen*—the offices of the local Chinese administration up to the British lease. The other public buildings in the walled city were a free school, whose building on the west side of the *yamen* still stands, occupied now by a complex of squatter houses, and a temple on the site of Kwong Ming Street to the east, which has totally disappeared. The former *yamen*, now a children's centre, was occupied for about fifty years by a Chinese Christian home for old women, which took its rise in evangelism among women and children squatting in the buildings, probably about 1900.

The *yamen* and former free school buildings face south on to Lung Chun Lou, which runs roughly east-west across the whole length of the walled city, and must have been the principal formal street. It is mostly about

6 feet wide. Another street, narrow and much interrupted, but still recognizable both on the modern map and on the ground, now for most of its length called Alms House Back Street, runs parallel to it behind the former *yamen* building. Four streets, regularly spaced, cross the city from north to south; two on each side of the *yamen* building. These streets also have a standard width of about 6 feet. The lanes which are tributary to the principal formal street, Lung Chun Lou, are numbered only; those which are tributary to the other streets are either numbered together with the name of the street, or have their own names.[13]

To judge from the modern map and the visual evidence, the street plan of the walled city appears to be corrupt in detail, but in general to preserve traditional layout with remarkable fidelity. It is notable that the rectilinear principle in layout is preserved practically without a break. On the modern map, there are very few building lines or other boundaries which are not parallel or at right-angles, or nearly so, with all the others.

This is remarkable and surprising, if it is true that there is no continuous history of occupation or even of building. It is the more remarkable, because the evidence which exists for the physical state of the walled city even before the clearances of the 1930s suggests only a very loose kind of street layout.[14]

One reason why the streets were physically degenerate must have been that they were not thoroughfares. The main gate lay to the south-east of the *yamen*, at the southern end of what is now Lo Yan Street.[15] (Plate 31.) This must have been the ceremonial main gate. The practical main entrance obviously lay at the south-east corner, from which the main village street led straight to the pierhead. The only other breaks in the wall, according to the Jackman map of 1925 and other early maps, were insignificant ones not linked to pathways. One was on the north side, formerly giving access only to the plots of land on the hillside within the salient; it is now the busy but steep and almost unbelievably narrow entrance to the darkest and narrowest part of the street network. The other was at the north-west corner, now represented by the entrance at the north end of Sai Sing Lu; it opened close to the pathway to the north-west called Chuk Liang Kai, but according to the maps did not give effective access to it. The walled city formerly had no effective access except at the south-east. Breaks through the former line of the walls now occur at both ends of all the north-south streets except one.

In the face of a situation like that which has been described, it is hard to be sure what continuity really means. In short, the contemporary situation appears to be remarkably traditional in form, more so in fact than the situation of two or three generations ago. At the eastern end particularly, where Kwong Ming Street now cuts through the site of the temple, the modern form is more 'traditional' than that of 1925 or 1903.

The physical layout of the villages area presents fewer puzzles. In essence, there are three groups of buildings: Tung Tau Tsuen, the old main Eastern Village; its peripheries and satellites, shading at the west end of the area into commonplace squatter settlements; and the straight numbered streets of Sai Tsu Tsuen just off the Carpenter Road fringe (Figure 22).

As has already been shown, Tung Tau Tsuen was formerly the principal settlement of the whole complex. Its main street, the chief route of access to the pierhead, was called Main Street (Tai Kai), as its remnant is still (Plate 33). It was apparently always an industrial village, and it has been a place of many vicissitudes. The Japanese clearances for the extension of the airport removed the pier and some of the village. Subsequently squatter fires, the resumption of land by the government for resettlement housing and access roads, and recently the traffic-road complex which occupies the bottleneck between the villages and the airport, giving main access to all north-east Kowloon and Kwuntong—all these have taken their toll of the old village land and the viability of the settlement. Tung Tau Tsuen is now no more than a group of shadows of its former self. But even in its present degenerate condition, several village streets and localities can be distinguished, with the help of local names. Among them are the old Main Street, in places only a few feet in width (Plate 33); Ta Tit Kai (Blacksmith Street), parallel to the coast and crossing Main Street, relatively wide and straight, the remnant of the main cross street; Hasapo at the seaward end (Sheungsapo seems to have disappeared altogether since 1940)—and at the walled city end, two or three streets of Hoklo Tsuen, now no longer a village of Hoklo people, but the main centre of the drug trade (Plate 32). There is still a good deal of worn-out but solidly-built property in Blacksmith Street, Hasapo and Hoklo Tsuen; but fresh deliberate clearances are now taking place, and there is now unbuilt land in the area which is not even occupied by dumps or stores. Tung Tau Tsuen and Hoklo Tsuen are visibly dying.

The western end of the villages area is much more loosely occupied. The extreme western edge, facing Junction Road, has small restaurants and shops, but the bulk of the area is very like an ordinary squatter settlement, with wooden huts and narrow footpaths. There are however some old villas, two small vegetable farms, and (where access is better) some big industrial premises.

The south-western group of villages, together with the Carpenter Road fringe, also has distinctive features. The north side of Carpenter Road is lined by wooden huts and other similar properties, most of them restaurants or shops. According to local accounts, Carpenter Road took its present form on the north side in about 1951 and 1952, especially at the western end, where the former village of Fuklo Tsuen, which lay to the south of Carpenter Road, is now represented only by a street-name. Until about 1947, there were still vegetable farms in the Carpenter Road area.

The two Sai Tau ('western') villages lie to the north of Carpenter Road. They comprise partly old-style stone-built village houses; partly straight streets like Sai Tau Tsuen First Street and Second Street, with property with three or four floors, and partly mixed squatter enclaves with wooden huts, such as Lung Yuen. All these streets lie some 10 feet below the level of Carpenter Road, with access by steps. These streets were probably built in the last years before 1941, in spite of local opinion that they are much older. Photographs taken early in this century show in this area only the few villa properties close to the walled city, which still exist.

LOCALITY STRUCTURE AND ECONOMIC LIFE IN THE WALLED CITY AND VILLAGES

The most marked feature of the present location of business in the city and villages is the strong tendency of the peripheries to separate themselves off from the rest. This situation has several phases. The most interesting is the big assemblage of dentists' and doctors' surgeries which lines the northern fringe of the walled city, along the south side of Tung Tau Tsuen Road, where the properties occupy the former site of the wall itself, and which extends into the eastern and south-eastern fringes of the walled city. These are practitioners who do not have the Commonwealth qualifications recognized by the government, and who are using the immunities of the walled city to protect their professional positions. The doctors mainly use rooms on the upper floors; the ground floor properties are mostly occupied by the dentists. With their shop windows full of artificial teeth, they form an impressive *ch'eng-shih* trading cluster as dense as any in the city, and those who do business there regard the assemblage in the same light as those elsewhere who deal in Chinese medicines or groceries. Before 1941, there were some dentists doing the same kind of business in Kowloon City, but no more than a handful, according to local account. Since Tung Tau Tsuen Road did not then exist, the businesses at the south-east corner of the walled city almost certainly represent the location of the trade at that time; however, the pre-war directories do not list any businesses at all in the walled city. The cluster has grown to its present size and importance alongside other features of Kowloon and Kowloon City. Dental treatment is cheap here, and patients are said to come from within a wide radius. But these premises have no running water supply.

The eastern fringe of the walled city is also a commercial area depending on access to the outside world, with dentists, furniture businesses and hairdressers. The whorehouses which proliferate in Lung Shing Road, the eastern periphery street of the walled city, also share the advantage of easy access from the outside world. Also depending on passing trade are the restaurants of the western and southern fringes of the villages area, especially the Carpenter Road fringe to the south.

The Carpenter Road fringe is particularly interesting. The property is low and shabby, but the whole frontage, from the extreme west almost to Lok Sin Road, is lined with shops and restaurants which show signs of much greater prosperity than there is evidence for in any part of the interior. At the western end, there is a well-known cluster of restaurants occupying shack property whose relation to their surroundings is identical with that of cooked-food-stall restaurants. Here there are thirteen restaurants in nineteen properties, as well as some places which sell soft drinks. The rest of the frontage is occupied by shops selling a wide range of day-to-day goods, which forms part of the Carpenter Road marketing assemblage—shops, hawkers, a cinema—which extends southwards into the neighbouring densely populated tenement streets. This whole business assemblage, which includes a small but lively night fair, is based in part on the official fish, meat and vegetable market hall in Nga Chin Wai Road close by.

In the numbered streets of Sai Tau Tsuen, tributary to Carpenter Road, low-grade shops rub shoulders with small workshops and cottage industries which occupy no more than a single family. The rest of the fringe areas are industrial. The most interesting is Tung Tau Tsuen, the remnant of the former principal village of the complex. Most of Tung Tau Tsuen has motor access, as well as excellent location in relation to main roads, and its uses are overwhelmingly industrial—timber businesses, textile, metal, food, plastic and engineering manufacturing. A good deal of residence takes place among the factories and inside them, and there is one big rambling lodging-house on the southern fringes which is said to house some 400 or 500 people in cubicles, but 70 or 80 per cent of the land area is in industrial use or in parallel uses like timber-yards. Tung Tau Tsuen has of course an industrial tradition of its own, especially in food industries, textiles and wood-yards, extending back before the war.

A very different industrial zone occupies quite a large area in the north-west, part of the district called Chuk Liang Kai. Here the land units are characteristically large—upwards of 10,000 sq. ft.—and access by lorry is possible, using the old footpaths, for up to about a hundred yards from the road. The industrial units which occupy these sites are also quite big by Kowloon City standards. One is a scrap-metal business, where until a few years ago there was a film-studio. Others are timber and bamboo-yards; and the one good building is occupied by a manufacturer of corrugated paper. Here too empty land is being kept empty by the government.

The south-western corner of the villages area is occupied partly by rather loose settlements in traditional-style houses, some of which appear on the earlier maps, and partly by a very untidy mass of squatters' wooden huts. These streets and courts are mostly residential, with only incidental domestic industries like chicken-roasting, but there are several rather big factories as well. There is also some open waste land. To the north of this corner lies one of the remaining two tiny vegetable farms, the villas which were mentioned earlier, and some very mixed property, mostly residential, leading up to Chuk Liang Kai and the second of the two little farms. All these kinds of land use seem to arise from the relatively plentiful land in this corner, distant from the old industrial village of Tung Tau Tsuen, and with poor access.

Before 1941, the main shopping street of the whole complex was the Main Street of Tung Tau Tsuen. There were three jewellers' businesses recorded there in 1927, together with other shops and some tea-houses. There is no sign of this kind of business in Tung Tau Tsuen now. In so far as there is now a shopping street in the city and villages, it is Lung Chun

Tou, the street which runs along the outer margin of the former south wall (Plate 31). The shops there are not impressive. Many are dirty and untidy, and in size and diversity of stock they compare unfavourably with the average grocery store in a working-class tenement area. Some of them open only in the evenings. There are also about twenty restaurants. In some of these people can eat dog, an illegal dish to which illegality lends special interest, but in other respects they are not remarkable; they have much the same relaxed, shabby appearance and style as most restaurants in standard squatter areas. Business in the shops and restaurants is stimulated in the evenings by the influx of customers to the disreputable entertainments of Kowloon City—drugs, gambling, blue film shows, and prostitution.

In the former walled city, apart from the old *yamen* and free school buildings, about one-fifth or one-sixth of the ground-floor property is in industrial use, and about the same proportion is in use by shops or restaurants. A few factories occupy upper floors in new buildings, but on the whole the upper floors are used for residence only, more or less cubicled. The range of industries in the walled city is not particularly wide. It includes rubber, plastic, rattan and bamboo, food, weaving, spinning and dyeing industries. Metal and engineering industries are scarce, except on the eastern periphery. Most of the factories are quite small, employing less than ten people. Most use electrical or hand power, and the physical conditions of both work and access are generally very bad. The bigger factories are mostly weaving sheds, but the machinery is invariably automatic, and employment is not large.

In the course of informal but repeated surveying on the ground in 1970 and 1971, about 3,500 legitimate jobs were counted in the city and villages. Sample checks performed in 1974 indicated that, if anything, jobs in Kowloon City had suffered less than in comparable areas elsewhere from the relative decline in economic activity at that time, though here as elsewhere the plastics industry seemed to have experienced the most contraction. There is very little skilled work in Kowloon City, and in common with most squatter areas the area is a net exporter of labour.

The chief employer is the textile industry, mainly in the interior districts of both the city and villages. Spinning, weaving, knitting, dyeing and finishing all take place here, but the biggest component is weaving. The next biggest employer is the shops, which are widespread throughout the area but most important in the Carpenter Road fringe. They, the dentists and doctors, and the timber businesses, are in their different ways natural occupants of the fringes. The restaurants are either of this 'fringe' kind, or else form part of the entertainment complex mainly in the walled city, and in that case occupy central locations.

All this tends to show that the economic structure of the city and villages, apart from the illicit trades, is not very different from that of other squatter areas in Kowloon—some manufacturing, the area's own service industries, a tendency to rely on passing trade at the fringes, and a high rate of commuting out.

Figure 23 represents a transect across the whole area from north to south, crossing both the villages area at Sai Tau Tsuen and the former city. The detail recorded shows clearly the range of businesses which occupy ground floor property in this area, and the sizes and layout of the premises. Illicit trades are not usual in the area covered by the survey.

THE ILLICIT TRADES

The centre of the drug business in 1974 and for a number of years previously has been in Hoklo Tsuen, just off Lok Sin Road (Plate 32). Both in 1970–1 and in 1974, it has been quite easy to find visible evidence that hundreds, even thousands, of people were supplied with drugs daily in this locality.[16] It was more difficult to find equivalent evidence for numbers in the tens of thousands. If the standard figure of 80,000 drug addicts in Hong Kong is correct—and it is usually thought to be much too low—and Kowloon City is one of a handful of major supply centres, it is necessary to think of Hoklo Tsuen as supplying perhaps 20,000 people daily. If each of these people called individually, this would mean visits by seventeen persons per minute throughout a twenty-hour day. (The serious estimate of a local addict in 1970 was that 100,000 people were supplied daily in this area.) By 1974 it was common knowledge that police pressure on the drug trade had greatly reduced the availability of drugs in other parts of the city, so that demand was increasingly channelled towards Kowloon City. At the same time, the police were putting intermittent but generally much increased pressure on Kowloon City itself. As a result, the Hoklo Tsuen supply centre was operating only discontinuously. It is fair to add that many people who take drugs do so only discontinuously.

In 1974 the price of an injection was said to be $50, and of a cigarette containing heroin, $20. On the showing of these prices and the figures suggested earlier for numbers of customers, the turnover of the heroin business in Kowloon City could not be less than $300,000 daily, and might well reach $500,000, or even more. This figure must be compared with the turnover of the textile industry in the city and villages, which must be between $15 and $25 millions *annually*, based on a total of about 1,000 jobs. Costs in the drug business are no doubt high, and Whisson is surely right when he says that the organization of the drugs business is diffuse and 'segmented',[17] but these are obviously very large sums.

Little of this money remains in Kowloon City. If one hundred men and women are employed in selling and packing drugs, keeping watch, and so forth, they are not likely to earn in aggregate more than $200,000 per month at a very generous estimate—say $2½ million per annum. What is certain is that if big money is made in the drugs business, very little of it is spent in Kowloon City. The status of Kowloon City in the business hierarchy is self-evidently low, and the income to the area from whatever traffic is done locally in drugs is also self-evidently low.

Both the gambling business and the sex films business are located within the confines of the walled city, towards the south-western corner. The rationale of money-making which has been built up for the drugs business appears to apply to both of these businesses as well. Employment in both is small compared with the money that both seem to make; and the contribution of either to the domestic economy of Kowloon City seems to extend no further than wages and rent. On this showing, only the drugs business seems likely to be bringing money into Kowloon City on a scale commensurate with the shops or restaurants (each employing some hundreds of people). Even the drugs business seems unlikely to be bringing as much money *into Kowloon City* as the textile industry.

POVERTY

Clearly Kowloon City is not simply one more squatter area in north-east Kowloon—it is special in a number of ways. There is one additional respect in which it is exceptional: it is much more squalid than other squatter areas, and there is an overriding appearance and tone of poverty about the whole place.

There appear to be several sides to this situation. Most of the people who work in the city and villages live within the area. Accommodation here can be very cheap—less than $100 a month for a cubicle which can house a family. Hence, low levels of wages are relatively easy to tolerate. Some local people say that they cannot afford to move out. Some people appear to live here for the sake of ready access to drugs.

Wages for both skilled and unskilled work are said to be generally low, and skilled jobs are not common. In the dental business, levels of skill and investment appear to be quite high, although the business works for low charges, but this fringe must be expected from the general judgement about poverty. There has been investment, and investment is still going on, in building and in manufacturing machinery. These investments must be related to the general climate for investment in these fields in Hong Kong at large. There is no sign whatsoever that the returns from these investments are spent in Kowloon City—much less than that the returns on private investment in the great industrial districts like Tokwawan are spent in those places. Retail business is very slow. There are virtually no shops which aim to furnish more than the minimal daily needs of the local community, except on the Carpenter Road fringe. A good deal of purchasing power must go outside, especially to Carpenter Road and the market to the south. It is remarkable, and another indication of poverty, that Kowloon City is practically free of hawkers.

The businesses which furnish illegal entertainment disconcertingly do not create the prosperity which might be expected of them. Apart from the drugs business, their customers are working men who come here for the sake of low prices. People with money who want these kinds of entertainment can readily find them in the fashionable districts, without experiencing the physical squalor and social stigma of Kowloon City. There is less visible vitality, gaiety and money in life at night in Kowloon City than in almost any other part of the city.

With this hypothesis of an overriding poverty, the general appearance of Kowloon City and the villages is wholly compatible. In areas both of high buildings and low, the place has a theatrical appearance of extreme antiquity, created by the narrow streets and narrower lanes, the frequent corners, the changes of level and short flights of steps in the streets, the open drains, the noise from factories, the piles of rotting refuse in unfrequented spots, and the lack of street lighting—in the villages, the irregular placing of the low buildings and the occasional patches of vegetation; in the city itself, the overhanging buildings and lack of light, the gentle curves in most of the streets, the high walls and gates of the *yamen* and temple buildings (Plate 30). Only the very loosely occupied section at the western end does not share this appearance of antiquity.

Yet it is clear that extreme antiquity is far from being the reason for all this. Especially in the walled city, most of the buildings are less than twenty years old, and many are less than ten. Only a minority of the buildings in any part of the area date from before about 1930. Poverty, conjoined with filth, is the reason for the physical appearance of Kowloon City. Both of these things arise from the underlying anomaly of status which is the walled city's distinguishing mark, and which in some degree extends to the villages. Because the city's status deprives it of social services, and forms a standing invitation to disreputable trades, Kowloon City has shared only indirectly and inadequately in the rapid rise of standards of life and expectation which has taken place for all classes of people in the rest of Hong Kong during the past generation, and the money which changes hands in the course of the drug trade in Hoklo Tsuen has little relevance to human conditions in the area itself.

1 The name *Kowloon* means literally 'nine dragons'. People usually explain it by a rather unconvincing count of a selection of the mountain peaks which line the northern side of the harbour. But this 'nine dragons' is a rather common name in China, often related to local myths about saints and dragons. (W. Eberhard, *The local cultures of south and east China* (Leiden, 1968), pp. 230–1.)

2 *Laws of Hong Kong* (1964), App. IV, L1.

3 A full account of the legal status of the walled city, together with its 'specifically Walled City system of law' is given by Peter Wesley-Smith in 'The Walled City of Kowloon: historical and legal aspects', in *Hong Kong Law Journal*, 1973, pp. 67–96; and of the administrative status of the Hong Kong government in the area in the same author's paper, 'Inside the Walled City of Kowloon', *Journal of The Royal Asiatic Society, Hong Kong Branch*, 1973. I am indebted to Mr. Wesley-Smith for copies of these two distinguished papers.

4 This was recorded by T'ang Chien-hsün, *Tsui-hsin Hsiang-kang chih-nan (Latest Hong Kong guide)*, (Hong Kong, 1950). These walls were quite formidable, standing twenty feet high. A walled salient extended to the top of the hill which overlooks the city to the north. The walls were completely pulled down during the Japanese occupation.

5 Shuang Yai, *Hsiang-chiang chiu-shih* (*Old Hong Kong*), (Hong Kong, 1969), p. 50.

6 Documented and discussed at length by Peter Wesley-Smith, especially in his *Hong Kong Law Journal* paper, op. cit., pp. 69–71.

7 Wang Ch'u-jung, *Hsiang-kang kung-ch'ang tiao-ch'a (Survey of Hong Kong factories)* (Hong Kong, 1947), *fu-lu*, Appendix, pp. 7–8. Casual enquiry reveals at least one case of a weaving factory whose early history is documented in this record, which started

life in 1931 in Tung Tau Tsuen, survived its removal under the Japanese, and now occupies some 20,000 sq.ft. of space, equipped with automatic looms, in a new factory building in Sanpokong.

8 Peter Wesley-Smith, *Hong Kong Law Journal,* 1973, op. cit., pp. 74–5.

9 The distribution of squatter settlements at any period is not well-documented, partly no doubt because of the government's insistence that they were temporary features. R.H. Hughes in 'Hong Kong, an urban study' in *Geographical Journal,* 117 (1951), facing p. 18, printed a valuable map of land use in the city in 1949, with interesting traverses and comments on them. He shows to the north and east of Kowloon City at that time a large area which he calls 'an extensive and ever increasing "shanty town" of temporary buildings housing refugees and other persons displaced by the war. It is without roads, water supply or adequate sanitation'. Hughes was right to call this area 'ever increasing'. It finally extended to cover all the 'agricultural land' which on his map of 1949 occupied the rest of the area to the north of Choi Hung Road, and in part it still does so. There is some evidence of a significant squatter population in north-eastern Kowloon before 1945, but it is neither plentiful nor conclusive.

The most important social group in Kowloon City comprises Ch'aochou people from eastern Kwangtung. It appears to be among these people that Chinese festivals, especially those connected with the dead, survive with particular vitality in Kowloon City.

10 A sub-standard block of flats was demolished on the orders of the government in 1973. This was in Lung Shing Road, to the east of the walled city.

11 Some people say that these buildings have no foundations. Some say that since bedrock is very shallow, deep foundations are unnecessary. The truth is no doubt that owners who intend to build cheaply can build without foundations if they so wish.

12 Peter Wesley-Smith, *Journal of the Royal Asiatic Society, Hong Kong Branch*, op. cit., pp. 5–6. Wesley-Smith considers that this figure is too small. Certainly it is easier to envisage revising it upwards than downwards.

13 The formal layout of Kowloon City, described here, closely resembles that of the *hsien* city, Hsin-An, as is indicated by the description and map of Hsin-An in the *Hsin-An hsien-chih* (Gazetteer of Hsin-An County). Ms dated 1818, Hong Kong University Library.

14 This evidence comprises a most interesting Public Works Department map dated 1925, on a very good scale, which is preserved in the Public Record Office in London. (P.W.D. Crown Lands and Survey Office. S.D. No. 1. *Kowloon City*. Signed, J.F. Jackman, 17.6.25. Scale: 64" to 1 mile (1/990). London, P.R.O., MR. 789.) This map appears to have been made as part of the preparations for the building of a dispensary (marked on the map) on the site of the temple on the east side. The dispensary was never built. This map is reproduced by Peter Wesley-Smith in *Hong Kong Law Journal,* 1973, pp. 72–3, with the date 1902, which may well be correct.

15 In 1970, two big Ch'ing cannon were found buried at a very shallow level close to the southern end of Lo Yan Street, and pointing south. These are presumably the cannon mentioned in T'ang's *Tsui-hsin Hsiang-kang chih-nan* (op. cit.), p. 101. According to the account of a local man who lived here during the Pacific war, recorded before the discovery of the cannon was made, a number of cannon were taken to Japan when the walls were removed, and some which were too big to move were buried on the spot. Local pride, and some touchiness about the status of Kowloon City, has resulted in the cannon being now kept embedded in concrete outside the wall of the former *yamen.*

16 For instance, during part of 1974, at certain times of day, a constant stream of taxis coming from the north brought people to a certain unprepossessing spot on the edge of Hoklo Tsuen.

17 In this respect it rather resembles Chinese business organizations in general, as has been shown. This must be one advantage which these businesses enjoy.

The standard discussions of the whole topic of drug addiction are by M.G. Whisson, 'Some sociological aspects of the illegal use of narcotics in Hong Kong', in L.C. Jarvie and J. Agassi, *Hong Kong. A society in transition* (London, 1969), and *Under the rug* (Hong Kong, 1965).

9 Squatter Villages

THIS chapter was written in 1970–1. In 1973–4 the Clearwater Bay Road villages were cleared to make way for low-cost housing, and the physical form of the valleys themselves was transformed in the process of site formation (Plate 36). Since this is the natural end of such villages, and the end which was looked towards in the original account, there seemed little reason to make any changes in the chapter as it stood. It is accordingly presented as written, without changes in tense.

In the years since 1971, squatting has become progressively less important in the urban area. Some conspicuous and notorious settlements, such as Lim Fa Kung on the hillside above Causeway Bay, formerly a centre of the drug trade, have been completely or almost completely cleared. A number of nibbles have been taken at the main group of squatter complexes in north-east Kowloon, of which the Clearwater Bay Road villages were part. In the rural New Territories, apart from prohibited areas such as the margins of roads, permission may now be given by district offices for the erection of temporary buildings; and there is some evidence that a considerable amount of such building has recently been done.

INTRODUCTION

In this chapter, approaches of two distinct kinds are made to the study of the squatters in and around the city. First, an attempt is made to show that squatting and other unauthorized kinds of land use have features in common, and to explore both their historic status and their present relation to the people's livelihood. Second, an attempt is made to describe and interpret present conditions and activity in one mixed squatter area in north-eastern Kowloon, the scattered, diffuse and varied group of villages lying to the south of Clearwater Bay Road. These villages, which have almost no pre-war history, are based partly on farming, partly on industry, and partly on government-organized settlement. In these villages, an attempt is made to explore the form and functioning of the localities, to demonstrate the rationale and consequences of spontaneous settlement in these particular areas, and to show in what ways these are related to the course of time and to official policy.

It will be helpful in the first place to state briefly what 'squatting' means in contemporary Hong Kong, and what is the present status of the squatter community.

'Squatting' is essentially a legal concept.[1] In Hong Kong it means the use of unleased public land for unauthorized private purposes, and it is against the law. However, almost the whole of the squatting at any moment is 'tolerated' squatting. This means that at one of the two official surveys of squatter 'structures', made in 1959 and 1964, or in the case of cultivation of land by squatters the survey of 1954, the government registered this illegal use of land, and accepted its existence for the time being. When the land is wanted either for private leasing or—more usually—for government purposes like housing, the government must offer 'resettlement'—'Group B' cheap residential accommodation—to all the people whose houses are cleared away, and also as households, though not as farmers, to the farming squatters. Squatter factories, if they are registered, and if they are not too big or engaged in unsuitable trades, are offered accommodation in resettlement factory blocks. These arrangements give squatters some degree of right, if not privilege, in the community, but it is right of a limited though assured kind: its time of maturity is unpredictable, it is limited to resettlement tenancy in an estate where at the time tenancies are available, and it accrues not necessarily to the owner of a tolerated squatter structure, but to the occupant at the time of the survey which precedes clearance.[2] Registration is strict and thorough. Structures are measured and their dimensions recorded, so that unauthorized additions cannot be made.

Untolerated squatting is that which has occupied fresh sites since 1964—or, in the case of farming, since 1954. In principle, and usually also in practice in the urban areas, such offending structures are removed, and the materials confiscated. Those who build them are not punished in any way but there is little inducement to take the constant risk of losing one's house and materials; and people who cannot find a cubicle, a government room, or a tolerated structure go to licensed areas instead. Here they are allocated a site, and allowed to build a hut.

SPONTANEITY, ENCROACHMENT AND DESTITUTION

In principle, spontaneous expansion by the people into unoccupied land cannot take place in Hong Kong. Land has always belonged to the Crown until leased—which is to say in effect that land in Hong Kong is and always has been nationalized.

In practice, spontaneous expansion has always been possible within limits. Squatting has a long history in the colony and the city.

> A Government proclamation was issued on 21st October 1844 calling attention to the fact that 'a great number of Chinese have, without permission and in direct opposition to Law and Custom settled themselves upon the Queen's Road and at diverse places along the coast of this Island', and called upon them to remove themselves forthwith, failing which they would be ejected. The constant reference throughout the years to trespassers and other illegal occupants of Crown land makes it clear that such encroachments have continued to occur.[3]

This is the essence of the squatter situation.

> Despite all the efforts that were made throughout the first half of the [twentieth] century, squatters continued to be an endemic problem and by 1950, as a result of

the incursion of great numbers of immigrants, very large areas of Crown land had been overrun.[4]

In addition to unauthorized squatting, there have been for the past century—indeed there have probably always been—arrangements for granting permission for temporary occupation of unleased land. Osbert Chadwick advised that around the infant town of Yaumati, 'roads should be laid out, before granting squatters licences'.[5] Draft 'Matshed Regulations' were proposed in 1902 to regularize the construction, occupancy rate, and so forth, of temporary matsheds for which the Building Authority might give permission.[6] It is recalled by people who knew Nathan Road before 1914 that unbuilt plots were occupied by matsheds. This kind of arrangement was the forerunner of the 'tolerated areas' for squatters of the early 1950s, and also of the present 'licensed' areas.

Chadwick also pointed out that the seashore gave additional opportunities for encroachment.[7] Private reclamation of stretches of the foreshore sometimes took place, and the use of boats for residence implied potential claims to the use of beaches and mud-flats where many boats were kept grounded. Permission for private reclamation has been given in various places even since 1945, under various conditions.

Farmland has relevance to spontaneous expansion in three ways. The first point is that the Crown Lands authorities have usually been more tolerant in practice towards squatter farmers than to other kinds of squatters, and the system of permits has gone much further.[8] A second is that in the 1940s and 1950s a great deal of properly leased farmland, particularly in north-east Kowloon, was sub-let to immigrants and others who were not farmers. Some old villages, such as Chuk Yuen in north-east Kowloon, attracted big hutment communities consisting partly of squatters and partly of sub-tenants. The third point is that in the expansion after 1947, the old rural villages close to the city were themselves assimilated to the way of life of the squatter communities by which they were surrounded. Moreover in many places the complex of situations which grew up in squatter settlements formed a continuum with village life. Villagers sub-let land and took industrial jobs even before the Pacific war, and many squatters kept pigs or village shops. The same adaptations are visible today further afield, in the rural villages and on the more accessible islands, such as Cheung Chau.

Chadwick also wrote:

> In short, the demand for house-room in Hong Kong vastly exceeds the supply. Every available space is at once filled and the overwhelming population overflows the dwelling into the street. The cook cannot find room or light in the cookhouse to chop wood, so he comes out into the street to do so, much to the detriment of the side-channel. Washing and other domestic operations are conducted on the sidewalk which, but for the vigilance of the police would very soon be occupied by artizans and small dealers. Indeed, in many cases the sidewalks are already occupied by huxters stalls.[9]

This is the basic statement of the basic realities of urban encroachment.

The butcher in contemporary Kwuntong who dismembers pigs' carcasses on the pavement each week follows precisely the same logic as Chadwick's cook.[10] Squatting in the usual sense was and is no more than a disproportionately publicized phase of a much wider and more momentous continuum of spontaneous expansion. At one end of this much bigger continuum are the hawker markets which a century ago dominated Wellington Street in Central District (Plate 1), which still dominate old streets like Graham Street in Central District, parts of Canton Road and many other streets in Kowloon, and flood the resettlement estates (Plate 28). In the middle (so to speak) are the squatters, urban or rural, residential or industrial. At the other end are the boat people who were one of the foundations of the city itself, who were one of the first squatter groups, and who form a part of the far wider continuum of colonization, fishing, mining, piracy, emigration and foreign dealing which distinguishes this remote and unorthodox southern coast of China. The squatters who create new fields or start piggeries, and the hawkers who open unauthorized markets, are less obviously but just as realistically numbered among the inheritors of the frontier of opportunity in Kwangtung which is as old as Chinese settlement itself. The canteens which encumber the entrances of industrial buildings in Taikoktsui are no less part of the same continuum of enterprise and work, and so are the plastic roofs and domestic impedimenta which convert stretches of footpaths in squatter settlements or in the countryside, or parts of alleys in the city, into a kind of private property. A brothel which unites the public hallway of the floor which it occupies in a high building with its private premises belongs no less to the same continuum, and so do the hairdressers who work on the pavement, and those who store crates of fizzy drinks there. When a householder with a flat of 300 sq. ft. has built roofed balconies enclosed with wire cages outside his windows to an area of 30 sq. ft., he has extended his flat by 10 per cent and created space worth a dollar a day, and has established his place within the same continuum.[11] Everywhere in this great city, in a limitless range of circumstances, the community has a limitless capacity for life and livelihood, and encroachment as well, wherever it finds security and opportunity.[12] Its standard means of doing so is to develop the infinite potential of the difference without a distinction.

What has so far been said about squatting and hawking lays emphasis on the opportunity side of these phenomena, and has been interpreted in terms of encroachment. There is another side to these situations, which might be called destitution. There have been times in the recent past of the city when for some poor people the creation of homes and jobs for themselves has been the only alternative to having neither. People destitute of other accommodation have entered the wooden hut areas as squatters, many of them not as immigrants but as a result of redevelopment and increased rents. Once there, they may seek to maintain themselves by keeping pigs or doing factory out-work. People destitute of other work have started to cook and sell bits of food on the streets to passers-by, or have started to cultivate fields on empty hillsides. The community has always had people who were destitute, but the post-war influx of people from mainland China enforced a radical reassessment of their position in the whole argument about spontaneous occupation, partly because of their numbers and partly because of the increasingly sensitive state of social conscience.

But the argument from destitution cannot be separated in real terms from the argument for opportunity. It was in the name of the argument from destitution that the government, in 1950–3, allowed the victims of squatter fires to build huts in the streets. Street huts then cost $30 to $40 to build, and they were rent-free, whilst squatter accommodation, less well-situated, cost typically $15 to $20 per month. 'Destitution' gave place to 'encroachment' when once this difference was brought to mind, even without any demonstration that some people might use destitution (i.e. homelessness) to create opportunities for encroachment.[13] A squatter who began by doing factory out-work may well end by owning a squatter factory, reflecting the highest credit on his tenacity, enterprise and skill, but far removed from his former state of destitution. A widow today can easily get a legitimate hawker's license from the government because of what is here called destitution—her lack of other support. If she finds that her pitch is a bad one which will not give her a living, or not a satisfactory living, she may illegally rent a better pitch from somebody else, or take up an illegal pitch, joining the community of encroachers and at the same time making herself liable to blackmail by the local police. In cases like these, and many others, the argument from destitution and the argument for encroachment converge and unite.

In principle, a squatter community, or any other community or household whose home or livelihood forms part of what may be called the spontaneous continuum, barters away legal status and the day-to-day advantages of city amenity such as effective sanitation, in return for freedom from rent, taxation and administration. In practice, especially after the passage of years or decades, the squatters may well be paying rent, are getting sanitation of sorts and a water-supply, to all intents and purposes administration, and quite possibly spasmodic blackmail as well. With the passage of time, much the same becomes true, *mutatis mutandis*, of the rest of the activities in the spontaneous continuum, such as hawking. What is then happening in practice is that the squatter (or hawker, or boat people) community draws enough advantage to maintain life at an adequate level month by month from the economic and geographical territory which lies between the opportunities created by the existence of the city, and the will or capacity of the city authorities to administer them fully. How wide this territory is, in either a physical or an economic sense, and how varied and productive, depends on both official policy and capacity to act, and the enterprise of the squatter or other encroaching individuals themselves. What kind of livelihood this territory yields to an individual family has also to take account of the degree of density of use of the opportunities which exist—that is, the intensity of competition. All this is equally true, whether the family is in a state of destitution or not. What is under discussion is the maintenance of life, *and* hopefully the foundation of prosperity, by the exploitation of the margin between opportunity and administration. But in this margin competition promptly rises to normal levels, so that the unconventional opportunities represent little more than a group of particular aspects of the economy of the whole city, and the economic territory available for spontaneous occupation represents no more and no less than an additional dimension in day-to-day life for some people.

THE SQUATTER EXPERIENCE

It has been shown that squatting was not in principle or in practice a new phenomenon in Hong Kong after the Pacific war. Yet the situation as a whole was new, and by 1950 very new. The essence of this novelty was, as it turned out, not simple but twofold. The first and obvious new feature was the great numbers of people involved. The second, which was not evident until some years had passed, and not really recognized until 1962, was the extraordinary capacity of the squatter community to maintain its numbers, and in some phases to increase them, whilst at the same time the government was actively clearing away squatter estates, and building resettlement accommodation hand over fist.

In 1949, there were thought to be 300,000 squatters in Hong Kong, against 30,000 two years earlier.[14] Twenty years later, with a million former squatters housed in resettlement, there were 400,000.[15] In 1963, at the peak of squatting and when 500,000 people already lived in resettlement estates, there were more than 600,000 squatters.[16] The reason for this remarkable elasticity in the supply of squatters is that, as Keith Hopkins puts it, 'the majority of the squatters have been emigrants from the city rather than immigrants from the countryside'.[17] The peak of squatting around 1963–4 coincided with a peak of approvals of new building projects, and hence of clearing of the tenements.[18] Immigration from China was no longer significant. The government's working party of 1963 on squatters and resettlement showed that people were becoming squatters for a variety of reasons: because of becoming homeless as a result of natural disaster or through the official demolition of dangerous buildings, usually very old tenements; as a result of eviction, with compensation, from a building where the landlord intended to rebuild; as a refuge from the acutely congested conditions in the tenements including those then being built, and because of natural increase and some immigration.[19] They realized, as most subsequent commentators have done, that the squatter townships form a continuum with the rest of urban Hong Kong. Squatters do not represent a special concentration of poverty, or of bad housing, and immigrants are not particularly common among them.

All this sets the post-war experience of the squatter communities aside from that of the pre-war years. Civil war and Communist victory in China stimulated vast immigration to Hong Kong in the years after 1947. This

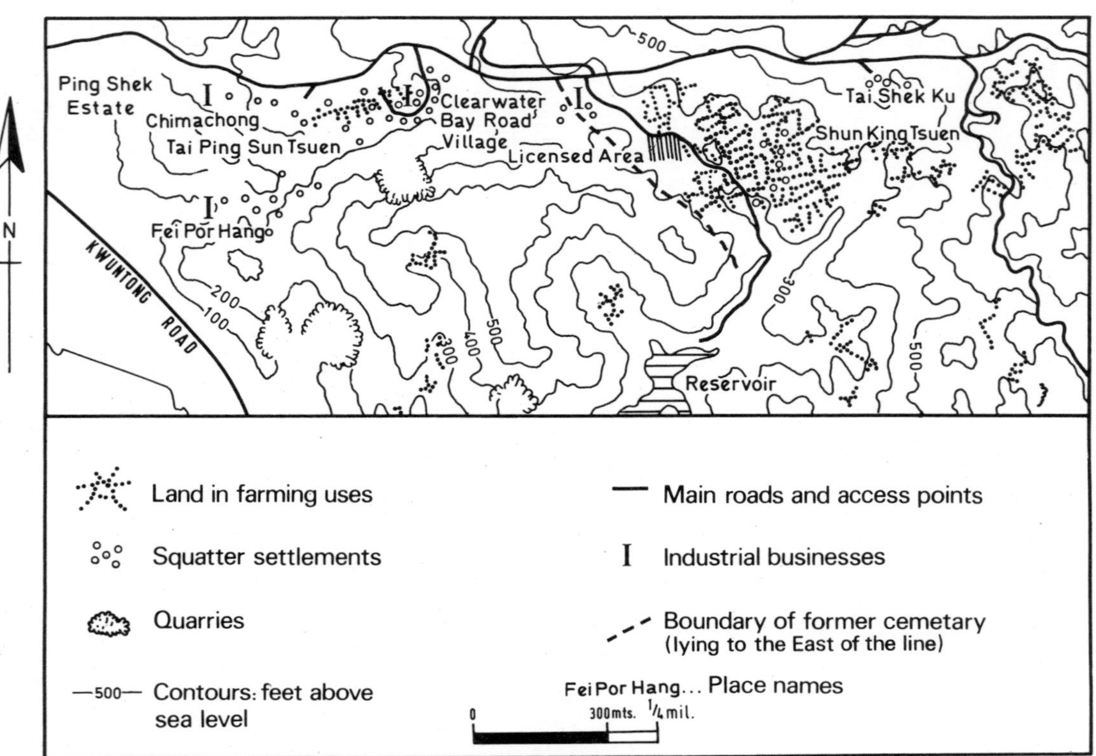

FIGURE 24

THE CLEARWATER BAY ROAD VILLAGES Scale: 1/10,000

immigration, together with other factors, stimulated the city into incontinent growth and a frantic programme of building and rebuilding. The squatter huts and villages represented temporary shelter for people who in one phase or other of these tremendous upheavals lost their homes. Factories and workshops appeared in the squatter estates almost as soon as the huts themselves, and these served for the re-creation of economic opportunity and the turning of the immense social growth then taking place in the city to business advantage, also on a scale wholly out of proportion with pre-war experience.[20]

THE CLEARWATER BAY ROAD VILLAGES

The villages which have been selected to illustrate the conditions and problems of squatter areas occupy parts of three different valleys, in an area which is topographically quite complex, and consequently rather difficult of access. This area is shown in Figure 24. The area comprises the upper part of the Jordan Valley; the whole of the valley of the unnamed stream in the north-western part of the map, which may be called the Tai Ping Sum Tsuen valley; and the little valley of the Fei Por Hang to the south of it. The main feature of resemblance among the villages is their joint dependence, apart from Fei Por Hang, on access from Clearwater Bay Road. Fei Por Hang is physically contiguous with part of this complex, and separated from other places by the big quarry to the south; formerly it extended southwards across the watershed.

Clearwater Bay Road here climbs steadily towards the east, running along the southern foot of Kowloon Peak. Four motorable short roads of various sorts lead off southwards into the valleys from the main road; and these are the main cause of local differentiation. All these roads, including that which serves the quarry, are for practical purposes *culs-de-sac*. There are also a number of access points apart from these roads, where lorries can draw off the main road to load and unload. These places, and to some extent the roads as well, serve as access points for transportation by hand inside the valley.

The total population of this rather ill-defined area, as shown on the map, was thought to be of the order of 5,000 in 1970. Parts of the valleys are fairly densely, but very discontinuously, settled; there are factories and workshops, a few places which sell drinks and a few shops, one or two primary schools, huts for residence, workshops, farms and piggeries. There is at most a handful of substantial buildings in the whole area, and none with more than two floors (Plate 34).

The most important settlement in the whole area is called Clearwater Bay Road Village (Plate 35). It lies on a short *cul-de-sac* road of its own, towards the top of the Tai Ping Sun Tsuen valley, and below the big quarry which occupies the north-facing slope. The centre of the village is a cluster of dyeing works, but there is also a varied scattered fringe as well, including both factories and houses. Most of the industrial firms have 'licensed' status, and hence have no tenure or resettlement rights, but pay very low rents.

There are about sixteen dyeing businesses in the village, mostly occupying adjacent sites in the middle of the valley, all with drying yards where yarn from the dyeing vats is dried on bamboo poles, with cover for wet weather. Local people say that the dyeing works have occupied these sites for only about six years. This is borne out by the aerial photograph of 1963,[21] which clearly shows the access road, but in which all the present industrial sites, except those very close to the main road, are farmland. Firms came here from Shumshuipo, Wong Tai Sin, Choi Hung and other places during the 1960s, generally forced to move by the government's taking over their previous sites—themselves usually squatter sites or those in earlier licensed areas—for housing purposes. Dyeing is greedy of space for drying grounds, and tends to occupy peripheral property with low land values, and hence to be perpetually at risk of displacement as commerical land values, and government land needs, rise. The advantages which this valley and this village offer to the dyeing industry are said by local people to be primarily water and land availability. Well-water is plentiful, and both cheap and unchlorinated. Transport is generally easy at this village, since most of the factories have direct access to the village road, which lorries can use. The few factories which do not lie adjacent to the road use steep footpaths and hand labour to get their materials and products to and from their sites. Some of the workmen live locally; some commute from other parts of Kowloon. Most of the commuters live in the big government estates relatively close-by, but a few travel from as far away as Tsuen Wan, nearly ten miles distant.

Dyeing is the chief industry in this little complex, but it is not the only one. One small firm makes metal window-frames. Another makes bean-curd, and sells its refuse to local pig-breeders, some in the same village, as pig-food. Beans are germinated for bean-sprouts, and there is a bakery and at least one plastic works. One or two firms use the residue of used ore from lead-smelting to reclaim metals which remain—lead, and also gold and silver. There are also a few iron foundries which use scrap iron to make castings. Almost all these are industries typical of squatter areas, requiring abundant space and little capital, and creating some degree of nuisance. The big quarry which overlooks the village produces mainly stone crushed to the fineness of gravel for use as building material. It is older and more highly capitalized than the little factories, and belongs to a different phase in the exploitation of the opportunities and resources of the valley.

What has so far been described is the rather tight-knit manufacturing village which occupies the central position in this group of valleys. This village has neighbours to the east and west.

To the west, towards the airport and the coast, the valley narrows. The industrial village gives way to a residential and farming squatter village called Tai Ping Sun Tsuen, built of individual wooden houses mostly on steep sites, to which access is had by crumbling earth, stone or wooden pathways, through a tangled low jungle of bushes. The people say that this village is between ten and twenty years old, according to locality, but most people have lived here for less than ten; twenty years ago there were only two or three families here, according to one early settler. Most of the village comprises residential huts, but there is also a little cultivation of vegetable and flowers, and some people rear pigs. People work locally in the valley factories or commute out. Many families have recently been resettled, and their huts have been pulled down or stand derelict. Some former shops have likewise been abandoned. This village is well on the way to its final dissolution.

Further west towards the coast, lie the lower part of the Tai Ping Sun Tsuen valley and, across a low watershed, the Fei Por Hang valley. Each of these valleys has its own character, though both are primarily industrial. The Tai Ping Sun Tsuen valley, emerging close to the junction of Clearwater Bay Road with the main Ngautaukok Road, has relatively big units of land at the bottom; here there is a big car-breaking business. The Fei Por Hang valley is smaller in scale, and less easy of access. Fei Por Hang is a rather isolated squatter village in its own right, the remnant of a much bigger place. There is some industry, occupying small to medium-sized firms—metal-working, dealing in metal drums, and the manufacture of cement bricks. There are now no shops at all in Tai Ping Sun Tsuen or Fei Por Hang. People walk down to Ngautaukok Road to buy household necessities.

Part of the former site of Fei Por Hang is now occupied by extensions to the big quarry which opens out southward at Ngautaukok. The extension of the quarry during the 1960s was not popular with the squatter residents, although resettlement was available. Squatter huts are often squalid, and a time of fire or flood may be disastrous; Fei Por Hang is also rather isolated. But squatter huts are extremely cheap to live in, with abundant space for people and children; and the present resettlement areas—the argument runs—are also isolated. For these reasons, squatter people may well be reluctant to move to resettlement blocks; much depends on their personal situation.

Moving eastward up the valley, beyond Clearwater Bay Road Village and beyond the access road and crushing plant for the quarry, the factories give way to scattered farming households with only footpath access, extending discontinuously over a hundred yards or more of rough and rocky ground, with scrub vegetation. One farming family here came to this place just after the Pacific war, and as squatters and pioneers made a farm on the open hillside, very close to the edge of the cemetery which formerly occupied all the land to the east. Now they keep pigs. Through this place, there is only footpath access to the east.

This patch of rocky ground is really part of the low watershed between the Tai Ping Sun Tsuen valley and that of part of the Jordan Valley headwaters. The Jordan Valley reservoir road enters the valley at this watershed, to serve a mixed group of settlements. Close to Clearwater Bay Road there is another small group of factories, served by this road. One is a sawmill, which imports, cuts and stores timber, mainly for furniture firms in Mongkok. This firm came to this place only three years ago from the urban area, after losing its former premises—also temporary ones—to low-cost housing. Here the firm now has a travelling crane and powered trolleys on rails. Two adjacent businesses make wooden chests. A neighbouring business which repairs oil-drums has been here for five or six years, the shop for ten. The scale of the shop business appears to be very small, but here as in the two parallel businesses in Clearwater Bay Road Village, there is a canteen side which is more important.

Beyond this place, the Jordan Valley opens out south-eastwards as a very handsome rural panorama. In the valley above the reservoir, there are broadly speaking two kinds of land use: residence and farming. There are also two kinds of locality, relatively level land which has reasonably good access by the reservoir road which crosses the valley to Clearwater Bay Road above, and hillside land which is much less accessible.

A prominent feature of the reservoir road area is a small government 'licensed area' for hut resettlement. In areas of this kind, people who are homeless are allowed to build huts of a specified kind on payment of the very low rent of $3 per month. This scheme amounts to a kind of licensed squatting, though without the right to ultimate resettlement. The Jordan Valley eastwards of the reservoir road was expected some years ago to be mainly occupied by the licensed area, but because of its poor location people are unwilling to live there, and the 'licensed' village remains small. It is not surprising that people who do live there work in a wide variety of areas.

Adjacent to the licensed area, and occupying the bulk of the flat land in the valley—some of it levelled by the government at the time the licensed area was planned, about ten years ago—is the squatter farming village of Shun King Tsuen. Opinions differ about the date of the beginning of this farming settlement, whether it was before 1945 or not; but the local consensus is that there was no farming settlement here before 1945.[22] A Chinese cemetery at that time occupied more or less the whole area eastward and upstream of the watershed; much later the cemetery was cleared away by the government.

Farming squatters whose farmland dates from before the aerial survey of 1954 are regarded by the government as 'tolerated'. Others are 'untolerated', although as residents or pig-breeders—that is, as occupants of buildings—they may have registered squatter rights up to the registration of 1964. Squatter farms begun after 1954 may or may not be tolerated in practice by local officials; in particular, if the farm is small and distant from the road, the responsible official may turn a blind eye to it—much more so, it transpires, than to squatter buildings. There are now about forty families in Shun King Tsuen, almost all occupied in vegetable farming or pig-breeding or both. There are also one or two small schools, and a café which performs some of the functions of a club.

Pig-breeding in squatter conditions, in the countryside or the urban area, is quite profitable. Clear profit per sow in 1970 was of the order of $800 per year,[23] which means that a family can live on the income from five sows. Some do so, together with other small income from chickens and so forth, even without a job; in a squatter area, living is in most respects extremely cheap. One farmer in this area has 14 sows, and so can make about $1,000 per month, about double an ordinary working man's wage. Another man has 3 sows but also has a lorry in which he does a pig-feed business. This man started as a vegetable farmer when he came to the valley in about 1962, but gave up vegetables because of the shortage of water.

Eastwards of Shun King Tsuen, the land climbs again towards the main headwaters of the Jordan Valley. Part of the upper end of this steep hillside was occupied until 1971 by a scattered village called Tai Shek Ku, which comprised about twenty households mainly dependent on pig-breeding. Here as at Shun King Tsuen, pigs and piglets were kept in sheds and yards and fed on town swill, which for Tai Shek Ku came in by lorry to the point of access on the main road above the village which is marked on the map, to be distributed by pail and yoke by footpath to the piggeries, together with paper cuttings and other industrial waste, used as fuel to boil the food.

Tai Shek Ku dated from about 1958, and originated as a squatter village. It was subsequently made into a 'permit' area for farming occupation, at a rent of H.K.$8 per acre per annum. The permit area was 'frozen' about 1964; nevertheless, at Tai Shek Ku in farming as at Clearwater Bay Road Village in industry, there was a tendency for the 'permitted' occupants to attract others who had no status. Tai Shek Ku was cleared away in 1970 and 1971 to make way for the new Shun Li Tsuen, a resettlement estate. *Ex-gratia* compensation was being paid by the government to the farmers up to a maximum of H.K.$2,500; and the people were to be offered resettlement accommodation. Those who wished to continue farming, and enter an established village community elsewhere, would generally be obliged first to seek and obtain the approval of the village concerned, in accordance with Chinese custom.

What fields there are on these steep hillsides are terraced. Their exploitation is obviously discontinuous and sporadic. Some old terraces have gone out of use; some terraces have been newly made; some are half-finished but abandoned. Some are partly planted in an amateurish way, but others bear every mark of careful and professional husbandry. According to local people, the determining factor for variations in the style of farming in the Jordan Valley is labour supply. Only families with plenty of labour can grow vegetables on a professional basis, mainly because of the plants' demand for water. This valley has a piped water supply from the storm dam at the top, which feeds the little cement-lined pools which the farmers use for watering their fields; but the work involved in watering the plants is still very great. Vegetables are taken on foot to the marketing organization in Ngauchiwan below the reservoir.

THE RISE AND FALL OF VILLAGES

The Clearwater Bay Road villages do not add up to a very big or very important squatter area; but from study of them an insight can be had into the side of Hong Kong life which is lived in squatter villages. There are three underlying realities: the need of people without homes or work to find or create both; the need of the government to regulate the use of public land; and the special conditions of each area which is taken up by squatters. All these have both short-term and long-term implications.

In terms of locality (to take the third point first), the Clearwater Bay Road villages are not strong. The area is distant from Old Kowloon, the topography is difficult, access roads are few, and the Clearwater Bay Road is not well served by public transport. When Shun Li Tsuen and its new access roads are built, the upper end of the Jordan Valley will still be distant, but its locational character will be greatly changed.

Government policy and the law draw sharp distinctions among unauthorized squatting, tolerated squatting, occupation of licensed and permit areas, and the holding of regular leasehold title to land, sometimes upon conditions and sometimes not. These distinctions are based upon various phases of administrative action now and in the past. On the ground, among the common people, these distinctions have two levels of significance. At one level, they are absolute but long-term. These distinctions do represent important legal and administrative realities; and in due course, when the government decides to resume the land, they will affect what happens to people, and the actions they will take. So by 'freezing' squatting in 1959 and 1964, and by establishing various administrative categories of licensed and permit areas, the government has established a comprehensive administrative and legal framework of relationships with those who are using this land. The people recognize these categories, and know their status and rights. But in this kind of area, until the land is resumed, in terms of the day-to-day social and economic life of the people, these distinctions are relatively narrow in their implications, and some are not important. This is the second level of significance.

It is true that even at this level, differences do arise. For example, squatter factories may not extend their premises by building on unbuilt land, but factories in licensed areas may do so. Sub-letting of licensed property is not authorized, but squatter property may be let or sub-let freely, and its use can be changed without interference—that is, a man may start a factory if he so wishes. Pigs may not be kept in a residential licensed area, but they may be, and are, kept by squatters, both farming squatters and others, and by lessees of farmland.

These are relevant differences. But there are more, and more far-reaching, resemblances, and these bring us to the first of the points mentioned above. Shops can be opened in all kinds of areas, and light hand-work such as the assembling of plastic flowers or toys can be done anywhere. For an established group of factories, whether its site is 'licensed', or 'squatter', or even leasehold in an old village, makes no day-to-day difference. Squatter farms do not differ in day-to-day ways from leasehold farms; the quality of the land, and access to water and transport, are the external fundamentals of their situation. In all these ways, it is most realistic to think of the licensed and squatter areas as forming a continuum with the old villages, united by impermanence, by a relatively rudimentary style of building, investment and public services, and generally speaking by occupying peripheral locations. Even in administrative terms, in this kind of area, regular leasehold land itself forms part of a continuum with squatter property, because the government can resume leasehold land as it chooses, on payment of proper compensation; and in places such as those which are discussed here, it is likely to do so.

On the ground, to the observer, squatter areas appear very complicated, partly because layout is irrational, and partly because land-uses and property-uses are mixed, with factories, houses, piggeries and shops occupying adjacent or the same properties. Land is also used for refuse and farming. In reality, squatter areas are not particularly complicated. People live in them, and earn their living either locally or outside. The same may be said of the old villages in the same localities. The style of economic and social life in a squatter area or a village differs from that in a working-class industrial area like Yaumati or Taikoktsui mainly in being less dense, because of course squatter and similar property is not high-built. At the highest, residential and population densities in squatter areas may approach or reach those of government resettlement housing at present levels, and employment may also reach resettlement estate levels—that is, levels much lower than those in mixed tenement areas. Economic life in squatter areas also tends to be less diverse than in the tenement areas, partly because it is less dense, partly because of isolation. The Clearwater Bay Road valleys and villages are unusually simple and narrow in structure as squatter villages go, but even much bigger and better located squatter villages are much less complex than tenement streets.

In the Clearwater Bay Road valleys, whose history of settlement is very short, the whole sequence of events in the history of occupation can be reconstructed. Pioneers entered the valleys to make farms in the years after 1945; in various parts of the valleys, there was already some settlement before 1945.[24] The farming communities expanded. Vegetable farming gave way to pig-keeping, except on the best land and that with best access to water; some of the later settlers always depended on pigs, and at the present time half or more of the total farming income of the valleys must come from pigs. Vegetable farming also gave way to factory industry, even on some of the best land. Six villages grew up in the valleys during these twenty years, as well as others in the south-eastern half of the Jordan Valley which is not discussed at all here. Of these six, one is industrial, one residential, and one pig-keeping; and the other three are mixed in various ways, one combining vegetable-farming with pig-keeping and two combining residence with various kinds of farming. During the decade of the 1960s, the government has interfered in various ways, earlier by introducing licensed residential settlement in one area and allowing 'licensed' industry to be set up; later by 'freezing' further settlement (after about 1964), and beginning to clear squatter communities; later still by resuming the land in the Tai Shek Ku area for low-cost housing, looking forward to complete clearance for a fresh cycle of uses. It is this last kind of interference which is permanent.

1 The Hong Kong Chinese term which translates 'squatting' is *kui-chü muk-uk k'ui,* which means literally 'living in a wooden hut area'. No Chinese term with a meaning equivalent to that of 'squatter' is in use in this context in Hong Kong, though equivalent terms do exist in Chinese.

2 'Occupants' include *bona-fide* lodgers. The checking of *bona-fides* is naturally an important aspect of these surveys. There is no obstacle to the sale or letting of squatter property, and some squatter huts are densely cubicled like tenement floors.

3 *Annual Report*, 1963. 'Review: Land', p. 35.

4 Loc. cit. More detail on these points, including some on the distribution of squatter settlements, appears in Luke S.K. Wong's article, 'Squatters in pre-war Hong Kong', in *Journal of oriental studies*, 8 (1970), pp. 189–205.

5 O. Chadwick, *Report on the sanitary condition of Hong Kong* (London, Colonial Office, Eastern No. 38, 1882), Para. 290.

6 *Report on the question of the housing of the population of Hong Kong* (1902), p. 79. As early as the *Blue Book* of 1845 (p. 119), 68 'wooden houses', some occupied by 'families', some by 'stone cutters' and others, are specified for Victoria, and 6 'builders of bamboo houses' are recorded. The specifying of 'wooden houses' suggests, though it does not prove, that some kind of squatter or permit status was involved.

7 O. Chadwick, op. cit., Paras. 291, 292, 299.

8 Since 1950, most fresh agricultural land has been leased not by auction, but by private treaty with farmers who have previously occupied and farmed the land for a period of years under permit. *Annual Report*, 1963, p. 18.

9 Chadwick, op. cit., p. 26.

10 In 1974 he does it no longer. The butcher's shop, in the very centre of Kwuntong, is now a supermarket. But the same practice can still be found in the city, for instance in Yaumati.

11 This practice, always of doubtful legality and in extreme cases threatening to make high buildings unsafe, has been stopped altogether, except with permission, since 1971, though older balconies remain.

12 It is not surprising to find that in Lienchiang, on the Chinese mainland in the no less unorthodox province of Fukien, in 1962–3, the Three Evil Tendencies included taking up excessive amounts of land as private plots, excessive opening of uncultivated land and usurpation of public land, emigrating, doing 'rat work' (odd jobs for money), and abandoning agriculture for peddling. (C.S. Chen, *Rural people's communes in Lienchiang* (Stanford, 1969), pp. 169–92.)

13 In fact, there was evidence that some squatter fires at that time were started deliberately (Commissioner for Resettlement, *Annual Departmental Report*, 1954–55 (the first of the series), p. 14).

14 Commissioner for Resettlement, op. cit., 1954. p. 1.

15 Commissioner for Resettlement, *Annual Departmental Report*, 1968–69, Para. 13, p. 5.

16 *Annual Report*, 1963, p. 35. The figure for 1973 is 275,000 (*Hong Kong 1974, Report for the year 1973*), p. 100.

17 'Housing the poor', p. 279, in K. Hopkins (ed.), *Hong Kong, the industrial colony,* (1971).

18 This peak in building was itself partly an outcome of the then imminent introduction of new and more restrictive planning regulations on building (*Annual Report,* 1963, p. 181; *Annual Report*, 1965, p. 123).

19 Hong Kong. *Report of the 1963 working party on government policies and practices with*

regard to squatters, resettlement and government low-cost housing, especially Part ii, pp. 4–13.

20 All this said about the specific conditions leading to the squatter experience of Hong Kong, it must be remembered that in the years since the Pacific war, most cities in poor countries have had some experience of squatting as a long-term institution, and in many, including places as far apart as Lima, Kinshasa, Ankara, Seoul and Calcutta, it has supplied a much bigger part of the city's experience and housing than in Hong Kong. A most interesting discussion of squatter settlement in general, conducted in the light of Hong Kong experience, is D.J. Dwyer, 'Attitudes towards spontaneous settlement in third world cities', in D.J. Dwyer (ed,), *The city as a centre of change in Asia* (Hong Kong, 1972), pp. 166–78.

21 Hunting Surveys Limited, London. Hong Kong, Run 6, Film 6, 5080, 5082, 5084, cover the area under discussion. These photographs are dated 25 January 1963. The G.S.G.S. map Series L8811 Sheet 19, based on air photographs of 1954 and a field check of 1956, also shows the access road and some settlement on the site of the village.

22 The local concensus may be mistaken. A little farmland and one or two houses are marked at Shun King Tsuen on the relevant sheet in the 1903 group of maps of Kowloon preserved in the Public Record Office in London (MP. H. 149. Map G). However this gives no assurance of continuity to 1945.

One government official whose responsibility is related to Shun King Tsuen is of the opinion that farming settlement on a small scale existed here before 1945.

23 'Unofficial' estimate kindly supplied by the Department of Agriculture.

24 It is natural to ask, what kind of process was this opening up of new fields, or building of suburban huts, by pioneer squatters? The answers of local people to questions on this point are limited and down-to-earth. Some have already been given. In the old cemetery, the pioneers were people who were not too much afraid of ghosts. In all areas, in the phases of active squatting, land was taken up individually by households or businesses, and apportioned among the people themselves as the process developed in each squatter area. It is said that if greedy people tried to take more land than others, or more than they needed, in the days when the squatter villages were growing up, the other people did not usually try to interfere, but simply sat out the situation.

10 A Hong Kong System

THERE is a characteristic scheme of Hong Kong life which may without hyperbole be called the Hong Kong system. The system has many features which in the nature of things have not been prominent in the discussion of individual localites, such as family life, the upbringing and education of children, social stratification and social groups, the organization of factories and other businesses, spending and investment habits within the community, and so forth. But many characteristic features of the system have emerged from the locality studies which have been made, and it will be of value to try to draw these threads together.

The central feature of the Hong Kong system as it emerges here, though not its most conspicuous, is the factories which represent its economic foundation. Hong Kong is not simply an industrial city; it is a city which is permeated through and through by industry. Industry represents the largest body of employment in the city for both men and women,[1] typically in small enterprises which occupy parts of shared buildings. Through the small factories, situated almost everywhere, and the out-work performed at home or in the street which they nourish, manufacturing industry permeates the community physically as well as economically.

The dominance of industry is recent, a development of the 1950s, but the origins of the industrial economy are as old as those of the city itself, contrary to conventional opinion. Until the 1930s, most Chinese industry was family-based and occupied standard tenement property which it shared with other uses. In property terms, mixed uses and multiple occupance including factory industry form the heart of the Hong Kong system in both past and present time. On the one hand, during the phase of massive expansion during the past generation, small industry in shared tenement premises has led through factory tenements to the high flatted factory buildings of the present, which are not only the solution to the problem of costly sites but also satisfy the community's need for means to perpetuate the system of multiple use. On the other hand, small industry continues to form part of the tenement complex of mixed uses. Since 1956 these mixed use assemblages have increasingly come to be housed not in traditional tenements of three or four floors each occupying a single address, but in bigger multi-storey buildings of more economical and more sophisticated design; but the practical content of these assemblages in new buildings differs little from that in old in most districts. Apart from good-class apartment blocks in good districts and new office blocks in districts which have central functions such as Mongkok and Sheung Wan, the separation of uses makes slow progress. The clearing of encumbrances from stairs and hallways and the cleaning of the public parts of mixed buildings, under the authority of recent legislation, may represent the start of more fundamental change, particularly if cleanliness and the separation of uses continue to be linked in the public mind with prestige and making money through the raising of standards of amenity.

Multi-storey buildings in mixed use cannot be separated from congestion, the most conspicuous feature of the system. It has been shown that congestion must not be confused with residential crowding, which is no more than one of its components. Congestion is a natural result of a social and economic system which seeks at all costs to unite diversity and specialization in one spot, where every successful economic activity invites others of the same and related kinds to settle in close proximity, and where the grouping of customers invites more traders, and the grouping of traders invites more customers. There is evidence that this kind of town rationale is rooted in Chinese traditional thinking and organization; in Hong Kong, the exceptional conditions of explosive demographic, industrial and physical expansion since 1947 seem to have led to exploitation of the latent possibilities of these traditional forms to an extent which might also be called explosive, and which is certainly unprecedented. A parallel reinterpretation of Chinese traditional forms on an unprecedented scale has guided the creation of the vast, sophisticated squatter and hawker communities. An even more momentous reinterpretation of the old Chinese forms of shared house-room led to the explosive development of the tenement and cubicle system in the years of most acute crowding. This kind of explosive reinterpretation of Chinese traditional forms, the course typically taken by the marked changes which the community has experienced without cease since 1945, is the principal historic dimension of the system.

One principal component of the general rise in densities of use throughout the city during the past generation has been ceaseless investment in new building. The system has accommodated the transformation of the fabric of the city whilst preserving with remarkable fidelity such apparently fragile institutions as specialist business clusters and the clusters of clusters which occupy important parts of the streets—and not only in traditional trades in an old district like Sheung Wan, but in engineering and related trades in relatively new streets. Business clusters, and the community cells out of which they arise, represent a tenacious tradition of internal self-management of parts of the community which is rooted in Chinese traditional experience. The same tradition is adapted to the self-management, or management by self-appointed organizations, of the Temple Street fair and many other phases of activity in the city.

The government's place in the Hong Kong system, as it affects the geography of the streets, is in part the negative one of interfering remarkably little with the people; in part the immense positive one of extensive creation of new sites, vast traffic works and ceaseless building. Over 40 per cent of Hong Kong people now live in government housing, and life in public housing, increasingly high-built and increasingly remote from the old city centres, has become a central feature of the Hong Kong system. In New Kowloon especially, extended public housing and the great new factory areas have together introduced a new scale and a new degree of social limitation into the built environments during the past decade. In new areas like Kwuntong, even more than in the squatter settlements which in part they replaced, pioneering on new sites represents a body of experience which stands opposite to that of the old business streets in districts like Yaumati, with their increasing densities of mixed uses, and each successive phase of investment leading to a fresh phase of intensification. In Kwuntong town centre the old multiplicity appears to be assembling itself: but in Kwuntong outside the business centre and in the great government estates throughout the city there are signs that the separation of uses will prevail. But in government housing Western solutions are already generating Western problems, notably the growth of crime in the big estates, together with isolation and the increasing burden of the journey to work and to school.

The choice between total congestion and the separation of uses is essentially a choice of evils; in this respect the community has not yet found means of harmonizing incompatible wishes and needs. Present government campaigns aimed at suppressing other evil but characteristic features of the Hong Kong system—dirt, corruption and crime—must be whole-heartedly supported, though it may be feared that crime and corruption are in some degree alternatives in so crowded and vulnerable a community. There must also be warm support for the slow but cumulative growth of government provision of social and recreational amenities for the people, such as sports stadiums and sports halls, swimming pools, properly organized beach facilities, and so forth—and for the planned establishment of countryside parks. Public gardens are now being planted, but too often only on traffic islands and other unsatisfactory sites; it may be hoped that soon the government will begin to plant trees and small gardens in crowded working-class districts like Yaumati, where room for them can be found on the sites of old tenements, at the sacrifice of a small part of the land revenue.

The Hong Kong system operates within a special and limited physical environment. One aspect of this is the profoundly familiar layout of land, sea, mountain and diverse localities within which (together with the diminutive countryside) the people pass their lives. Isolation from Kwangtung and China is a feature of the system which is new since 1949; before that time Chinese people travelled freely to Canton and elsewhere by both rail and water. It is not compensated for by either the elevation of the city to be a major focus of international air traffic, or the self-conscious and uneasy journeys which many Hong Kong people, especially working-class people, perform from time to time to places in Kwangtung to visit relatives.

The second aspect of the environment is the emphatic procession of the sub-tropical seasons, punctuated by the Chinese festivals and the arrival of the seasonal foods—the steamy heat of August, when food and bottles of brandy are offered even by poor households to the hungry ghosts, and bonfires of paper presents to the dead dot the streets among the parked cars: or the bright sunshine and clear air of winter, when people eat fatty sausages and other warming foods, bringing in the Chinese New Year, the principal public holiday, with peach-blossom and visits to relatives, and for most employees, a bonus equal to a month's wages.

The Hong Kong system is overwhelmingly a Chinese one in language, social habit both public and private, and the social consciousness of the people. The Chinese community enjoys a high degree of cultural protection from the difficulty which foreigners experience in learning Chinese. Within the protection afforded by the Chinese written and spoken language, the community can and does conduct its affairs virtually impervious to foreign scrutiny, except that of the government. Within this protection thrive many informal Chinese business institutions whose purpose is typically the regulation of parts of the community to the advantage of the professional participants. Many other internal Chinese organizations, such as the locality organizations based on common origins in mainland China, extending in many cases into business and industry, enjoy the same protection. The same protection is also enjoyed by other, less wholesome institutions, such as the black societies of the hawker streets, the resettlement estates, and Kowloon City.

But apart from language, and these special institutions, must the system be thought of as essentially Chinese? The question tries to separate inseparables. The city is Chinese certainly, in many respects which can be named; but it is unlike other parts of China, assuredly. Kwangtung itself is Chinese but unlike other parts of China; and since the day it was founded, Hong Kong has shared and extended this quality of Kwangtung, using and developing the British and international connexion to a point where the city and community cannot well survive without it. Throughout its history, Hong Kong has had the distinction of adding a fresh dimension to the vast diversity of southern China. During the past thirty years, because of accidents of history and through immense investment of capital and labour, it has risen from a distinction which was regional to one which is international.

1 Commerce, transport and all services taken together employ slightly more men than industry, but slightly fewer women.

Index

Where one reference is of particular importance under a certain heading, it is given in **bold**.